Writing with an Accent

Contemporary Italian American Women Authors

Edvige Giunta

palgrave

For Louise DeSalvo, Joshua Fausty,
and Cettina Minasola Giunta

and for my children, Emily and Matteo,
with love and gratitude

First published in 2002 by
PALGRAVE™
175 Fifth Avenue New York, N.Y. 10010 and
Houndmills, Basingstoke, Hampshire, England RG21 6XS.
Companies and representatives throughout the world.

PALGRAVE™ is the new global publishing imprint of St. Martin's Press
LLC Scholarly and Reference Division and Palgrave Publishers Ltd.
(formerly Macmillan Press ltd.).

ISBN 0–312–22125–8 hardback
ISBN 0–312–29469-7 paperback

Library of Congress Cataloging-in-Publication Data
Giunta, Edvige, 1959-
Writing with an accent: contemporary Italian American women authors/
Edvige Giunta.
   Includes bibliographical references and index.
   ISBN 0-312-22125-8 (cloth) / ISBN 0–312–29469-7 (pbk)
   1. American literature—Italian American authors—History and
criticism.   2. Women and literature—United States—History—20th
century.   3. American literature—Women authors—History and
criticism.   4. American literature—20th century—History and criticism.
5. Italian American women—Intellectual life.   6. Italian Americans in
literature.

PS153.I8 G58   2002
810.9'9287'08951073—dc21

2001048209

A catalogue record for this book is available from the British Library.

Design by Letra Libre, Inc.

First edition: January 2002
10 9 8 7 6 5 4 3 2 1

Printed in the United States of America

Contents

Acknowledgments   v

Preface   *Writing with an Accent*   ix

Introduction   What's in an Accent?   1

Chapter 1   Of Women, Writing, and Recognition   15

Chapter 2   Immigrant Literary Identities   35

Chapter 3   "A Song from the Ghetto"   53

Chapter 4   Speaking Through Silences,
               Writing Against Silence   71

Chapter 5   "Spills of Mysterious Substances"   93

Chapter 6   Forging Public Voices: Memory, Writing, Power   117

Epilogue   Coming Home to Language   139

Notes   145
Bibliography   169
Index   189

*Ma fino a quando si può chiedere alle cose che ci stanno intorno,
di rimanere forestiere, perfettamente comprensibili e remote nella
loro indecifrabilità?*

*(But for how long can she expect things around her to remain for-
eign, perfectly intelligible, yet far away and impossible to decipher?)*

—*Dacia Maraini*, La lunga vita
di Marianna Ucrìa (The Silent Duchess)

❧   ❧   ❧

A lingua ni tagghiaru quannu vinemmu ca.

(They cut our tongues out when we came here.)

—*Rose Spinelli*, Baking Bread

❧   ❧   ❧

Everything my American friends say sounds like a translation.

—*Carole Maso*, The American Woman in the Chinese Hat

Acknowledgments

Since 1992, I have been writing and giving papers and lectures on Italian American women at conferences, universities, bookstores, and community centers. Some of these writings have become part of this book. Earlier versions of chapters two and three appeared as afterwords to the reprints of Helen Barolini's *Umbertina* (1999) and Tina De Rosa's *Paper Fish* (1996) (New York: The Feminist Press, CUNY). Earlier versions and sections of Chapter 4 variously appeared in the following articles: "Speaking Through Silences: Ethnicity in the Writings of Italian/American Women" in *Race and Ethnic Discrimination in American Literature*, edited by Michael Meyer (Amsterdam and Atlanta: Rodopi Press, 1997); "Narratives of Loss: Voices of Ethnicity in Agnes Rossi and Nancy Savoca" in *The Canadian Journal of Italian Studies*, Special Issue on Italian American Culture 19 (1996); "Reinventing the Authorial/Ethnic Space: Communal Narratives in Agnes Rossi's *Split Skirt*" in *Literary Studies East and West. Constructions and Confrontations: Changing Representations of Women and Feminisms, East and West* 12 (1996). A section of Chapter 5 appeared as "'Spills of Mysterious Substances' or Making One's Own History: Tina De Rosa, Louise DeSalvo, Sandra Mortola Gilbert, and Rose Romano" in *A Tavola: Food, Tradition, and Community Among Italian Americans,* edited by Edvige Giunta and Samuel J. Patti (Staten Island, NY: American Italian Historical Association, 1998). Finally, sections of Chapter 6 appear in an article entitled, "Where They Come From: Italian American Women Writers as Public Intellectuals," included in a forthcoming volume edited by Phil Cannistraro and Gerald Meyers, *The Lost Radicalism of Italian American* and in the following articles: "Teaching Memoir at New Jersey City University," published *Transformations* 11.1 (Spring 2000), "Writing Life, Writing History: Italian American Women and the Memoir." *Italian Americana* 18.1 (Winter 2000); and "Figuring Race in Kym Ragusa's *fuori/outside,*" included in *Shades of Black and White: Conflict and Collaboration Between Two Communities.* Proceedings of the 30th Annual Conference of the American Italian Historical Association, edited by Fred Gardaphé, Dan Ashyk, and Anthony J. Tamburri (Staten Island; American Italian Historical Association, 1999).

The writing of this book has been made possible by colleagues, students, friends, and family who have continuously sustained my work. John Paul Russo first believed that I should write about Italian American literature and pushed me to do so long before I became an Italian American. My students in Italian American literature and film classes at Union College in the early 1990s first witnessed and shared my passion for Italian American studies. The NEH Seminar on "Emerging American Literatures" run at Baruch College by John Brenkman in 1995 provided me with many opportunities to explore issues that are central to this book. At New Jersey City University, I found a welcoming and supportive academic home that treated my work as worthy and important. By granting release time through a Separately Budgeted Research Grant, the University helped me as I sought vital time to complete this book. I am grateful to my colleagues at New Jersey City University for their support and to Ansley LaMar for valuing and sustaining the memoir project, which has deeply influenced my work on Italian American women writers. My gratitude also to Larry Carter and Jo Bruno for their support. My memoir students at New Jersey City University, who have taught and continue to teach me about keeping one's commitment to one's writing in the most difficult circumstances, have helped shape this book—especially the last chapter—through their insights, their writings, and their community-building. I am especially thankful to the students whose writings are quoted in this book.

My gratitude to Jean Casella and Florence Howe, current and previous directors of the Feminist Press, for having believed in and supported my work since we first met. I wish to acknowledge Fred Gardaphé, Paolo Giordano, and Anthony Tamburri for their important work in Italian American studies and for the consideration and support they have given to my own work in the field. Peter Covino's poetry and his friendship have inspired me; I only regret that the subject of this book did not allow any lengthy discussion of his remarkable contribution to Italian American literature. I also wish to acknowledge Stefano Albertini, Maura Burnett, Ernie De Salvo, Maria Vittoria D'Amico, Carlos Coello, Michael Eskin, Lisa Vanderlinden, Barbara Stacy, Deborah Starewich, Laura Lawrie, Regina Tuma, Nino Camuso, Eric Bulson, Caterina Romeo, Bob Viscusi, Ben Lawton, Peter Carravetta, Carol Bonomo Albright, Anthony Valerio, and Phil Cannistraro. My colleagues and friends, Fawzia Afzal-Khan, Kym Ragusa, and Jennifer Guglielmo, read some of the chapters and offered exacting and astute criticism: I am deeply grateful for their help and friendship, as well as for the inspiration their work has provided. My gratitude to Audrey Goldrich for her unfailing encouragement and confidence in my work. Thank you to Rosette Capotorto, Mary Cappello, Maria Mazziotti Gillan, Gioia Timpanelli, Rita Ciresi, Marisa Labozzetta, Nancy Caronia, Agnes Rossi, Sandra M. Gilbert, Mary Saracino, Nancy Azara, Nancy Savoca, Adele Regina La Barre, Franca Barchiesi, Joanna Clapps Herman, Mariarosy Calleri, Phyllis Capello, Annie Lanzillotto, B. Amore, Carole Maso, Maria Fama, Mary Russo Demetrick, Vittoria repetto, Dorian Cirrone, Loryn Lipari, Flavia Rando, Maria Laurino, Jeanette Vuocolo, Luisa Pretolani, Giuliana Miuccio, and all my Italian American sisters, who have believed in and helped make my work possible.

I have been fortunate enough to have Michael Flamini as an editor: I am grateful to him for his enthusiasm about and commitment to this project; my thanks also to Amanda Johnson, Amanda Fernandez, and Donna Cherry at Palgrave for their invaluable help.

My gratitude, also, to the Giunta, Minasola, Urbano, Ossip, Forster, and Fausty families—my Italian and American families—for their love for me and their faith in my work. Among family members, Irwin Forster has been a sharp and devoted reader, whose opinions and insights I will always cherish. I am grateful to Al and Andy Ossip for their loving support and for rescuing my children—their grandchildren—when I locked myself in my office to write or when I needed to get a breath of fresh air. The history lessons of my father, Vincenzo Giunta, were very much on my mind while writing this book. Claudia Giunta, loving sister, brilliant lawyer, fellow immigrant and Italian-American-in-the-making, has given me her friendship, insight, and humor when I needed them most.

My mother, Cettina Minasola Giunta, who saves all my letters and always believed I should write, came to my rescue when the deadline was looming; she continued to be by my side—even six thousand miles away—as did my grandmother, Nunziatina Nuncibello Minasola.

I thank Louise DeSalvo for her friendship, for her work, and for her extraordinary generosity; for *Vertigo,* a book that has transformed lives, including my own and those of many of my students; for reading and responding to portions of the manuscript; for helping me see (and feel) that my work is important; for our many enlightening conversations about Italian American literature, especially in a multicultural and feminist context; for being my guiding light as I have ventured into the territory of memoir reading, writing, and teaching; for cooking gourmet meals for me when I was beaten down and had no strength or will to cook, much less to keep writing; for acknowledging the struggles of her own life, which has been contagious and healing; for our daily conversations which, whether we are talking about tomato sauce or our writing, have sprinkled my life with pleasure; for her wisdom and her strength; for her courage; for her example.

My husband, Josh Fausty, has traveled with me through each stage of this book since its inception and has known it in each of its incarnations.

I am grateful to him for his countless readings, his patience, his cooking and his cleaning, his love, and, most of all, for being with me throughout this book's journey and our own. Finally, I thank my 12-year old daughter, Emily Giunta-Cutts, the youngest Italian American woman writer I know, and my 2-year old son, Matteo Giunta Fausty, who have lived with this book and who fill my life with joy. They are two of the greatest pleasures of my life between cultures and languages; for this, and for them, I will always be grateful.

Edvige Giunta
Teaneck, New Jersey

Preface

Writing with an Accent

Jersey City, early July 1998. I am sorting clothes and books, packing for a month away from the place that I currently call home, getting ready to return to Italy, my other home. I linger by the neat row of Italian books, right next to the bookshelf that holds my Italian American collection, and pull out a couple of books from the odd assortment of Italian writers that includes Verga, Maraini, Leopardi, Messina (both Maria and Annie), Ariosto, Cutrufelli, La Spina, Lampedusa, and, of course, Dante. What better time than my upcoming stay in Italy to read the batch of recent Italian books I had asked my mother to send me a while ago and that have been waiting patiently for my attention? What better time—and place—to reread Leonardo Sciascia's *La Sicilia come metafora* or Pirandello's *Uno, nessuno e centomila?* In Italy, I will be able to hear my voice speak without any trace of the accent that, as I often say half-seriously, I cultivate with daily devotion in the United States. In Italy, my cultural identity and the way in which I articulate it will be transparent, uncomplicated. After all, I am Italian: Born in Italy, I lived in that country for the first 25 years of my life; I have returned there many times; most of my family and many of my closest friends live in Italy. I maintain, to this day, my Italian citizenship, even though in 1999 I also became an American citizen. Should not my Italian identity be clear and simple?

However, I regard myself as an Italian American, too, although I am not exactly sure when I became one. It was long before I became an American citizen. I began to call myself Italian American when American English no longer felt clumsy and hard on my tongue; when I stopped shuttling back and forth between Italy and the United States, and did not go back to Italy for five years; when I started feeling kinship and solidarity toward the descendants of earlier Italian immigrants in the United States. In some ways, my choice to call myself Italian American is political, a response to those who claim that I do not fulfill their expectations of

Italian Americans. Because my social and educational experience and background are different from those of most Italian immigrants from the nineteenth- and early-to-mid-twentieth century, I wish to challenge quintessential notions of Italian American identity. What does it mean to be Italian American? Does it mean to be Italian *and* American? A particular kind of Italian or a particular kind of American? Either? Neither? I have become increasingly more Italian American—and presumably *less* Italian— as I have distanced myself, at least geographically, from my country of origin, and as I have begun to feel closer to the country to which I emigrated about 16 years ago. Becoming Italian American: a process of splitting and joining, blending but not melting, absorbing but not assimilating; a negotiation with cultural identities and languages that I often perceive as at odds with each other; a rethinking of the question of—and the quest for— origins.

☼ ☼ ☼

Late July 1998. I am in Italy now. In a moment of distress I call my younger sister, who lives in Washington, and beg her to speak to me and let me speak to her in English. The sounds of English have a soothing effect, and my body relaxes as the words once foreign to me unroll smoothly off my tongue, slip into my ear.

I live in the United States. I have spent most of my adult life here. I work, love, cook, write, mother, read, teach in this country. But I also have done most of these things in Italy, the country where I became an adult. A hybrid, an inhabitant of cultural borders, I am one of those who feel at home and in exile on both sides of the border. When I return to Italy, I experience a sense of intimacy toward and estrangement from the places and the people. As Eva Hoffmann puts it, in her memoir *Lost in Translation,* there is pain in departure, even for those who want it. And so for me. Recently, while I was in Italy to give lectures on Italian American women authors at the University of Rome, a faculty member there introduced me as "la collega italo americana." The appellation surprised me, even as I have been calling myself Italian American in the United States for years, and even as I have been referred to jokingly as "l'americana" by family and friends in Italy ever since I left to come to the United States in 1984. These days, I would not quite know how to describe my national and cultural identity in a brief and uncomplicated way.

The Italian accent in my spoken English remains the most recognizable sign of my foreignness, a mark of origin that sticks to me like a second skin. No longer self-conscious about my accent, these days I would quickly dismiss the suggestion given so many years ago by a well-meaning friend to hire a speech pathologist to help me rid myself of my accent. At one time, I did consider such a suggestion and went as far as calling a number of "experts" to find out about possible "cures." But if mine is a pathology, it is one that I embrace willingly and consciously, for it is in this linguistic difference that I nestle—if not always comfortably—and begin to trace the slippery contours of cultural identity.

Language is a manifestation of cultural identity. My languages are diverse and interconnected: English (which I first learned and spoke in its British form), Italian (which evolved from the regional Tuscan dialect), Sicilian (a hodgepodge of Italian, French, Spanish, Arabic, and Greek, among others), Latin (which I began studying in middle school, like all Italian children of my generation), Greek (another ancient "mother language" that I studied in high school), and Spanish (yet another ancestral linguistic layer for Sicilians, which I chose to study in college, in homage to the dreams and memories of my grandfather who, as a young man, emigrated to Argentina and, even in his old age, spoke with fluency and affection a language with which he had no direct contact for over 50 years). Brief excursions into other languages did not last: English, so foreign to my immediate cultural experiences and origins, would become my language of choice, and as such it would come to permeate my sense of cultural and binational identity.

If the inflections in my Italian occasionally reveal that I am Sicilian, those in my English shout the unambiguous fact that I am, and remain, Italian. Accents bespeak geographical and class origins but also that transitional quality that characterizes cultural hybrids such as myself. How can I *not* write with an accent?

❧❧❧   ❧❧❧   ❧❧❧

Jersey City. Early July 1998. I hold *La Sicilia come metafora,* skim through its pages, reread a couple of passages I have marked previously. Then I put it back on the shelf. I should not take any books. I should just plan on reading the Italian books I want to buy in Italy. Travel light for a change. Yet baggage reassures me, especially on returning to the United States from Italy, when I will carry with me a wealth of objects that embody Italy: oregano and rosemary from my parents' orchard; *limoncello* (a sweet liqueur my mother makes with pure grain alcohol and a special variety of small Mediterranean lemons); *torroncini* (almond candies of Arabic origin, coated with an exquisite glaze in many flavors: orange, vanilla, chocolate); colorful and shapely marzipan fruits, like those that adorn the windows of the best Sicilian *pasticcerie,* particularly in early November, when the Day of the Dead is celebrated; my mother's homemade orange marmalade; and more: embroidered linen, family recipes and photos, Caltagirone and De Simone ceramics, pictures and icons of Sicilian Madonnas and saints, small Greek clay masks I hang on the walls of my American home for good luck. It is material culture that speaks most powerfully to those who are separated from their homeland. I am, predictably, an immigrant, notoriously and inevitably attached to baggage, the physical embodiment of a home that needs to be portable.[1] The suitcases I drag from one port to another counteract the odd lightness of migrancy, that which lifts the immigrant and throws her around, without direction or roots. For this trip, I will anchor myself down with books, bricks of an imaginary home I can pack and unpack at will.

I pick three: Mary Cappello's memoir, *Night Bloom,* still in galleys; a collection of essays edited by Mickey Pearlman, *A Place Called Home: Twenty Writing Women Remember;* and Layne Redmond's *When the Drummers Were Women: A Spiritual History of Rhythm.* Mary Cappello, a fellow Sicilian American, has just returned from Sicily: Her book will serve as a tangible sign of her presence, for I need a traveling companion who understands the impact of repeated cultural crossings. The memoiristic meditations on home—homes lost, acquired, forgotten, remembered, craved, dreaded, imagined—in *Remembering Home* will help me face my own sense of homelessness and the longing to search for and create a home wherever I go. I am especially fond of one piece, "The Shelter of the Alphabet," by Carole Maso, fellow Italian American: "I am a wandering soul—but not an aimless one," she announces as she writes of the need "to imagine a home that might be moveable. . . . a home that can be conjured within. . . . [Home is] Where language trembles and burns" (182–3). I understand this trembling, this burning: It occurs in the space where one's languages and identities meet and conflate, momentarily without discord. Lastly, I pack *When the Drummers Were Women,* a book I hope will reveal to me more about the *tarantella* and *tammurriata,* ancient dances of Southern Italy I have been learning in the crypt of St. John the Divine in New York, with my nine-year-old daughter and a handful of Italian American women—friends and fellow writers—under the guidance of Alessandra Belloni, musician, dancer, singer, and cultural traveler extraordinaire. This book will help my feet balance and move at ease, following ancient rhythms, on the soil of the island to which I am about to return.

These books—although meant to facilitate my journey to Italy—are all written in English. I have come to realize that, while in the United States I hold on to my Italian identity, in Italy I will need to hear my voice filtered through the now familiar and comforting sounds of English. I will need to hear English mingle with Italian. I will need to speak, read, and write with an accent "here" as well as "there." This is a necessity that, as a perpetual traveler, I cannot—and will not—avoid.

❧❧❧   ❧❧❧   ❧❧❧

It is the coming to consciousness of this necessity that has led me to write this book. *Writing with an Accent* is the result of work I have been doing in the last decade to help the literature, film, photography, painting, and sculpture of Italian American women gain visibility and recognition. I came to Italian American studies through indirect, unexpected routes. After studying English and American literature at the University of Catania, Sicily, where I wrote a thesis on Lewis Carroll, in 1984 I came to the United States to study in the graduate program in English at the University of Miami, Florida. As a graduate student eager to immerse myself in—and, indeed, to be assimilated into—American culture, I shied away from any involvement with Italian American communities, despite the frequent encouragement to explore scholarly venues in the field offered by my mentor and friend John Paul Russo. At that stage, I was fully invested in adjusting to my new environment and too absorbed by my anxieties about navigating American language and culture as a whole. Italian Americans were both foreign and too close to me: What could I learn from them that could be of relevance to me as I tried to understand how to exist within U.S. culture? They did not seem to fare well in terms of cultural respect. I was also at that time invested in emphasizing that I was Italian and not Italian American, keenly aware, I realize in retrospect, that a class distinction existed between the two and I had nothing to gain from aligning myself with these people toward whom I felt a strong but uncomfortable sense of kinship. I did gravitate toward Italian Americans who had and maintained close intellectual and linguistic ties with contemporary Italy: people who had traveled to Italy, people who spoke Italian and not some degenerated form of dialect. Yet, I spent my first Christmas in Flushing, Queens, with an Italian American family I knew from Italy. The strong Sicilian inflection and the Neapolitan dialect overpowering their mix of English and Italian comforted me as much as the foods they fed me, foods that tasted of a distant home.

Intellectually, I wanted to be what in Italy would have been described as an "Anglista": I wanted to study authors who were unequivocally "English," whether on the American or the European side. Yet I sank my teeth into the esoteric writings of H.D. and Joyce, an American expatriate and an Irish exile, respectively, who, in different ways, epitomized the benefits and liabilities of living between cultures. That Joyce spoke Italian with his family—he was always "nonno" to his grandson Stephen—and that H.D. traveled to Greece and Sicily—and made the rewriting of ancient Greek mythology central to her work—strangely did not seem to strike a chord with me at the time, at least not consciously. The modernist concentration of the graduate program at the University of Miami and the fortunate confluence in the English department of a number of Joyce scholars made my choice to write a dissertation on Joyce and Lewis Carroll at once appealing and wise. In 1991, when I completed my Ph.D. and was offered a teaching position in a college of liberal arts in upstate New York, my career as a Joyce teacher and scholar seemed laid out in front of me.

Being a Joycean enabled me to reconcile the contradictions inherent in my position as a woman, Italian-born, and Sicilian at that, on the one hand, and as a student of English and American literatures in the United States, on the other—one who hoped to teach at an American university. Joyce's linguistic experimentalism had endeared him to me. The challenges that *Finnegans Wake* posed for me were not any greater than those they posed for my American peers. If anything, my multilingualism and accent served me well as I made my way through the foggy paths of the *Wake*. And, as a male writer, Joyce placated my predictable yearning for a confrontation with a powerful paternal figure. Call it anxiety of influence or anxiety of authorship, Joyce did fulfill the ambivalent function of literary forefather.[2]

While I was not alone among the Italian college graduates of my generation to come to the United States, most of them ended up in Italian departments, although they, too, held English literature degrees from Italy. I had considered taking and had been advised to take a Ph. D. in Italian or Comparative Literature because that would improve my job opportunities: I was told that my Italian accent would probably not serve me well in an English Department, while my Italian—not Italian American—background would constitute an asset in Comparative or Italian Literature Programs. I decided against both options, however, as I felt they would seriously undermine my goals. I very much wanted to continue to study and write about literature written in English (and that is, in many respects, still true, although my understanding of what English languages and cultures are has since considerably changed). As a graduate student, I also had little interest in contemporary American literature: I had not been really exposed to it through course work, but perhaps I also felt safer with authors who were close enough to me historically, but not too close to push me to explore issues I was not quite ready to address.[3]

Working in English departments, first as a graduate student and a teaching assistant, later as a faculty member, has forced me never to forget my foreignness, even as I have become more connected with American culture than I would have had I chosen to study and work in an Italian department. I spent years clearing my English writing of those idiosyncrasies that betrayed my foreign accent. If I spoke with a heavy accent, I did not want traces of my Italian identity to emerge in my writing. My writing, on Joyce and other authors, did not reveal any such traces. I developed a clear, limpid, almost aseptic style. I managed to make Joyce's lesson my own by disappearing behind my work. But Joyce does not truly become invisible, as I instead did, following the imperatives of "objectivity" in critical writing and the demands of cultural assimilation. But I would soon discover that reading and writing about Joyce did not enable me satisfactorily to articulate my unquestionably Southern Italian voice.

A change of direction was triggered in 1992 when I taught a course on Italian and Italian American cinema during my first year of full-time teaching. I had begun reading Italian American authors a year earlier and I was also avidly reading Zora Neale Hurston, Alice Walker, Toni Morrison, Ana Castillo, and Sandra Cisneros.[4] I wrote an article on the filmmaker Nancy Savoca, which developed from that teaching experience, and presented it at the 1992 American Italian Historical Association Conference.[5] Teaching enabled me to travel, with my students, from the worlds of Rossellini's *Roma, città aperta,* De Sica's *La ciociara,* Wertmuller's *Pasqualino Settebellezze,* to those of Scorsese's *Raging Bull,* Coppola's *The Godfather,* and Savoca's *True Love:* This stirred my silenced Italian voice. Writing about Savoca, an American filmmaker of Sicilian and Argentinean ancestry, opened up possibilities for a new kind of critical reflection. It allowed me to examine something that was simultaneously familiar and foreign. Once I started discovering the work of other Italian American women and met many of them, I became both aware of and indignant at the critical silence that enveloped these remarkable authors like a thick fog. This fog, unlike that of the *Wake,* had lethal consequences that needed to be challenged. I decided to dedicate my energies to writing about them and helping their work to receive due recognition.

There is nothing selfless about my dedication to Italian American women and my abandonment of Joyce: This work was right for me, an Italian woman, Sicilian immigrant and, more recently, an American citizen who, although economically privileged by comparison with earlier generations of Italian immigrants to the United States, carries to this day the baggage of cultural marginalization linked to her ethnicity and gender. Although I do not want to frame and explain my scholarly choice entirely within the bounds of identity politics, the personal and cultural pull that Italian American studies held for me did act as a catalyst.

But what really prompted me to abandon Joyce and to embrace a completely new field immediately after the completing my Ph.D.—perhaps not a wise venture for a young, untenured academic—was the sense of urgency I felt in the face of this literature and its cultural and historical contexts. In the late 1970s, I had been involved with the feminist movement in Sicily: I had been part of a consciousness raising group, attended meetings at *il Collettivo la Maddalena* in Catania, run feminist programs at Radio Gela in my hometown, gone to marches, participated in the campaign for the legalization of abortion and for gay rights. Years later, thousand of miles away, I found myself faced with an opportunity for my feminist activism to reemerge. The literature of Italian American women, unlike Joyce's opus, risked disappearing before it fully emerged. Here was a group of women, most of Southern Italian origins, whose voices and stories resonated within me. Like Joyce, these women also experimented—although along different lines—and wrote from the position of exiles, the colonized, the marginalized. That they did so as American *and* Italian women mattered immensely to me. These women wrote with an accent and, in choosing to write about them, I, too, could begin to infuse my writing—both critical and creative—with my accent, the marker of my cultural difference. It also was important that I become part of the diverse community of Italian American women authors participating in the development of a movement that embraced Italian American identity as a contradictory, often uncomfortable political—feminist—position. These women wanted to assert their cultural identity while also staying away from quasi-patriotic, unquestioning, even self-righteous celebrations of all-things-Italian that characterize the agenda of too many Italian American organizations.

In 1995, Fred Gardaphé, Paolo Giordano, and Anthony Tamburri, editors of *Voices in Italian Americana,* invited me to serve as guest editor of a special issue of their journal on the subject of Italian American women. That proved to be another turning point as I formally surveyed the state of the field and worked even more closely with a growing community of Italian American women writers.

In 1996, Louise DeSalvo, a well-known literary critic and Virginia Woolf biographer, published a memoir, *Vertigo,* which dared to demystify with unprecedented candor the myth of the Italian American family as a safe and sacred haven.[6] DeSalvo's work has been tremendously influential on mine: Here was an Italian American woman writer who wrote eloquently of traditionally unspeakable subjects and who did not hesitate to discuss and embrace gender, ethnic, and class identity—and to view them from an unambiguously political and feminist perspective.

Literary history is not made in the ethereal world of ideas alone. It requires, particularly in the case of women and minority writers, a grassroots commitment on the part of literary critics as well as collaborative work among scholars, writers, teachers, literary agents, editors, publishers, and, of course, readers. In the last several years I have been involved, for example, with the recovery of texts by Italian American women first undertaken in 1995 by Feminist Press with the reprint of Tina De Rosa's *Paper Fish,* a book that I brought to attention of the press with Fred Gardaphé, and for which I wrote the afterword. In years to follow, several books by Italian American women were reprinted. Witnessing how the reissuing of these texts has positively affected Italian American women's literary history has had a profound impact on what I choose to write about, how I write about it, and on the work I have done and continue to do as a cultural worker. Such work entails, in my mind and experience, building bridges between creative individuals and organizations as well as communities. Over the last several years, in addition to writing about Italian American women, I have been actively involved, with a group of Italian American women, organizing cultural events—from bookstore readings to workshops, conferences, and performances—that have addressed nonacademic audiences at least as much as, if not more than, academic audiences. Such events have opened up new forms of collaboration, awareness, and transformation and have encouraged community-building as well. The work of the literary critic, I firmly believe, cannot take place in the silence and isolation of a secluded library, nor in the brief social respite of academic conferences. Working closely with publishing houses, for example, can prove central to achieving the goal of building a *new* kind of public, as do speaking and writing for audiences that are not exclusively academic.

What underscores my work and those of many of the people—men and women—involved in this burgeoning movement known as Italian American studies is the questioning and expanding of the significance of "Italian American" and, on a broader level, the creation of new perceptions about cultural and gender identity, especially as they intersect with race, class, and sexuality. I have been concerned with helping to dispel the myth that a particular identity equals a particular political position and with affirming the importance of diversity. While my interest lies specifically in Italian American women authors, it will become clear throughout the book that the implications of this concern resonate with other ethnic groups as well, particularly in the wake of recent cultural and political conversations on multiculturalism.

Teaching in an urban institution like New Jersey City University, with its large, highly diverse population of working-class, often first-generation, immigrant students, has shaped in fundamental ways the work I have been doing as an Italian American cultural worker. Teaching memoir, for example, and working closely with so many extraordinary students, has given me insights into the links between class issues and literature that no book could ever have provided. Conversely, the intellectual and practical insights that this kind of cultural work affords have directly influenced my understanding of the teaching I do as politically and culturally relevant. I am committed to an acceptance and appreciation of difference and, perhaps more important, a recognition of self-difference. Because selves are never unproblematic, I believe in cultivating a certain skepticism, even distrust, for simplistic ideas about ethnic identity, ideas that are at the root of a lot of misguided, ethnocentric cultural work that tends to isolate and ghettoize instead of opening up creative and intellectual opportunities on an ever-widening cultural and political scale.

The Collective of Italian American Women is one outcome of the work I have done and continue to do in collaboration with a handful of brave and resourceful women such as Kym Ragusa, Rosette Capotorto, Maria Mazziotti Gillan, Joanna Clapps Herman, Nancy Azara, Jennifer Guglielmo, Phyllis Capello, Annie Lanzillotto, Jean Casella, Loryn Lipari, Mary Ann Trasciatti, Suzanne Iasenza, and others. The work of many of these women appears here as my inspiring subject matter. Creating progressive initiatives revolving around the work of Italian American women has been the mission of this grassroots organization, which is serving as a catalyst for the tireless efforts of several Italian American women to form a movement that would build a space for their ideas. In the year 2000, the Collective organized, in conjunction with Casa Italiana and the Department of Italian at New York University, a series of events on the theme "Italian American and Italian Women 2000: Cross-Disciplinary Narratives." This series brought together, for the first time, sister writers, scholars, filmmakers, and artists from Italy and Italian America in a face-to-face conversation.

This event, and many others that have occurred in the last several years (for example, the Conference on the Lost Radicalism of Italian Americans, which took place at the Graduate Center, City University of New York, in 1995; the Conference on Italian Americans and Publishing organized by Maria Mazziotti Gillan at the Paterson Museum in 1995; the Conference on Italian Americans and African Americans organized in Cleveland in 1997 by the American Italian Historical Association; the series "The Journey of Emigration," cosponsored by the Collective and Com.It.Es., in 1998–9; and the many important readings and events organized by Bob Viscusi and Vittoria repetto with the Italian American Writers Association) have added a new complexity and depth to the question of Italian American identity. These events, and the people who have lent their energies to creating them, inform this book and have contributed to the creation of a climate in which it could be written—and published.

§§§   §§§   §§§

In 1996, a few years after I had started writing about Italian American women and had become an active member of this burgeoning cultural movement, I began writing poetry and memoir, which up to then I had never envisioned myself capable of or interested in doing. I showed a brief essay I had written about my lost childhood diaries to Anthony Valerio, author of such books as *The Mediterranean Runs Through Brooklyn* (1982), *Valentino and the Great Italians* (1996), and *Anita Garibaldi: A Biography* (2000). He recognized the voice and the story of the Italian American cultural worker in the autobiographical recollection of Sicilian childhood and suggested I use the piece as an introduction to the special issue of *Voices in Italian Americana*. While I did not follow his suggestion, Valerio pointed out an important connection, one that would help open my eyes to new possibilities and ventures. In that essay, I wrote: "I never thought I could be a writer. . . . I guess I am the first writer in my family." I did not at first realize how much the private, intensely personal predicament I described in my autobiographical piece was one that I had already been exploring for a few years in the works of writers who, as some senior colleagues in the college where I used to teach put it, are not "household names in English departments."[7] That comment, meant to dissuade me from pursuing research in a field that those colleagues—and many others—did not recognize as worthy of attention, only served to spur me on. I have been trying to make these writers "household names in English departments" ever since. I hope this book will help me to accomplish just that.

Edvige Giunta

ACCENT. The mode of utterance peculiar to an individual, locality, or nation, as "he has a slight accent, a strong provincial accent, an indisputably Irish, Scotch, American, French or German accent." . . . This utterance consists mainly in a prevailing quality of tone, or in a peculiar alteration of pitch, but may include mispronunciation of vowels or consonants, misplacing of stress, and misinflection of a sentence. The locality of a speaker is generally clearly marked by this kind of accent.

A touch of colour or light which serves to bring the features of a structure into relief or furnishes a contrast in a scheme of colour.

To mark emphatically or distinctly; to heighten, sharpen, or intensify; to make conspicuous.

—Oxford English Dictionary

Introduction

What's in an Accent?

Italian American ethnicity transcends, for the authors who appear in this study, the restrictive bounds of identity politics. While Italian American identity is not, as such, a political choice, the authors I write about treat ethnic identity as political by underscoring the impact of class, race, gender, and sexual orientation on their self-identification. Italian American identity is called into question by writers who are uncomfortable with any prefabricated or reductive notion of identity. I use the denomination "Italian American" as a lens through which to investigate certain features of this literature. This lens, molded according to different criteria for defining identity itself, also helps me to put under scrutiny the unquestioned reliance on the term "Italian American": I am interested in the status of the term and the multiple—at times contradictory—ways in which these authors engage Italian American identity.[1] While I reject, as do the authors I focus on, any essentializing notion of identity, I believe that terminology is politically relevant.

One must recognize that, as is the case for other ethnic groups, the term "Italian American" may turn out to be—specifically in the contemporary context—rather "empty," up for grabs for anyone interested in ascribing certain political beliefs and agendas to ethnic identity. In some ways, this study wants to rescue the work of some Italian American women authors from any oversimplification and distortion that the use and misuse of "Italian American" may have bestowed on them. Ultimately, what interests me is not Italian American identity per se, but what forces are at work in this literature and how the label "Italian American"—and its concomitant historical ramifications—have led to the reliance on certain literary and political strategies by these authors.

Their continuous engagement with issues such as public health, gender, race, class, and sex discrimination demonstrates that for these women the choice to be a writer cannot be separated from the choice to live according to one's sense of social and political responsibility and activism. In identifying a literary tradition that has been blossoming in the last few years into a cultural movement, *Writing with an Accent* addresses the lack of recognition for Italian American women authors in the latter part of the twentieth century and how such lack resonates within their works in terms of literary strategies and political stances. A highly politicized awareness of Southern Italian identity underscores the interrogation of the politics of class, race, and gender, particularly in the works of authors of Southern Italian ancestry, who constitute a majority of the authors in this study.[2] These authors write with an awareness of the history of political and economic oppression as well as the racialization of the Italian South.[3]

An accent is not a single, easily identifiable element or a definite linguistic device—although actual bilingualism and the interjection of "foreign" words represent recurring strategies used by those who write with an accent.[4] I use the word "accent" to refer to a series of elements—narrative, thematic, and linguistic—that, collectively, articulate the experience of living between cultures. Such an experience and the modes of its expression vary according to the chronological proximity of one's generation to the departure from the country of origin, the relationship between one's culture of descent and the culture of ascent—to use Werner Sollors' distinction[5]—as well as one's sense of allegiance to and/or disconnection from one's ethnic community, and other biographical, geographical, social, and cultural factors. This experience of living between two cultures has been eloquently articulated by Eva Hoffman in *Lost in Translation,* a memoir that explores the many implications of living in more than one language, Gloria Anzaldúa's *Borderlands La Frontera: The New Mestiza,* and Cherríe Moraga's *Loving in the War Years: lo que pasó por sus labios,* key texts of reflection on the political significance of linguistic and cultural crossings. Recollecting her family's departure from Poland in 1959, Hoffman describes her experience of a "severe attack of nostalgia, or *tesknota*—a word that adds to nostalgia the tonalities of sadness and longing," a feeling that comes on her "like a visitation from a whole new geography of emotions, an annunciation of how much an absence can hurt" (4). In the autobiographical essay "La Güera," Moraga poses the following question: "What is my responsibility to my roots: both white and brown, Spanish-speaking and English?" She proceeds to describe herself as "a woman with a foot in both worlds. I refuse the split" (*Loving* 58). A perpetual sense of loss, of absence, but also a stubborn determination to live—culturally, linguistically, creatively—in both worlds characterize the creative process and product I refer to as "writing with an accent."

A marker of difference, a vestige of otherness, an accent signals marginalization and separation. This is particularly true in the works of writers who have deliberately incorporated bilingualism in their writings as a political gesture through which to legitimize diversity and who proclaim that multilingualism is central to their experience as well as the North American cultural experience as a whole.[6] In *The House on Mango Street,* Sandra Cisneros negotiates the line of cultural/linguistic division and connection through the reflections on language and identity of young Esperanza Cordero: "No Speak English" is the title of one of the vignettes of the novel. At its center is *Mamacita,* the woman who never leaves her third-floor apartment because, Esperanza believes, "she is afraid to speak English and maybe this is so since she only knows eight words" (77). Julia Alvarez's novel *How the García Girls Lost Their Accents* similarly foregrounds the intersections of gender, language, ethnicity, and identity, although Cisneros highlights the relevance of class identity more sharply than Alvarez. These writers deliberately do not provide a translation of the "other" language for the uninformed reader in order to portray, on the written page, a more accurate sense of life within a truly multilingual and multicultural world. This literary tactic legitimizes, much like Zora Neale Hurston's use of the vernacular in *Their Eyes Were Watching God,* their particular cultural experiences, and confers on those experiences political as well as literary dignity.

The literature of Italian American women mirrors, in its own distinct way, the phenomena of bilingualism and biculturalism in other U.S. literatures. Like writers from other ethnic minorities, Italian American women authors have explored the sometimes labyrinthine routes of the linguistic and cultural journeys of immigrants. Giuliana Miuccio, an Italian poet who has lived in the United States for the last three decades and who writes in Italian as well as in English, describes, in the poem "Apolide," a predicament shared by many immigrant writers:

una volta sola
terra madre
t'ho tradito
lasciandoti

ogni istante
terra matrigna

ti tradisco

restando.

(Miuccio 6)[7]

The speaker juxtaposes "terra madre" and "terra matrigna"—motherland and step-motherland—to articulate her simultaneous cultural allegiance and betrayal, significantly experienced through language. The two terms, related through the speaker's double betrayal, establish not a binary opposition but an exchange, an endless—and fruitful—negotiation through which the speaker seeks to fashion her identities. Many Italian American women authors speak from this space of displacement and belonging, of betrayal and allegiance, of nostalgic evocation and biting attack. It is in this space that one's accent can be spoken and heard.

Through linguistic recovery and acquisition, but also refusal of and escape from stifling cultural codes, Italian American writers often articulate a dislocation that is linguistic, geographic, and cultural. Giuliana Miuccio and other bilingual authors demonstrate that Italian language is not just a language from a remote past for contemporary Italian American women writers. That Italian American authors are revisiting Italy, literally and metaphorically—and writing about these "returns"—signals an important moment in the development of Italian American literature.

Like Barolini in *Umbertina* and several of her essays ("How I Learned to Speak Italian," "Turtle Out of Calabria," "The Finer Things in Life"), or Maria Famà and Mary Russo Demetrick in their coauthored book of poetry, *Italian Notebook,* Rose Romano examines the reverse movement, back to Italy, of the descendants of earlier immigrants—a return home that for Romano crystallizes the dual displacement she experiences as an Italian American woman in the United States and an insider/outsider in Italy, as demonstrated in the poems "Native Language Conversation: Intermediate I" and "A Little Spaghetti."[8] Maria Laurino, in her memoir, *Were You Always an Italian? Ancestors and Other Icons of Italian America,* undertakes a cultural journey that leads her to decode, for the first time, the mysterious language spoken by her family, an Italian American adaptation of Southern Italian dialect, and to "read" cultural artifacts, from Armani and Versace to Peg Perego strollers.[9] Such decoding and reading enable the author to gain a better understanding of the cultural politics governing the relationship of the Italian North and South and the history of immigrants of Southern Italian ancestry. The returns of Adria Bernardi, Mary Caponegro, Theresa Maggio, and Gioia Timpanelli appear to be of a different nature, chronologically as well geographically: The Italian Renaissance is the backdrop for Caponegro's *Five Doubts* and Bernardi's *The Day Laid on the Altar,* while Sicily is at the center of Maggio's and Timpanelli's work. The former focuses on the ritualistic killing of the tuna—the *mattanza*—in *Mattanza: Love and Death in the Sea of Sicily;* the latter turns to a Sicily suspended between history and myth in *Sometimes the Soul: Two Novellas of Sicily.* Filmmakers such as Renata Gangemi, Rose Spinelli, and Gia Amella have literally traveled back to Sicily to search for the images and the language through which to articulate their artistic vision, a vision that is inextricably linked to immigrant history. Their videos and films follow the complex trajectory of the return to the homeland of their ancestors: This return is bound to be partial, incomplete, even as it becomes a powerful creative source.

⛑ ⛑ ⛑

I chose *Writing With an Accent* as the title for what I initially intended to be a book on contemporary ethnic American women writers that would include only a chapter on Italian American women. The term "ethnic" is, of course, highly problematic if used etymologically, for who is not ethnic? I use the word, however, to signify cultural minorities, groups that, even when and if many of their members have acquired some kind of social and economic status, are perceived and perceive themselves as culturally marginal.[10] It took a couple of years for me to realize that what I wanted to write and had been writing was instead a book that focused primarily on the literature of Italian American women and described that literature as legitimately belonging within the multicultural tradition both for historical reasons and for the literary and political choices made by a large group of Italian American women authors.[11] These were writers who, like me, were inspired by contemporary women writers from ethnic minorities who, in my mind, wrote with an accent. Like these writers, Italian American women creatively articulate the tension that arises out of their multiple cultural identities and produce narratives that simultaneously signal acculturation and cultural displacement, affiliation and separation. Both echoing and resisting the sounds and signs of the various cultures simmering in their works, they speak—and write—in a variety of accents.

Indeed, the literature of American minorities has been instrumental in helping me identify, examine, and understand the literature of contemporary Italian American women. Writers such as Gloria Anzaldúa, Cherríe Moraga, Alice Walker, Audre Lorde, Toni Morrison, Joanna Kadi, Ana Castillo, Sandra Cisneros, Sapphire, Julia Alvarez, Esmeralda Santiago, Leslie Marmon Silko, Cristina Garcia, and Edwidge Danticat have helped me, and other Italian American women, to listen to our voices, our accents, our stories, and to put them into our writing. In the process of creating literature, these authors have forged and strengthened community bonds.[12] The ways in which they have sustained and inspired each other's work have inspired Italian American women and taught them strategies vital to establishing a literary tradition. Louise DeSalvo claims that her own encounter with the literature of African American, Asian American, Native American, and Latina women alerted her to the fact that there was something with which she, as a feminist critic, biographer, and writer, had not dealt: her Italian American identity.[13] She would write about that in *Vertigo* (1996), a memoir that in turn alerted other Italian American women to what they themselves had not dealt with: their ambivalent relationship to a culture beloved but also dreaded. In telling her story, DeSalvo constructs an "unlikely narrative": that of a "working-class Italian girl who became a critic and writer" (*Vertigo* xvii). The publication of *Vertigo* marks a key moment in Italian American literary history because of the way in which it foregrounds the politics of gender, class, and ethnicity within family, community, and country.

Other Italian American women besides DeSalvo claim a kinship to other minority writers who have served as mentors and models: Rosette Capotorto dedicates "Bronx Italian" to Audre Lorde, whom she acknowledges as her teacher and mentor; Nancy Caronia claims Toni Morrison and Maya Angelou as her models; Mary Cappello acknowledges the influence of women filmmakers such as Julie Dash and Cheryl Dunye and of writers such as Alice Walker, Toni Morrison, Gloria Anzaldúa, Jewelle Gomez, bell hooks, and Gayle Jones;[14] Jennifer Guglielmo speaks of the political and cultural affinity she has felt toward Chicana women.[15] Recognizing the crucial role in her creative, intellectual, and political formation of Joy Harjo, Jamaica Kincaid, Theresa Hak-Kyung-Cha, Audre Lorde, and Trinh T. Minh-ha, the filmmaker Kym Ragusa claims: "These authors helped me to understand the complexity of my own racial and class history. That they placed their experiences within history was very important for me, as was the fact that they were able to embrace all the differences within themselves. . . . [I learned that] you can use the multiplicity of your differences in creative ways, instead of accepting the invisibility that accompanies them."[16] Italian American women writers have consistently turned to authors from other ethnic minorities to affirm the importance of solidarity and to seek an affirmation of their own political and literary choices. Mary Saracino affirms with conviction the influence of Toni Morrison, Audre Lorde, Amy Tan, Sandra Cisneros, and Jessica Hagedorn: "What has continually drawn me to these writers is their unfailing courage to tell the truth, to address difficult issues and break silences around the realities of the lives of women of color in America. They don't flinch, they don't apologize. They witness and reveal and give voice where voice is most needed."[17]

Conversely, the experiences of Italian American women have been meaningful to women of other marginalized groups. Calling Helen Barolini's *The Dream Book: An Anthology of Writings by Italian American Women* (1985) "a book of heroic recovery and affirmation," Alice Walker acknowledged the connection between the work of African American and Italian American women writers.[18] In an essay on Asian American women published in 1987, Amy Ling writes that the introduction to *The Dream Book* "resonates" for her "in many ways, for Italian American women have suffered similar oppression from the men of their own culture, a similar sense of alienation from the dominant Anglo-American traditions, and the same affinity with black women writers that Chinese American women feel" (740). Indeed, the stories that Italian American women tell and the issues they explore reverberate well beyond the confines of their ethnic group exactly because they do not shy away from exploring the often contradictory position of describing oneself as Italian American in a historical climate in which that term can be read in multiple and contrasting ways, and connotations of racism as well as political conservatism and disengagement have been attached to it.

My interest lies not in *all* Italian American women authors. Most of the authors I discuss are either of working-class origins or infuse in their writings working-class consciousness. Janet Zandy emphasizes the connection between class and accent, and the concomitant links with shame, passing, and assimilation for working-class people:

> What we call "English" has many accents. . . . The working-class intellectual must decide how to negotiate the linguistic border between these languages of home and the official language of the academy and publishing institutions. She or he could take speech and attempt to pass linguistically. (*Liberating Memory* 5–6)

But, Zandy notes, there are tremendous risks involved in the assimilationist undertaking, namely "the loss of contact with the mother tongue" (6) and with those who speak it. Regional provenance and accent are of paramount importance to Italians in Italy, particularly because of the diversity among the Italian regions and the North/South dichotomy with its class implications.[19] The status of Southern Italians as the poor of Italy and the interface of class and race continue to be addressed in Italian politics, literature, and popular culture.[20] My own position as a first-generation Sicilian immigrant with firsthand experience of the complexities of race, class, and regional identity, my recent acquisition of American citizenship, and my long-standing feminist politics have led me to an interest in Italian American women authors who view ethnicity neither as an accident of birth nor a source of patriotic pride but, rather, as a complicated site for the articulation of a politicized and progressive Italian American positionality. Community-building as well as the creation of alliances within the multicultural spectrum are at the center of these women authors' choices and understanding of what it means to be Italian American at this particular time in U.S. history.

Since the roots of the Italian experience in America are primarily working class, my focus on authors who are, for the most part, of Southern Italian ancestry is useful in terms of a retrospective exploration of the paths that have led to the creation of Italian American literature. The authors I am interested in are concerned with questions that are literary *and* political. They engage issues such as public health (DeSalvo in *Breathless* and Sandra M. Gilbert in *Wrongful Death*[21]), domestic violence (Cara De Vito's *Ama l'uomo tuo*), exploitation of domestic workers (Renata Gangemi's *Talking* Back), racism and classism (DeSalvo, Mary Cappello, Rosette Capotorto, Janet Zandy, Luisa Pretolani, Kym Ragusa, Penny Arcade). In asserting and defending difference, these authors write in accent-inflected voices. Those who appear in this study—some prominently, some tangentially, albeit not less significantly—speak in voices that, in the diversity of their accents and the stories they tell, resonate with—and even echo—each other.

The six chapters into which the book is divided cover primarily the literary production of Italian American women in the last two decades of the twentieth century: 1979 and 1999, the respective dates of the publication and the reprint of Helen Barolini's *Umbertina*. While I discuss at length works written in the late 1970s—Helen Barolini's *Umbertina* (1979) and Tina De Rosa's *Paper Fish* (1980)—I focus primarily on the literature of the mid-to-late 1980s (*The Dream Book* was published in 1985) and 1990s, a period in which many Italian American women authors have written with alacrity, have had their books released by well- and lesser-known publishing houses, and have begun to see themselves as actively participating in the making of a literature that is simultaneously Italian American *and* legitimately American.

The year 2000 has been an unprecedented year for the publication of works by Italian American women, signaling the beginning of a new phase, much as the year 1996—the year of the reprint of Tina De Rosa's *Paper Fish* as well as of the publication of *Vertigo* and the special issue of *VIA* on Italian American women authors—marked a moment of renewed confidence and development in the field. I find it necessary to discuss Barolini and De Rosa, and the history of their works and careers, because that history sheds light on Italian American women's literary history as a whole. Indeed, it *is* the history against which we must examine more recent books. I also discuss other cultural texts—in film, art, and music—to place the literary production of contemporary Italian American women in the wider context of a burgeoning artistic and intellectual movement. Each chapter cuts across chronological and genre lines in order to outline a literature embodied in the works of authors who, while often producing their oeuvres with little or no awareness of the existence of other Italian American women authors, nevertheless have been at work on a collective project, cohesive in its diversity. To illustrate the collective nature of this project, even as it focuses on individual authors, *Writing with an Accent* moves back and forth through a variety of texts and authors.

Chapter 1, "Of Women, Writing, and Recognition," maps out Italian American women's literary history and focuses on cultural and literary issues concerning its relatively recent origins, its rapid development in the mid-1990s, and the central question of what makes an author Italian American. Within this context, I examine some of the literary strategies used by Italian American women in dealing with issues ranging from the mafia to the environment. While it is my intention to emphasize the extreme diversity among these authors, I also wish to underscore how certain commonalities can be identified. Such commonalities evidence the existence of Italian American women's literature.

The following three chapters focus primarily on three authors, Helen Barolini, Tina De Rosa, and Agnes Rossi, as case studies that help to trace and define the development of a canon of contemporary Italian American women's literature. I am not so much interested in author studies per se as in using these authors as exempla to illustrate what is involved in the making of this literature.

Chapters 2 and 3, "Immigrant Literary Identities" and "'A Song from the Ghetto,'" examine *Umbertina* and *Paper Fish,* two texts that document the history of a literature that has developed despite *and* as a result of significant struggles and impediments. Barolini and De Rosa entered a world that stood in contrast with what many viewed as the reclusive and non-political haven of Italian womanhood. *Umbertina* and *Paper Fish,* two *bildungsromans* that occupy, in the Italian American canon, a place comparable to that held by *The Color Purple* in African American literature and *The House on Mango Street* in Chicana literature, were published in 1979 and 1980 respectively, although they quickly went out of print and have come forcefully to the attention of a wide and diverse audience after their respective 1999 and 1996 reprints. Along with Barolini's *The Dream Book* (1985), *Umbertina* and *Paper Fish* could be regarded as *ur*-texts for the Italian American women who would produce, in the following two decades, works infused with a rich, albeit often ambivalent and certainly more complicated sense of Italian American identity. But what must be emphasized, aside from any literary value readers and critics choose to attach to these texts, is the groundbreaking fact that these authors wrote them—and managed to publish them—at a time when Italian American women had no publicly recognized literary existence.

Chapter 4, "Speaking Through Silences, Writing Against Silence" explores assimilation, self-silencing, and passing as three interconnected strategies in the writings of Italian American women who, whether consciously or not, camouflage their ethnic identity, at times to the point of seemingly erasing any ethnic traces in their writing. While the primary focus is on Agnes Rossi, this chapter also considers several other authors who, in diverse yet comparable ways, are relevant to the issues I address here. Many of the literate children and descendants of Italian American immigrants, thrown into a world in which their culture does not receive recognition, have often hidden their ethnic and class identities. The question I pose is: What happens to the voices of those who surrender to the seduction of assimilation and the self-silencing it entails? Writers such as Maria Mazziotti Gillan, Louise DeSalvo, and Maria Laurino foreground the question of silence as they reclaim and remake their cultural identities. Others, including Carole Maso, Kim Addonizio, Cris Mazza, and Agnes Rossi, are seemingly less concerned with these issues and yet they, too, relentlessly examine the relationship between silence, language, and identity. The question of ethnic self-representation is complicated, as this chapter underscores, by the often troubled relationship that women maintain with Italian American culture, within which they have historically occupied a subservient position. The ethnic tapestry Italian American women writers weave becomes even more complex when factors such as ethnic and racial crossing and sexual orientation enter the picture, as is the case with African American and Italian American filmmakers Kym Ragusa, Giannella Garrett, and Lilith Dorsey; Argentinean American and Italian American filmmakers Nancy Savoca, Renata Gangemi, and Liliana Fasanella; and for lesbian writers such as Rose Romano, Mary Cappello, Mary Saracino, and Vittoria repetto.

Through discussions of Italian American women's literary representations of material culture—primarily food and religion—the fifth chapter, "'Spills of Mysterious Substances'," examines contemporary Italian American women authors' struggle to negotiate between their often devastating critique of Italian American culture and their urge to defend and preserve the very traditions they seem to oppose. The previous chapters touch on the subject of material culture because I wish to emphasize the interconnections between the making of literature and the material texture of people's lives. The fifth chapter, however, underscores with greater deliberation and focus how material culture speaks powerfully of and to the experiences and histories of Italian Americans, whether it is the recipes interspersed in the writings of so many Italian American women, the Madonna of 115th Street in Italian Harlem—the subject of a study by Robert Anthony Orsi and a documentary project by Kym Ragusa—the monumental sculptures and wood carvings of Nancy Azara, the transformation of public spaces such as the Arthur Avenue market in the Bronx by performance poet Annie Lanzillotto, Adele La Barre's *biancheria* (needlework) project, or Joseph Sciorra's research on *presepi* (nativity scenes).

The last chapter. "Forging Public Voices: Memory, Writing, Power," discusses the routes followed by Italian American women authors to become public intellectuals—and what such a phrase has come to signify for many Italian American writers. As for many contemporary feminist memoirists, the motto *the personal is political* has not exhausted its radical potential, and indeed it constitutes a vital operative political and creative stance for writers such as Louise DeSalvo, Maria Mazziotti Gillan, Annie Lanzillotto, Mary Cappello, and Rosette Capotorto. This chapter focuses on writers who engage public issues and, in doing so, both foreground ethnic identity and transcend the limitations of ethnic celebration and self-valorization. In the conclusion to this chapter, I explore the pedagogical power of the memoir and, in general, teaching, as tools for radical social transformation.

❦ ❦ ❦

I would like to conclude by addressing the importance of the critical work that a number of critics have produced during the last decade. The literary criticism written not only in response but collaterally to the emergence of Italian American women's literature possesses an intellectual and creative integrity of its own. This is true especially in light of the circumstances in which, like the literature it advocates for, the literary criticism has been produced, in academic settings unfriendly to or, at best, disinterested in Italian American women authors. In her essay "Reintroducing *The Dream Book*," a revised, updated version of the classic introduction to the 1985 anthology, Helen Barolini claims Italian American women writers can and do react to the fact that their work is not taken "seriously" "by becoming themselves the teachers and critics of their experience" (*Chiaroscuro* 196). What Barolini does not acknowledge in her otherwise inspiring claim, however, is the contribution of a handful of devoted literary critics and editors to the affirmation of Italian American women's literature.[22] If for a long time Italian American women writers have had to produce the critical narratives that would legitimize their existence—as has certainly been the case for Barolini early on in her career—during the last several years a greater interest in the subject has begun to develop, testifying to the commitment of a growing number of individuals to the recording of the long overdue history of this literature. As I have noted, in the not-so-distant past, the obstacles encountered by literary critics of Italian American literature have been, in many ways, comparable to those encountered by the authors themselves. The emergence of Italian American critics and writers as public intellectuals engaged in issues that transcend the limits of a narrowly conceived ethnic narrative is another fact that must be, like the literature itself, recognized and documented.

For Italian American women to write about Italian American women authors does not mean merely to choose to write intellectual and literary history. Writing is at times an act of defiance. Writing might require daring to write, directly or obliquely, of one's own life. It might mean asserting the right to break the silence imposed from the inside—by communities that often sacrifice their own in the name of a misguided sense of respectability and self-preservation—and from the outside—by American culture and media willing to accept and reproduce only stultifying images of Italian American womanhood. It often means shaping a place in-between, a "*spazio*/space"—to use Miuccio's bilingual juxtaposition—that cuts across the hyphen, a space the elusive borders of which fluctuate between the real and the imaginary: a space continuously reinvented by a community of writers, artists, critics, and readers working to nurture the birth of works that resonate with powerful accents.[23] Yet, it also means writing about an intellectual and artistic community that often reproduces the very insidious dynamics that come under attack in the works of contemporary Italian American women. It means writing about authors who wear the Italian American hat for reasons of convenience, and then discard it when it no longer seems to serve their purpose. It means embracing a community as fraught with contradictions as the works it produces. It means embracing advocacy, which is what this book is about: the need for advocacy, the need for the recording of cultural history, and for a recognition of the many ways in which the making of books and authors shapes and is shaped by that history.

⠶⠶ ⠶⠶ ⠶⠶

They were poor, they had "accents," the children went to state schools.

—The Guardian, *5 October 1962*

⠶⠶ ⠶⠶ ⠶⠶

Chapter 1

Of Women, Writing, and Recognition

For publication means the breaking of a first seal, the end of a "no-admitted" status, the end of a soliloquy confined to the private sphere, and the start of a possible sharing with the unknown other—the reader, whose collaboration with the writer alone allows the work to come into full being. Without such a rite of passage, the woman-writer-to-be/woman-to-be-writer is condemned to wander about, begging for permission to join in and be a member.

—*Trinh T. Minh-ha,* Woman, Native, Other

And it was then that my father's Italy became a place imprinted on the platen of my soul.

—*Flavia Alaya,* Under the Rose: A Confession

Last year, my mailman delivered a package containing a book; on the cover, a color photo revealed the author, a woman, youthful despite her white hair, standing against a green and mountainous background. This unexpected gift came from a writer I had never heard of: Filomena Lo Curcio Stefanelli. She had read an article about my work on Italian American women writers that had just appeared in the *New York Times* and felt compelled to write to me.[1] Writer, historian, archivist, and photographer, Stefanelli self-published, in 1998, *The Stromboli Legacy: My Voyage of Discovery,* an evocative exploration of the author's cultural and geographical connection to the rocky island off the coast of Sicily where her parents were born. Stefanelli wanted me to know about her book—perhaps she knew I would let others know about it, too.

Reading the letter that accompanied the book, I was struck by the fact that, having been born in Brooklyn in 1916, this 84-year-old was the oldest living Italian American woman writer I knew of. When I called her to thank her, I was surprised to hear a feeble, tremulous voice. I had expected an assertive, robust voice: This was, after all, the woman who only two years earlier had had the energy to self-publish her book. We did not have much of a conversation. As her husband—who picked up the phone after a few minutes—told me, his wife could not hear well.

How auspicious that I would receive a letter from an Italian American woman writer who was born almost a century ago just as I was completing my book on contemporary Italian American women writers! And yet how sad that we could not speak to each other: I wanted her to hear my words, to know that I had "heard" her.

Nevertheless, I couldn't but appreciate the serendipity of the fact that this foremother—and nevertheless contemporary author—still seeking recognition managed to reach me, with a book she herself published at the close of the twentieth century, at the very moment I was pondering what it means to be a contemporary Italian American woman author at the turn of the century. That she was a fellow Sicilian who spoke the ancient Aeolian dialect seemed to bear some link with the title of my book, *Writing with an Accent*. How many languages, how many different accents were in the writing of this American writer who claimed Stromboli as the place of her cultural and linguistic origins?

Stromboli: a volcanic island off the coast of Sicily, surrounded by its equally stunning sisters, the Aeolian islands—Lipari, Alicudi, Filicudi, Salina, Panarea, and Vulcano—named after the king of winds, Aeolus, who gave Odysseus a gift of a bag of wind to speed his return home. But this mythical island is not as well known in the United States as Strombóli (with the accent on the second "o," instead of the first), baked pizza dough filled with cold cuts and cheese, an Italian American version of fast food. The placement of an accent marks and makes the difference: It is, among others, what differentiates Italian and Italian American last names. My own divided national and linguistic identity leads me to appreciate, even seek out, that difference.

The fate of the places, stories, and artifacts of Italian American memory seems to become oddly diminished, as they are turned into grotesque versions of themselves, incorporated into an American imaginary that often has little if any respect for the intricacies of the cultural inheritance of U.S. minorities. Thus, Santa Lucia is commonly associated with the soundtrack of those too-often-loaded-with-stereotypes movies and commercials featuring Italian American stick-figures, instead of the haunting iconography of the Sicilian patron saint of eyesight, who lived in the fourth century A.D. and is characteristically represented holding her eyeballs on a small platter; in the United States she is certainly not associated with the imposing cathedral devoted to her in her hometown of Syracuse, built on the surviving structure of the temple of Athena. And few in the United States are familiar with the folk tales she inspired and that survive in the repertoire of contemporary Italian American storyteller Gioia Timpanelli. When it comes to reading the Italian American experience, the range of popular references is frighteningly poor. Sharp differences mark the media's responses to Italian Americans and those contemporary Italians (some of whom have even taken up residence in the United States) who are considered celebrities here.

A few years ago, Gianni Versace's murder triggered an outpouring of media attention in the United States that glorified this icon of contemporary Italian fashion. The contrast with the disparaging depictions of ordinary Italian Americans is blatant.[2] The sorrowful tone of the reporters was a far cry from the treatment the same press bestows on Italian Americans, usually depicted as mobsters or as pizza and macaroni eaters: both types are considered semiliterate, inarticulate, loud, often violent, and always, *always,* preposterously passionate. These supposedly brainless buffoons make up, in the American imaginary, the core of one of the largest ethnic groups in the United States. If Italian icons such as Gianni Versace, Giorgio Armani, Gianfranco Ferrè, Sofia Loren, and Luciano Pavarotti stand for a contemporary, fashionable, artsy Italy, John Gotti and his acolytes personify an Italian America petrified in time and occupation. It is an old story, insidious and resilient, and its effects have been devastating.

The mafia exists, historically but also in the realm of its creative representations, as an almost exclusively male phenomenon, with Mama Corleone and Connie serving, in the 1970s, as the reductive models of Italian American femininity, and the Soprano women as its latest incarnations.[3] The lack of diverse critically and historically founded—but also creative— alternative accounts of the mafia has been destructive for Italian American culture. Italian Americans—particularly those who have very little to do with the mafia (most of them by far)—often decline to discuss organized crime, as if a willingness to make any kind of pronouncement on the subject could be interpreted as the acknowledgment of some form of collusion.[4] While the subject of this book is not forms of organized crime associated with Italian or Italian American groups, I am compelled to acknowledge this topic, albeit briefly, rather than letting it hang dangerously over my subject. I do believe that Italian Americans, and the United States in general, would benefit from a historically grounded and politically insightful conversation on this subject that would include the perspectives of Italian politicians such as Giovanni Falcone, but also Italian writers such as Leonardo Sciascia and Maria Rosa Cutrufelli, and artists such as Roberta Torre, who have examined the mafia with a depth, rigor, and political and artistic integrity that is lacking in the representations offered by Hollywood and U.S. popular culture and the media.

Even Spike Lee, with his seeming concern for speaking out against
racial and ethnic discrimination, has created Italian American characters
who are nothing if not trite stereotypes. In *Jungle Fever,* Annabella Sciorra
plays the part of a lower-working-class, poorly educated Italian American
from Bensonhurst, who takes cares of her abusive widowed father and her
uncouth brothers, and is beaten by the former for her sexual escapades
with an African American architect from the office in which she works as
a secretary.[5] This overly simplistic tale in which Italian Americans are fea-
tured as ignorant, racist, and violent, is one that audiences have been
trained to expect. The unfortunate alternative has been the emptily celebratory and overly sentimental mode of films such as *Moonstruck* and of
pasta and olive oil commercials.[6] Hollywood and mainstream American
media consistently have failed to provide rich and complex alternatives to
this culturally vapid range of plots.[7]

Writing of the devastating consequences of racism not only on African
Americans but also on the U.S. social fabric generally, Patricia J. Williams
calls attention to "the distance between the self, and the drama of one's
stereotype. Negotiating that distance is an ethical project," she argues, "of
creating a livable space between the poles of other people's imagination
and the nice calm center of oneself where dignity resides" (*Seeing* 73).
Stereotypes and ethnic bias against Italian Americans have made it impossible for Italian American women writers to achieve the kind of recognition that the quality of their work, its innovation, and its power should
grant. If stereotypes are damning, so is the lack of a critical examination of
stereotyping and of a recognition of the social and cultural circumstances
that produce the stereotypes themselves. It is only recently that filmmakers and writers have begun using stereotypes creatively and critically, em-
ploying a variety of strategies to break out of ideological "containment."[8]

I do not use the term Italian American as a rigid epithet but, rather, as a
problematic designation for a diverse group of authors who adopt and challenge ethnicity and envision it as a problematic and mutable terrain for creative and political inquiry, often not even addressing ethnicity, per se, in their
texts.[9] Carole Maso, Cris Mazza, Kim Addonizio, and Dalia Pagani, for example, hardly touch on their Italian ancestry in fictional texts inhabited by
a wide range of characters, from the junkie to the expatriate to the mountain wanderer; Nancy Savoca's films *Dogfight* and *The 24 Hour Woman* explore gender relations but could not be easily classified as Italian
American;[10] Maria Maggenti's film, *The Incredibly True Adventure of Two Girls
in Love,* foregrounds questions of class, race, gender, and sexuality but not
Italian American ethnicity; Louise DeSalvo's *Breathless: An Asthma Journal*
and Sandra M. Gilbert's *Wrongful Death: A Memoir* address issues of public
health rather than ethnic roots; Regina Barreca's *They Used to Call Me Snow*

White . . . But I Drifted contextualizes humor from a broad feminist perspective; Kym Ragusa's video *Passing* focuses on her African American grandmother's experience of racism while traveling in the South in the 1950s; Loryn Lipari's memoir "Cracked" deals with drug addiction and does not address ethnicity in an explicit way; in her art work, JoAnne Mattera creatively incorporates the cultural inheritance of her family of tailors and seamstresses; Lina Pallotta's photographs have Mexican women as their subject; Nancy Azara's sculptures evoke the cults of ancient goddesses; Liliana Fasanella's video *Women Forward, Mujeres Adelante* focuses on the women's movement in Chiapas, Mexico; Rachel Amodeo's film *What About Me?* is about the homeless in New York; Luisa Pretolani's video *Things I Take* focuses on the experience of Indian women immigrants to the United States; and the list grows and grows. Are these authors *not* Italian American? They certainly are, I would argue, and rather than scrutinizing their work through the myopic lens of a reductive ethnic-as-immigrant narrative, we should expand the interpretive range of that narrative to incorporate the diverse ways in which ethnicity and the immigrant experience are played out in the texts of contemporary Italian American women.

In this chapter, I will identify some of the writerly strategies employed by these authors, while also discussing vital concerns and themes some of these writers have begun to develop in defiance of stereotypes. In paying attention to their aesthetic choices as well as thematic and political concerns, we can far more thoroughly and accurately trace the outlines and intricacies of an Italian American female literature.

Nancy Savoca has astutely used humor, historically a radical weapon of oppressed groups, to work subversively against the very stereotypes her films—particularly *True Love* and *Household Saints*—present.[11] In addition, Savoca provocatively foregrounds the invisibility of working-class experience in films that combine the realist and the mythical (*Household Saints*) as two effective strategies adopted by minority authors.[12] The social and interpersonal interaction between apparently stick-figure characters produce the suggestion of a dynamic life that offers glimpses of their humanity and an awareness of the ways in which individuals can be straight-jacketed by stereotypes. The audience is thus led to question for whom these stereotypes work and what political purposes they serve.

In addition to filmmakers such as Nancy Savoca and Stanley Tucci, other Italian American authors have recognized the power of humor as a vehicle to help write "the self" in new, challenging ways. Some examples are: Christine Noschese, in her video *Mary Therese* (1977); Daniela Gioseffi, in her novel *The Great American Belly Dance* (1977); Louise DeSalvo, in her novel *Casting Off* (1987) and in her memoirs *Vertigo* (1996), *Breathless: An Asthma Journal* (1997), and *Adultery* (1999); Regina Barreca, in *They*

Used to Call Me Snow White . . . But I Drifted: Women's Strategic Use of Humor (1991); Marisa Labozzetta's *Stay with Me, Lella* (1999); Rita Ciresi in *Mother Rocket,* and *Sometimes I Dream in Italian* (2000), and, to a lesser extent, in *Blue Italian* (1996); Giose Rimanelli in *Benedetta in Guysterland* (1993); Maria Laurino in *Were You Always an Italian? Ancestors and Other Icons of Italian America* (2000); Penny Arcade in her theater performance *La Miseria* (1991); and Kim Addonizio in *The Box Called Pleasure* (2000). "Humor," writes Barreca, "doesn't dismiss a subject but rather often opens that subject up for discussion, especially when the subject is one that is not considered 'fit' for public discussion. Humor breaks taboos by allowing us to talk about those issues closest to us" (201).

This is the case with DeSalvo's cultural and personal exploration of adultery and illness. In *Adultery,* she offers a series of provocative reflections on the significance of adultery in American culture, drawing from literature, politics, and the personal account of her own husband's affair early in their marriage. She recounts considering, on discovering the affair, whether or not to commit suicide by ingesting the only stash of pills she kept home, a year's supply of birth control pills (the free sample her doctor husband had received from a pharmaceutical company):

> I figured, though, that the way my luck was running, I might grow some hair on my chest, but that I probably wouldn't die. . . . So I decided I would go back to graduate school, get a Ph.D., and become a college professor. (110)

DeSalvo's seemingly light-hearted tone does not dismiss the seriousness of adultery, in her life but also in contemporary American politics (the Clinton-Lewinsky scandal serendipitously exploded as she was completing the book); rather, it helps the author catch the reader off guard, as her narrative twists and turns in a tragic and comic roller-coaster ride, drawing the reader into a persuasive, demystifying analysis of the extramarital affair.[13]

DeSalvo employs a similar tactic in *Breathless,* in which the gravity of her own health condition, and her understanding of its many psychological and political ramifications, lead her to a series of hilarious reflections about her illness. Here, for example, is a list of the various ways in which she considers telling people of her asthma:

> I have asthma
> I am asthmatic.
> I am an asthmatic.
> I am a person with asthma.
> I suffer from asthma.
> I get asthma attacks.
> I have asthma attacks.
> I have asthmatic episodes. (73)

DeSalvo's self-parodic tone heightens rather than diminishes the serious-ness of her discussion of asthma and its political contexts, particularly in re-lation to environmental racism and classism.

In *The Politics of Postmodernism,* Linda Hutcheon argues that, "as a form of ironic representation, parody is doubly coded in political terms: it both legit-imizes and subverts that which it parodies" (101). Thus, she believes, with Dominick La Capra, that parody is a vehicle of political engagement as op-posed to a sign of political disengagement (Hutcheon 100). Hutcheon's the-ory, which can be used to "read" the works of, among others, Italian filmmaker Roberta Torre, whose mafia musical *Tano da morire* subverts the glorification of organized crime, offers important insights into the potentially subversive power of the use of stereotypes in literature and film, as opposed to their widespread bigoted use in those same media.[14] The kind of humor pursued by authors like Savoca and DeSalvo is particularly effective in chal-lenging preconceived notions about subjects such as the notorious mafia phe-nomenon, revitalized in Louisa Ermelino's *Joey Dee Gets Wise* (1991) and Giose Rimanelli's postmodern "liquid novel," *Benedetta in Guysterland.*[15]

If humor enables writers to address traditionally unspeakable subjects—such as illness, violence, family secrets—assimilation, another strategy central in the work of many Italian American women authors, operates both as a lit-erary device and as an important thematic component. Assimilation into a certain social reality—and the ethnic self-silencing that it entails—can lead to the suppression of a group's cultural identity.[16] Because of their problematic status as white ethnics, Italian Americans do not easily fit within the category of minority groups. Although they have not gained acceptance into the cul-tural mainstream as the members of northern European groups have—and al-though, according to one study,[17] they continue to represent a large portion of high school drop-outs in the New York area (where there happens to be one of the largest, if not the largest, concentration of Italian Americans in the United States)—many have made a seemingly successful, if not smooth, tran-sition into the white middle class.[18] Such a transition has required the sup-pression of working-class and ethnic origins, with devastating consequences in terms of self-perception as well as cultural and political identity.

If the social and cultural status of a group is linked to that group's capac-ity to produce a literature that will tell its stories and record its past, then the status of Italian American literature bespeaks the multilayered and contradic-tory history of the ethnic group that has produced it. In a key essay on eth-nicity and class published in 1993, the historian Rudolph Vecoli, a pioneer in the field of Italian American studies, rejects the classification of Italians as "white (or persons of non-color) sans ethnicity," and argues that such a clas-sification overlooks the "significance of class in human society" (296). Vecoli thus addresses the classic and historically tainted, as well as theoretically sim-plistic, dichotomy between European and non-European groups, a dichotomy that ignores historical, geographical, and social circumstances—such as those of emigration and assimilation of specific groups.[19]

Italians came to the United States from different regions, speaking different dialects, driven by dreams of success, and, for the most part, by extreme poverty. Many, however, also left for political reasons. And in the earlier part of the twentieth century, Italian immigrants were involved in labor activities in the United States, contributing significantly to the history of the American working class, including the women, whose radical activism also translated into the production of writings, for the most part in Italian, that appeared in newspapers and magazines, as Jennifer Guglielmo's groundbreaking work of recovery has illustrated.[20]

In an essay on Italian women garment workers and political organizing between the 1890s and the 1940s, Guglielmo notes that

> The social and cultural world that first and second generation Italian American women created to nurture dissident political activity has remained invisible to scholars of U.S. history. . . . The stereotype of Italian American women as docile workers, bound by patriarchal traditions, and confined to their homes to suffer in silence, continue to dominate narratives of U.S. history. ("Lavoratrici coscienti")[21]

It comes as no surprise, then, that such a radical history has been, until recently, ignored or suppressed in favor of images of Italian Americans as foolishly romantic—and thus politically disengaged—or closed-minded, clan-oriented conservatives. And if living examples of the above certainly exist, they do not cancel out the radical political and cultural commitment of other Italian Americans. While ethnicity does not define or generate politics, identity is often understood to lie at the intersection of mutable cultural constructs such as gender, ethnicity, race, nationality, class, sexual orientation, and disability.

Yet one must also not forget that the long-standing tradition of Italian American radicalism unfortunately has been replaced—particularly among some members of the upper middle class and, tragically, among members of some of the most disenfranchised Italian American communities—by an insidious concoction of economic and political conservatism, accompanied by a form of empty patriotism that has little to do with an appreciation for, or cultivation of, culture—be it Italian or Italian American. Then, there is the controversial history of Bensonhurst, subject to all sorts of sensationalized and vilified representations by media little willing to examine the multiple, complicated forces at work in episodes of racial violence. Maria Laurino and Marianna De Marco Torgovnick have written about Bensonhurst from perspectives that pay attention to such forces, while the filmmaker Kym Ragusa offers, in her video *fuori/outside,* yet another view, from her own uneasy, albeit rich and politically insightful, viewpoint as an Italian American *and* an African American.[22]

What must be emphasized is that Italian Americans do not constitute a homogenous group in any way—in terms of regional origin, social and economic status, or political perspective.While contemporary Italian American women authors cannot be regarded as a homogeneous group any more or less than the group at large can, it also is true that one can recognize certain trends, literary *and* political, in the writings that many of these authors have produced in the last two decades of the twentieth century.

Mocking and rejecting facile racial, ethnic, and class labels, in a poem entitled "Mutt Bitch," Rose Romano, one of the most polemical figures on the Italian American literary scene in the early 1990s, declares:"I'm not/oppressed enough. I/haven't been conquered/enough. I'm not Olive/enough. I may as well/be Italian" (*Vendetta* 38). Romano's cutting verse expresses indignation for the incapacity of American culture to recognize the position Italian Americans occupy in the ethnic panorama and its failure to pay attention to the intersection of ethnicity with race and class, an intersection that produces various forms and degrees of discrimination.[23] Ever since they began producing fictional and autobiographical accounts of life in their communities, Italian American women authors such as Romano have questioned stereotypical representations and created works that deconstruct the notion of a monolithic, quintessential Italian American identity. In the same poem, Romano offers an outrageous "inventory" of herself:"woman," "contessa," "contadina," "skilled blue collar worker," "poet," "dyke," "single working mother."And if "All this stuff doesn't add up to/just/one/person," she concludes, "Fuck it" (*Vendetta* 39). Through her juxtaposition of titles indicating radically different levels of social status, Romano rejects a simple definition of social identity and class. At the same time, she claims validation for her personhood, one that explodes the strict boundaries of identity implied by the notion of a singular self.

Romano is one of a handful of writers who have spoken out against the prevailing narratives on Italian Americans. Louise DeSalvo, Sandra M. Gilbert, Helen Barolini, Lucia Chiavola Birnbaum, Daniela Gioseffi, Tina De Rosa, Maria Mazziotti Gillan, Nancy Caronia, Rosette Capotorto, Mary Cappello, Mary Bucci Bush, and Maria Laurino are some of the writers who also have written eloquently on the subject of discrimination in works that have contributed to the creation of a richly diverse literature. A retrospective reading of the works produced by some of these and other authors will show how Italian American women writers have moved from working within isolated contexts to conceiving of their work as belonging to a fast-growing literature, a literature that articulates, *with an accent,* the many ways one can exist and write as an Italian American woman at the close of the twentieth century and the beginning of the twenty-first. The work that contemporary Italian American women writers and critics have produced in the recent past is retroactively making a literary history possible: Through their work, these women are sanctioning the literary existence of authors from a more distant past; in doing so, they are also validating their work as well as the work of other Italian American women in the future.

Excluded from both the literary mainstream and the margin, for years Italian Americans have occupied an ambivalent position, complicated by their connection with a humanistic tradition to which the majority of Italian immigrants seemingly had no direct access.[24] Nor could they count on an already established literary tradition from which to draw to articulate their issues and conflicts, or to legitimize their cultural identity.[25] Nevertheless, after some fifty years or so of solitary struggles, in the last decade of the twentieth century, Italian American literature has flourished and numerous authors have actively engaged in the work of cultural reclamation that also has characterized the literature of Latina, African American, Native American, and Asian American writers, to cite those ethnic groups whose literature has risen to some level of prominence in the latter part of the twentieth century. It took over a century for a fully-fledged literature to finally emerge, and when it did, it expressed, in story and in language, a past of often silenced struggles. While Italian American male authors have had to struggle to achieve recognition, the problem of invisibility has been far more extreme for their female counterparts, as it has indeed been for all women writers, especially those from minority groups.[26] From Frances Winwar, born Francesca Vinciguerra, who anglicized her name at her publisher's request, to Rita Ciresi, Agnes Rossi, Carole Maso, Cris Mazza, Lucia Perillo, and Kim Addonizio, contemporary writers who inscribe an internalized sense of cultural invisibility in texts that at times expose but most often suppress ethnic identity,[27] for almost three-quarters of a century Italian American women have waged a war against silence, a war fought through written words that articulate a diversity of experience and that only recently have begun to reach large and diverse audiences.

What Barolini called, in 1985, "The Historical and Social Context of Silence" (*The Dream Book* 3) lies at the core of the literary production of many Italian American women. Like other Italian American authors, Barolini has emphasized the contradictions of growing up Italian and American in a culture in which Italian immigrants and their descendants felt—and often continue to feel—like outsiders, which in turn has led to the devaluing of education, reading, and writing, and to various forms of self-hatred. In "Becoming a Literary Person Out of Context," Barolini writes that her aspiration to become a writer was "outlandish" in her Italian American milieu, and she highlights the link between writing and class, indicating that it was "primarily the uneducated masses who migrated to America" (266). Barolini attributes the difficulties Italian American have encountered in gaining access to literature to the absence of an inherited literary right. Yet, these "uneducated masses" carried with them oral traditions and evocative rituals and customs that, through storytelling and song, would be passed on to the new generations. Many contemporary Italian American women writers have been engaged in the recovery and creative transmutation, in contemporary contexts, of these stories, traditions, rituals, and customs.[28]

A number of Italian American writers, male and female, have lamented the lack of support within the family for fledgling writers, as does Rita Ciresi in the autobiographical essay "Paradise Below the Stairs": "Reading—which subsequently led to writing—has always been an act of rebellion for me, against Catholicism and other aspects of Italian American culture" (21). Similarly, writing of her own unlikely journey from the Italian American, working-class neighborhood of Hoboken, New Jersey, to becoming a literary critic, biographer, and writer, DeSalvo, too, expresses the long-lasting effects of culturally induced self-doubt: "Even as I write, though, I am wary of what I am writing. I come from a people who, even now, seriously distrust educated women" (*Vertigo* xvii).

While common to many male and female Italian American writers, the story of a family hostile to literature and culture is not shared by everyone. The storyteller and author Gioia Timpanelli recounts growing up in a house saturated with love of culture and literature, in which her Sicilian grandparents spoke to each other in Latin.[29] Other stories are told by more recent immigrants, who come from a more economically developed Italy, from a nation that in the last few decades of the twentieth century aggressively promoted literacy (with very few exceptions, universities are state-sponsored and thus affordable to most), and that has a number of university graduates so vast to warrant the use of the phrase "intellectual unemployment." The United States and Italy have allowed, since about a decade ago, dual citizenship: Being both Italian and American further complicates national identity. Such issues must be taken into account if one is to present a literary history that rejects easy generalization and elementary notions of ethnic identity and culture.

A deeply internalized and complicated self-deprecation—even, at times, self-hatred—that haunts the works of many Italian American writers, particularly those of working-class origin, stood for a long time in the way of the development of a literary tradition, even after literacy became available to the children of immigrants. This is evident in Marianna De Marco Torgovnick's *Crossing Ocean Parkway,* in which she examines the conflict-ridden relationship between the "I" and the "we" that epitomizes an American "tradition of active intellectual life which has no branch marked Italian American and female" (150). In an essay published in 1980 in *Attenzione,* "An Italian-American Woman Speaks Out," Tina De Rosa voiced her exasperation at the sense of displacement that she experienced as the "educated" granddaughter of Italian immigrants, "an educated lady who came from the streets of a ghetto, who didn't blink twice at fistfights, or horse shit—or *the* word" (38).[30] Dorothy Bryant explores an analogous sense of cultural disorientation through another "educated lady" from the ghetto, the protagonist of *Miss Giardino* (1978). In Anna Giardino, Bryant, as Janet Zandy explains in the afterword to the 1997 reprint of the novel, presented ethnicity not "as fixed identity or cultural celebration, but rather the forging of a class position out of migration, relocation, brutal work, and—for Anna's parents—the undelivered promise of America offering a better life" (166).

Other writers—DeSalvo and Mary Cappello, for example—are preoccupied with the effects of such "undelivered promise" on the immigrants but also on their sometimes wealthier descendants. Thus, in her essay "Digging Deep," DeSalvo recollects the overwhelming experience of finding herself, on her way to Colby College, where she was to give a series of lectures on Virginia Woolf, flying above the tracks of the Maine Central Railroad, the very place where her maternal grandfather worked at the beginning of the twentieth century. The dramatic contrast between her own economic condition and that of her ancestors provokes a reflection on the history of poverty and exploitation suffered by early Italian immigrants and her choice, as a working-class intellectual, to teach working-class students. Cappello, as she engages in a work of creative and intellectual recovery of the past lives of her ancestors, claims, in *Night Bloom,* that she must "produce warmth" with her words if she is "to coax" them "out of their shadows, because what is most apparent about the trouble they are in is that it chills them" (31). The exquisite metaphor employed by Cappello is all the more poignant because the chill she refers to is the literal cold that reigns in the house of the poor. Similarly, the title of DeSalvo's "Digging Deep" both alludes to her creative and intellectual project and literally describes her grandfather's manual labor.

For these authors, language is not an esoteric literary device but an instrument that roots literature in the life experiences of working-class people. The predicament described by DeSalvo and Cappello is not unique, of course, to Italian Americans, as Zandy shows in her groundbreaking anthologies of working-class writers, *Calling Home* and *Liberating Memory:* "Many of us are able to speak at all because we got lucky. . . . We were not killed or severely disabled on the job. We haven't given birth to children year after year and watched some of them die. We haven't been so ex-

hausted from work day after day that we were robbed of the right to develop our humanity" (*Liberating Memory* 8).

It is only when all these voices are heard, and when other voices reply,
that a literary tradition truly reflective of the diversity and complexity of
Italian American women's writing can be identified. Whether it is Tina De
Rosa speaking of her response to reading Carole Maso, toward whom she
feels a sense of literary kinship, or Louise DeSalvo writing about *Paper Fish*
and how it inspired her to memorialize her grandmother,[31] or Helen
Barolini gathering, in the early 1980s, the fiction, poetry, and nonfiction of
56 Italian American women with the combative purpose of demonstrating the existence of an Italian American female literary tradition, there is
no doubt that recognizing oneself as part of a literature contributes to an
author's sense of self-legitimization.

Writers from other cultural minorities have long known this. Joanna
Kadi argues that anthologies such as her *Food for Our Grandmothers: Writings by Arab-American and Arab-Canadian Feminists* (1994) "help record a
community's history and spirit. They are valuable maps in our struggle for
liberation, offering the hope and information, sustenance and analysis, ed-
ucation and challenges that we need so desperately" (Kadi xvii). The same
can be said of Gloria Anzaldúa and Cherríe Moraga's *This Bridge Called My
Back: Writings by Radical Women of Color* (1981), and Anzaldúa's *Making Face,
Making Soul: Haciendo Caras: Creative and Critical Perspectives by Feminists of
Color* (1990), *Making Waves: An Anthology of Writings by and about Asian
American Women* (1989), edited by Diane Yen-Mei Wing and Emilya
Cachapero, *Aiiieeeee! An Anthology of Asian American Writers* (1991), edited
by Frank Chin, Jeffrey Paul Chan, Lawson Fusao Inada, and Shawn Hsu
Wong, *Home Girls: A Black Feminist Anthology* (2000), edited by Barbara
Smith, Janet Zandy's anthologies of working-class writings (1990 and
1994), and, with specific regard to Italian Americans, the recent antholo-
gies, *Curaggia: Writing by Women of Italian Descent* (1998), edited by Nzula
Angelina Ciatu, Domenica DiLeo and Gabriella Micalef, and *Hey Paesan!
Writings by Lesbians and Gay Men of Italian Descent* (1999) edited by Gio-
vanna (Janet) Capone, Denise Nico Leto, and Tommi Avicolli Mecca.

Barolini well understood this function of literature in helping authorial
legitimization when, in reaction to the critical silence surrounding her
own novel *Umbertina* (1979), she collected the writings of authors as diverse as Sister Blandina Segale, Frances Winwar, Antonia Pola, Mary Gordon, Dorothy Bryant, Sandra Mortola Gilbert, Leslie Scalapino, Louise
DeSalvo, Anna Monardo, Daniela Gioseffi, Diane di Prima, Tina De Rosa,
Phyllis Capello, Maria Mazziotti Gillan, Gioia Timpanelli, and many others. She entitled the collection *The Dream Book* because she wished to connect her work to the past (by acknowledging a group of women

immigrants who used, collectively, a dream book to interpret their dreams) and to project it into a future—a dream to be realized. Lamenting the general exclusion of Italian American women authors from the literary canon, Barolini described *The Dream Book* as her "literary manifesto," through which she wanted to ensure that "some acknowledgment be given to Italian American women writers, that their names be part of the literary record, that redress be made for having neglected and overlooked a whole segment of writers" (Bonomo Ahearn 47).

The Dream Book opens with its editor's indictment of those forces, in academia and in the publishing world, that have thwarted the creation of a literary space for Italian American women. Barolini argues that it was not only the lack of publication that kept Italian American women writers in obscurity but also their blatant absence from libraries and curricula. She notes that, when they do finally get published, these writers "must confront an established cadre of criticism that seems totally devoid of the kind of insight that could relate to their work" (45).[32] This seems to be the case even for recent works, for example, Flavia Alaya's memoir *Under the Rose* (1999), attacked in a review by fellow Italian American writer Barbara Grizzuti Harrison on moral as well as aesthetic grounds. It is perhaps no coincidence that Agnes Rossi's autobiographical novel, *The Houseguest* (2000), which delves into the history of the Irish side of her family, was similarly criticized by another reviewer for a lack of conventional morality in portraying a father's abandonment of his daughter (Ferriss). Should Italian American women be held to strict moral standards? Does the retrograde concept of honor still apply to this ethnicity?[33]

One cannot begin to discuss the formation of a literature without taking into account the politics of the publishing world—of publication, distribution, and critical reception.[34] Whether it is the need to resort to a masculine pseudonym—as had been the case for a number of nineteenth-century European writers, from George Sand to the Brontë sisters—or abiding by the request of a publisher to anglicize a much too ethnic name—as was the case for Frances Winwar—or to assume the non-Italian last name of a husband—as was the experience for Sandra Mortola Gilbert, Dorothy Calvetti Bryant, and Marianna De Marco Torgovnick—the relationship that women writers have maintained with the publishing world, from the outset, has been fraught with difficulties that have further complicated their access to literature and other forms of creative public expression.

Legitimizing one's existence as an author through a critical narrative, in the face of the silence of the critics, has been a strategy employed by writers such as Helen Barolini and Daniela Gioseffi.[35] Several Italian American women writers have resorted to self-publishing to put forth their works. This has been the case with Dorothy Bryant's Ata Press, Rose Romano's malafemmina press, Nancy Caronia's Women's Words, Mary Russo Demetrick and Maria Famà's Hale Mary Press, Filomena Lo Curcio Stefanelli's Stromboli American Heritage Society, Camille Cusumano's Legas, Sadie Penzato's Penzato Enterprises, and Giovanna (Janet) Capone, Denise Nico Leto, and Tommi Avicolli Mecca's Three Guineas Press. Each of these publishing enterprises testifies not only to the determination of Italian American women to assert their presence in the publishing arena, but also to a long-standing tradition of cultural activism, for a number of these writers also have used their presses to publish other writers, Italian American and not. "I believe that part of women's work is to record stories," writes Nancy Caronia in "Setting the Table," the introduction to her multivoiced, self-published women's anthology *the girlSpeak journals:* "To record means publication. It is our responsibility to publish the stories we write" (x).

That so many works by Italian American women writers remain, to this day, unpublished or out of print is a practical matter: If books are not available, they are not read, taught, or written about. Many authors have remained unknown, often publishing nothing beyond a first book. This issue resonates forcefully in the literature itself, often leading many writers to silencing—whether consciously or not—that accent that signals one's ethnic origins; claiming an Italian American identity did not seem, for a long time, advantageous to many of those with literary aspirations. Such self-silencing in turn leads to the mistaken assumption on the part of many scholars and readers that there are no Italian American women writers. And the vicious cycle continues until there is, finally, a break, a crack that triggers change: a voice from the past (Tina De Rosa's *Paper Fish*), a defiant contemporary voice (Louise DeSalvo's *Vertigo*), a chorus, diverse and controversial (the women of *Curaggia*)—and things begin to happen.

As a conversation is finally developing among Italian American women, we can begin to conceive an imaginary and a language to articulate the complexity and variety of our experiences. The critic Julia Lisella writes of her hunger "to locate an Italian-American poetic response to the Depression" (Giunta and Patti 115). Yet, this is not a search devoid of contradictions for, as Lisella points out, in tracing the story of Rosa Marinoni, a forgotten poet of the 1930s, she has begun to "question this essentializing gesture to identify particular ethnic voices for the sake of collecting such voices."[36] It is imperative that we continue to reexamine the changing place and significance of ethnicity in literary as well as sociopolitical terms.

If one thinks of the importance of Zora Neale Hurston for Alice Walker and other African American women writers, one can begin to appreciate both the courage necessary to write in isolation and the necessity to undertake a systematic work of recovery and reprint.[37] Walker claims that she realized her "need" for Zora Neale Hurston even before she knew

Hurston's work "existed" (*In Search* 83). Indeed, Hurston's relatively recent canonization has consolidated the sense of a tradition for African American women authors, as Maxine Hong Kingston has done for Asian American women writers or Leslie Silko for Native American women. During the 1990s, not only did many Italian American women writers publish their first works, but a number of books also were reprinted, for example, Tina De Rosa's *Paper Fish* (The Feminist Press 1996), Diana Cavallo's *A Bridge of Leaves* (Guernica 1997), Dorothy Bryant's *Miss Giardino, Confessions of Madame Psyche,* and *Ella Price's Journal* (The Feminist Press 1997), Helen Barolini's *Umbertina* (The Feminist Press 1999), *Rosa,* the transcription of Rosa Cassettari's oral narrative by Marie Hall Ets (The University of Wisconsin Press 1999), Josephine Gattuso Hendin's *The Right Thing To Do* (The Feminist Press 1999), Barolini's *Chiaroscuro: Essays of Identity* (The University of Wisconsin Press 1999), and *The Dream Book* (Syracuse University Press 2000). This unprecedented project of recovery of out-of-print works by Italian American women writers has contributed to the process of legitimization of these writers, but also to the actual making of this literary tradition.

Before Barolini and De Rosa, other women authors had written about Italian America between the 1940s and the 1960s in narratives filtered through the lens of their gender: Mari Tomasi in *Deep Grow the Roots* (1940) and *Like Lesser Gods* (1949), Julia Savarese in *The Weak and the Strong* (1952), Antonia Pola in *Who Can Buy the Stars?* (1957), Diana Cavallo in *A Bridge of Leaves* (1961), Octavia Capuzzi Waldo in *A Cup of the Sun* (1961), and Marion Benasutti in *No Steady Job for Papa* (1966). All of these works, with the exception of *Like Lesser Gods* and *A Bridge of Leaves,* are currently out of print. That many of these authors told in their books of the struggle for survival of Italian American workers—be it in the city, as in *The Weak and the Strong,* or in the granite mines of Vermont, as in Tomasi's fiction—suggests the extent to which the combination of working-class consciousness and ethnicity in literature has not been palatable to mainstream U.S. publishing.

That many Italian American women authors never published a second book (if they ever published a first one) signals the fragility of a tradition that lacked a community that could sustain and nurture its growth. This is the case, for example, of Antonia Pola, whose novel *Who Can Buy the Stars?,* although steeped in the traditions of the immigrant plot and the romance plot, challenges both conventional narratives in original ways, by casting as its protagonist Marietta, an Italian immigrant who becomes a shrewd entrepreneur (much like Barolini's Umbertina). Pola's character yet pursues romantic dreams that are doomed to be shattered: class and gender politics shape a book by an author about whom we have little if any knowledge.[38] Other important books by Italian American women published between the 1970s and the 1990s are waiting for receptive publishers: Daniela Gioseffi's *The Great American Belly Dance* (1977), Anna Monardo's *The Courtyard of Dreams* (1993), Louise DeSalvo's *Casting Off* (1987) and *Vertigo* (1996), and Susan Caperna Lloyds's *No Pictures in My Grave* (1992). Earlier writers, including Sister Blandina Segale and Rosa Marinoni, are beginning to receive some critical attention, which might in turn lead, one hopes, to the reissuing of their forgotten works.[39] A reprint of selected works by Frances Winwar also represents another vital step in this necessary work of the construction and reconstruction of Italian American women's literature.

But even more writers still lay hidden in the obscurity that only systematic research will lift. Mary Jo Bona's recently published study surveys Italian American women's fiction from 1945 to the present and thus reasserts, through the analysis of a number of novels—including out-of-print novels that Barolini had excerpted in *The Dream Book*—the existence of a 50-year-old tradition of Italian American women's novelists.[40] The historian Jennifer Guglielmo has uncovered the writings of several Italian immigrants who were actively involved in labor organization and anarchist groups and who wrote, as well as published, in Italian language newspapers in the earlier part of the twentieth century. Guglielmo's valorous work of historical and literary discovery defies skewed representations of Italian women immigrants as a homogeneous group made up solely of housebound, subservient, illiterate women. Martino Marazzi's research on Italian immigrants in the United States who were writing in Italian between the end of the nineteenth century and the first decades of the twentieth has uncovered the writings of several women, for example, Caterina Maria Avella, Dora Colonna, and Clara Vacirca. Ellen Nerenberg's essay on the filmmaker Ida Lupino and Julia Lisella's work on the poet Rosa Marinoni give a sense of some other exciting avenues that current critics are pursuing, avenues that both question and expand—through the lens of the politics of gender—the notion of Italian American identity and culture. Gioia Timpanelli's invaluable work on folk tales, particularly on those from Sicily and Southern Italy, which she revitalizes in her spellbinding storytelling, constitutes yet another facet of a large project of cultural excavation, affirmation, and reinvention of cultural origins and identity undertaken by Italian American women authors.

When Helen Barolini undertook the task of searching for Italian American women writers as well as legitimizing her own position as a writer, she was asking that the existence of a literature of which she was part be recognized. Some of the contributors to this historical anthology have leapt beyond its bounds and done much to strengthen the position of Italian

American writers in American and world literature. Maria Mazziotti Gillan, who in 1985, the year of publication of *The Dream Book,* had published only a chapbook, has since published several books of poems and co-edited, with her daughter, the literary critic Jennifer Gillan, three important anthologies of multicultural literature, *Unsettling America* (1994), *Identity Lessons* (1999), and *Growing Up Ethnic in America* (2000), that include Italian American writers in the multicultural spectrum: Diane di Prima, Justin Vitiello, Lawrence Ferlinghetti, Grace Cavalieri, Jennifer Lagier, Vittoria repetto, Rachel Guido DeVries, and Maria Famà, among others. Through these and many other cultural initiatives, Gillan has importantly contributed to the recognition of Italian American authors. Sandra M. Gilbert, at the time already known for her groundbreaking work as a feminist critic, has published, since the mid-1980s, several books of poetry, a book-length memoir, and essays that deal with Italian American identity. Gilbert has established herself not only as a key figure in American poetry, but also, more openly, and even more aggressively, one might say, as an Italian American author. DeSalvo, already an acclaimed literary critic and biographer, has become, since the publication of her memoir *Vertigo* in 1996—and three other works of memoir/nonfiction in the following years—one of the most outspoken and politically minded contemporary Italian American women authors.

If it is true that in the 1990s Italian American women have written with more openness about their culture, it is also true that many publishing houses—and their marketing departments, as a result of the increasing recognition of a demand for these books—have not stayed away from titles, blurbs, and descriptions that highlight the ethnic background of the authors in question. The subtitle of Gioia Timpanelli's *Sometimes the Soul* is *Two Novellas of Sicily.* Jay Parini's blurb on the back cover of Cappello's *Night Bloom* reads: "Her book both modifies and extends the tradition of Italian-American literature in important ways." The subtitle of Marianna De Marco Torgovnick's *Crossing Ocean Parkway* is *Readings by an Italian American Daughter.* The University of Wisconsin Press describes Barolini's *Chiaroscuro: Essays of Identity* as a book "of crucial importance in establishing the contours of an Italian American tradition." In the year 2000, titles such as *Were You Always an Italian? Ancestors and Other Icons of Italian America* (Norton) by Maria Laurino, *Mattanza: Love and Death in the Sea of Sicily* (Perseus) by Theresa Maggio, *Black Madonna* (Simon & Schuster) by Louisa Ermelino, and *Looking for Mary* (Viking) by Beverly D'Onofrio evidence not only less reluctance on the part of publishers to issue books by Italian American authors, but also, and more important, an interest in Italian American stories and voices that defy conventional wisdom and challenge the devastating anti-intellectual stigma that has for too long crippled the growth of Italian American women's literature and arts.[41] Sympathetic publishers and shrewd editors have recognized and promoted these important changes: Jean Casella and Florence Howe at The Feminist Press, Rosemary Ahearn at Penguin, Alane Salierno Mason at Norton, and Deborah Chassman at Beacon, are among those who have contributed to making the 1990s a decade of emergence—but also rebirth—for Italian American women's literature.

During this decade, a new generation of authors—Agnes Rossi, Donna Masini, Mary Cappello, Kim Addonizio, Cris Mazza, Carole Maso, Rita Ciresi, Mary Saracino, Anne Marie Macari, Renée Manfredi, Kathryn Nocerino, Maria Laurino, Anne Calcagno, Susanne Antonetta, Dorothy Barresi, Dalia Pagani, Mary Caponegro, Theresa Maggio, Louisa Ermelino, Adria Bernardi, Beverly D'Onofrio—have joined authors who published in the 1980s—some even earlier—such as Sandra M. Gilbert, Tina De Rosa, Louise DeSalvo, Helen Barolini, Daniela Gioseffi, Diane di Prima, Dorothy Bryant, and Maria Mazziotti Gillan—in questioning and redefining, in unexpected and probing ways, traditional representations of Italian American women. Many of these authors have shown little interest in the predictable immigrant plot. In their works, being Italian American matters, but in new, often humorously self-deprecating ways. While many of these writers began working with little, if any, knowledge of a literary enclave in which they might claim membership, and even less of the tradition out of which, in theory, their own work emerged, it is certainly important, at this point in Italian American literary history, to examine the work of contemporary writers in relationship to their predecessors. The cultural conversation that Italian American women authors have engaged in at the close of the twentieth century problematizes historical boundaries. The question of a literary lineage in which to place oneself is fraught with conflicts and contradictions for Italian American women. These authors have engaged in a search for sources and ancestors but not necessarily models in a journey that cuts across geographical, national, linguistic, and historical boundaries.

Critics have recently begun to turn to the more remote past, to open the doors of archives, and to discuss the possibility of creating such archives.[42] But while it is of vital importance to turn back and consider what lays undiscovered, in this book I wish to focus on the present, and the very recent past, to pay tribute to the work of living writers who are making it possible to uncover the work of those who came before them, for it is today's feminist awareness and growing sense of literature as a collective effort that nurtures the discovery of the works of the past.

※ ※ ※

What this poor unfortunate man spoke, was so indistinct, and in such broken accents.

—*Jonathan Swift*

※ ※ ※

Chapter 2

Immigrant Literary Identities

> . . . *This is the city*
> *of grandparents, immigrants, arrivals,*
> *where I've come too late with my name.*
>
> —*Kim Addonizio, "Generations"*

> . . . *in search of my mother's garden, I found my own.*
>
> —*Alice Walker,* In Search of Our Mother's Gardens

The scarcity of published writings by Italian American women in 1979, the year of publication of Helen Barolini's *Umbertina*, places this novel in a complicated position with regard to issues of literary tradition, genre, and authorship. One of the first Italian American novels to explore the immigrant experience from a female perspective, *Umbertina* was published at a time in which, with the exception of a few devotees, Italian American authors in general, and Italian American women writers in particular, were virtual unknowns to the academic as well as lay readership. If examined in conjunction with Barolini's *The Dream Book: An Anthology of Writings by Italian American Women* (1985) and some of the essays reprinted in *Chiaroscuro: Essays of Identity* (1998), *Umbertina*'s literary history sheds light on the challenges and conflicts involved in becoming an Italian American woman writer in the late 1970s and early 1980s.

"I've never seen the name of an Italian woman on a book cover before, so I had to buy your book" ("Becoming a Literary Person" 271). This excerpt from a letter written by a reader of *Umbertina* to Helen Barolini underscores the absence of Italian American literary women, both as authors as well as fictional characters. In "Becoming a Literary Person Out of Context," an autobiographical essay published in 1986, Barolini maintains that for an Italian American woman to become a writer means "to be self-birthed, without models, without inner validation" (263). She goes on to assert that, in the absence of books that would tell her who she was, she would "write those that did" ("Becoming a Literary Person" 265). This claim is helpful when one tries to define what kind of relationship Barolini has fashioned with American literary history as a reader, a translator, a literary critic/historian, and, ultimately, as an author.[1]

Helen Barolini's journey began in 1925 in Syracuse, New York, where she was born into a second-generation middle-class Italian American family: Her mother's parents had come from Calabria; her father's parents were from Sicily. After attending Wells College and Syracuse University, where she majored in English, Barolini traveled to Italy in 1948. There she met and married the Venetian poet Antonio Barolini, with whom she had three daughters. The family lived both in Italy and the United States. Following her husband's death, Barolini moved back to the United States permanently in 1973. Her bicultural experience shapes her first novel as well as the work she has produced in the last three decades: a book of poems she coauthored with her husband entitled *Duet* (1966), *Umbertina* (1979), *The Dream Book* (1985), the novel *Love in the Middle Ages* (1986), *Festa: Recipes and Recollections of Italian Holidays* (1988), a book on the fifteenth-century Italian scholar-publisher Aldus Manutius entitled *Aldus and His Dream Book* (1991), *Chiaroscuro: Essays of Identity* (1997), a radio drama on Margaret Fuller, essays, stories, poetry, and translations from Italian and English published in periodicals and anthologies.

In her effort at self-valorization, Barolini compresses the undertakings of the literary critic, the essayist/autobiographer, and the cultural historian. The cultural historian emerges, for example, in the Introduction to *The Dream Book* and in essays such as "Becoming a Literary Person Out of Context" and "*Umbertina* and the Universe." In *The Dream Book,* Barolini makes evident her concern not just with her emergence as a writer but with fashioning a literary tradition that would valorize her work. Although she does not include her own work in this anthology meant to legitimize Italian American women writers, by assuming the posture of the literary historian, Barolini accomplishes her own self-legitimization as an Italian American women writer and adds another feature to the authorial persona that she has been painstakingly constructing. In "Becoming a Literary Person Out of Context," the initial use of the third-person pronoun, chosen to refer to the Italian American woman writer as a figure in the making, is replaced by the first-person pronoun, an "I" voice that, though "besieged by doubts" ("Becoming a Literary Person" 263), chooses to tell a story— *her* story—and demands to be heard. Recounting her own emergence as an author while living in Italy in the 1950s and 1960s, Barolini calls attention to the diversity of her literary production, which is linked to her struggle toward authorial self-creation:

> I wrote about the Italian poet, Lucio Piccolo, and about *Giacomo Joyce;* I wrote stories about displaced Americans in Rome and this time the displaced people were Anglo-Americans, not Italian Americans. ("Becoming a Literary Person" 269)

Fascinated by displacement, Barolini vicariously examines the implications of existing on the margins. Translating *Giacomo Joyce*—the persona of James Joyce, writer and Irish exile—Barolini could begin to explore life lived between different worlds and languages. The stories that she wrote, as she herself notes, were about the displacement of Anglo-American expatriates, not Italian American immigrants. Not quite ready to delve into the class issues that need to be part of any investigation of immigrant history, Barolini traveled the more glamorous territory of expatriation and exile, focusing on the ventures of those who can afford lofty ideals and are not plagued by the urgency of economic survival.

Later, Barolini's interest in displacement leads her to title her anthology of Italian American women writers after a "dream book" that Italian immigrants in Telluride, Colorado, consulted and shared:

> On a front page, in awkward uphill handwriting was the Italian notation of one Angela Zecchini who, with many misspellings and an incorrect date for the inception of World War I, recorded this terse account of her life.(*The Dream Book* xii–xiii)[2]

These writings, produced within a private space, deprived of access to the realm of "public" discourse, and seemingly addressing a self-selected, "private" audience, typify the cultural heritage of marginalized groups. They represent, like other writings produced within the domestic space, women's early literary production, and thus formulate notions of art, authorship, and audience not traditionally sanctioned as "literary."

In *The Languages of Patriarchy,* Jane Marcus questions traditional methods of literary history and claims that

> in the case of Virginia Woolf, very often the drafts and the unpublished versions seem "truer" texts. . . . Perhaps it would be true of all women writers. Perhaps it would be true of all oppressed people's writings, of blacks and lesbians, that the published text is *not* the most interesting book. (xii)

Marcus contends that different forms of censorship are at play in texts that camouflage the identity of the authorial voice. As a result, constructing the literary history of "oppressed people" necessitates a search for unofficial texts and sources. Over the last few decades—thanks, for the most part, to feminist and working-class scholars—we have learned to draw on unpublished, often unfinished, autobiographies, letters, memoirs, and also nontraditionally "literary" texts, such as cookbooks—and "dream books"—in order to reconstruct a marginal author's history. As it happens, it is within the parameters of this history that we can better comprehend Barolini's own literary career as well as the development of Italian American women's literature in general.

In 1969, Barolini began to work on a story inspired by her own maternal great-grandmother, although she did not work actively on what would become *Umbertina* until 1976, when she received a National Endowment for the Arts fellowship. Originally, Barolini conceived the project as two separate parts—a novel that included the "Umbertina" and "Tina" sections, and a novel entitled *The Last Abstraction,* containing the core of Marguerite's story. Following her publisher's suggestion, she merged the two novels into one, organized around three sections—one devoted to each woman—with a prologue from Marguerite's perspective. The result is a genre that is a mélange of social, familial, and personal histories.

In preparation for the book, Barolini conducted archival research on the Great Migration of the nineteenth century as well as an oral history project with Italian American women. She integrated the results of this research into her fictional account of family history (Interview with Bonetti). Through her choice of women's names as titles for the novel and for each of its three sections, the author underscores the need for Italian American women's stories and languages to be heard. Indeed, there is an almost calculated defiance in the choice of a name such as Umbertina, so unquestionably Italian—the kind of Italian that resists domestication by English pronunciation.

The history of Helen Barolini's first novel is sadly typical among works relegated to the category of "women's novels." At the same time, *Umbertina*'s history epitomizes the predicament of Italian American literature, which has been relegated to a similarly marginal status—particularly women's literature.[3] Undoubtedly, *Umbertina* suffered an unfortunate history due to misguided positioning by its publishers. First published in 1979, *Umbertina* has been reprinted three times, but only the third reprint, in 1999, gained the novel significant attention by critics and readers.[4] But even more essentially, it suffered at the hands of a literary establishment unable to conceive of a novel dealing with women's experience in general, and Italian American experience more particularly, as worthy of serious critical attention or a lasting place in American letters.[5]

Women writers from various ethnic groups—such as Toni Morrison, Alice Walker, Maxine Hong Kingston, Amy Tan, Cristina Garcia, Joanna Kadi, and Leslie Marmon Silko—have shown that the telling of multigenerational stories helps the uprooted, displaced, and oppressed, to position themselves with dignity and a sense of cultural belonging and legitimacy. The first novel by an Italian American woman to explore, in depth, intergenerational female relationships in an Italian immigrant family, *Umbertina* is set in both Italy and the United States, and explores life between different cultures and countries. Written in the 1970s, a time of ethnic revival as well as feminist awakening, *Umbertina* is concerned with ethnicity and gender, but it also tells the stories of those who recognize themselves as the poor and disenfranchised, as well as those of their economically more fortunate descendants. The novel shows that their conflicts are related to class as well as geographical mobility. *Umbertina* foregrounds the cultural and social implications of uprooting by situating its characters' lives against clearly outlined historical events: the unification of Italy, the Great Migration out of Southern Italy, the two world wars, the Great Depression, and the economic boom in postwar Italy. The novel privileges the stories of the quotidian struggles of immigrants that have been traditionally left out of official historical narratives and, most significantly, foregrounds the voices and perspectives of women.[6]

   Umbertina obliquely calls attention to the history of its creation as an ethnic female *bildungsroman* and *kunstlerroman*.[7] By telling the story of Marguerite's lifelong and unsuccessful search for her artistic talent, and the story of her daughter, Tina, including Tina's encounter with her great-grandmother Umbertina's bedspread and her decision to become a scholar of Italian literature, Barolini examines the routes leading to, or thwarting, the creation of an Italian American woman author. In an essay published in 1990, Anthony Tamburri, one of the first critics to write about *Umbertina*, argued that Barolini's novel departs from traditional representations of Italian American femininity: "The novelty of *Umbertina* lies precisely in Barolini's treatment of women as individuals, who, at one point or another in their lives, become aware of their true plight—the duality of gender and ethnic oppression—and . . . attempt to free themselves from the prison-house of patriarchy" ("Gender/Ethnic" 42–3). Tamburri highlights a predicament common to many Italian American women authors, who must negotiate their authorial voice and power out of a cultural experience that has oftentimes historically worked to repress that voice and that power.

   By opening the novel with Marguerite's need to remember her maternal grandmother,[8] the author articulates the central concern of *Umbertina* to pull together the threads of the stories of women immigrants and weave them into a narrative tapestry, one that will "last forever," like Umbertina's "coperta matrimoniale" (44), the bedspread she takes to America in the bundle of the family's few belongings. The novel unfolds chronologically and thus follows a traditional narrative trajectory, unlike De Rosa's pseudo-modernist experiment in *Paper Fish;* at the same time the reader must consider the three stories as the interconnecting pieces of one design, even though the Marguerite section occasionally disrupts the linear narrative. While the placement of this section in the middle of the book clearly places the novel in the tradition of social realist fiction—the linear narrative focuses on development, influence, and continuity between characters and events—Marguerite is also the figure who unravels the repressed and unspoken immigrant narrative and thus contributes in fundamental ways to the creation of the novel's overall structure and story.

With an abrupt chronological—and geographical—shift, clearly announced in the dates of Umbertina's birth and death—(1860–1940)—beneath the title of the first section, Barolini transports the reader from the fashionable world of bourgeois Rome and Florence of the early 1970s, which constitutes the setting of the prologue, to the rough peasant life in the small village of Castagna, in the Sila mountains, in Calabria, circa 1876, of the "Umbertina" section. Skipping the second generation (Carla), which Barolini seems to have found less interesting because more comfortably assimilated and Americanized (Greenberg 95), Barolini devotes the following sections to the third and fourth generations.

Umbertina's determination to leave a world of oppression, deprivation, and hopelessness leads her to accept willingly and without hesitation marriage to a much older husband, Serafino Longobardi, whom she does not love romantically but grows to care for as the trusted companion of her life. The illiterate Umbertina starts out by selling freshly made *panini* and pizza to her husband's coworkers, keeping "the men's orders in her mind" thanks to her "great powers of concentration and a memory that took the place of reading and writing" (94). Encouraged by the profits her hard work reaps, she opens "a space—a *spaccio,* as it was known in the old country" (95) in a storefront. After leasing a piece of farmland to grow her own provisions and purchasing a horse and wagon, Umbertina shrewdly transforms the *spaccio* into the Longobardi *groceria,* and later creates an importing business, a steamship agency, and a bank. Managing to build an economic security that protects her family even from the devastation of the Depression, Barolini's character follows a rags-to-riches journey, fulfilling—to all appearances, at least—the American Dream. Yet, after Serafino's death, she has to face, with bitterness and disappointment, the fact that her husband is the one commemorated for the family's economic success, while she is only mentioned as his "good companion" (128), not even a partner in the enterprise of Serafino Longobardi & Sons, which she single-handedly masterminded. The anxiety over women's lack of recognition thus emerges as an underlying theme of Barolini's work.[9]

Umbertina, the goat girl of the Calabrian mountains, views her bedspread as the embodiment of her struggle to extricate herself from the entrapment in a world in which people are resigned to poverty. It is significant that the bedspread has not been passed down to Umbertina by a mother or grand-mother, who never could have afforded such a luxurious item. Instead, it has been especially made for and sold to Umbertina by Nelda, the housekeeper of Don Antonio, the village priest. A huge class gap exists between Um-bertina's family and Don Antonio, who enjoys living conditions as foreign to people of Umbertina's class as the mythical New World to which she sails with her husband and their three children. Umbertina purchases the bed-spread as a beautiful object she has desired but also—and especially—as the sign of her belief in the possibility for better living conditions. For the same reason, she asks Nelda for rosemary from Don Antonio's garden, not in the traditional belief, voiced by Nelda, that women are strong in the houses in which the herb thrives but, rather, aspiring to use rosemary as a condiment for the meat that she hopes she and her family will one day be able to af-ford. Yet, the tradition voiced by Nelda will be passed down to, and remem-bered by, her great-granddaughter as she plants rosemary in the garden of her future husband's family home. Nelda's words strike a chord in Umbertina, who the people in Castagna say had "character right from the womb," and is destined to be "the man of her family" (23). This prediction of Umbertina's strength and power, however, also clearly exposes the patriarchal politics that haunt and hinder the full development of Barolini's women characters on both sides of the Atlantic.

Wary of nostalgia, and paying attention to the historical circumstances out of which the stories of her characters are born, Barolini recognizes the social inequities that motivate her characters' emigration: Perhaps one of the book's greatest merits is that it refuses to see anything romantic about poverty. Yet, Umbertina's longing—which surfaces in the form of scattered memories of the homeland towards the end of her life—paradoxically re-sists even the recognition of, and consequent resentment for, the fact that Italy has not been generous to her or to the millions of its children forced to leave by devastating poverty, malnutrition, and disease.[10]

The apparent promise held by the Italian nationalists who had fought to expel foreign rulers and unify Italy came to nothing for impoverished South-ern Italians like the peasants of Castagna. While Umbertina is considered an Italian when she comes to the United States, she is one of many Southern Italian immigrants who had been baffled by the Italian citizenship thrust on them in 1860, the year in which Umbertina was born. In any case, her new status as a citizen would have made little difference in her life, for the newly born Italian government failed to deliver "the poor of the earth" from their oppression and suffering. It is no wonder that Umbertina and many of her fellow immigrants feel no allegiance to the new Italian nation, with the ex-ception of the socialist Domenico Saccà, a character who testifies to the fact that people left Italy for political as well as economic reasons.[11] Even if

Umbertina shows little understanding of Italian politics, she is well aware that the lives of people like her are considered trivial and of little value. With the intuition of one who has experienced exploitation, Umbertina does not fail to recognize the similarity between the oppression suffered in the archaic Calabrian countryside, with its feudal social structure, and that of the modern New World, with its aggressive capitalism, perpetrated by the American *padroni* (masters), both "living and getting rich off the labor of others by taking from them part of what they worked for" (59).

Umbertina's bedspread, then, stands as a figure for this multigenerational story, for the structure in which it is embedded, and for the intersecting senses of longing and loss that both drive and thwart the lives of the characters. The artifact of Southern Italian American culture functions as a catalyst for the conflicts and ambiguities underscoring Umbertina's journey as well as the journey of her female descendants. In these journeys, home becomes increasingly undefined and unreachable, expressing the perennial displacement experienced by those who leave their homeland. Umbertina is forced to sell the bedspread that adorned the gloomy tenement room and showered it with a wealth of light and beauty from which the inhabitants of slums are normally excluded. As Anna Giordani, the social worker who sells it on her behalf, sharply reminds her, Umbertina must make the unavoidable choice of the poor, who cannot afford luxuries. It is not until near the end of the third and final section of the novel that we learn that Giordani herself had purchased the bedspread and later donated it to the Museum of Immigration. As the story of the bedspread suggests, while Umbertina's practical wisdom and economic astuteness enable her to prevail over the grim, fatal life of the tenement in New York, to move her entire family upstate, and to build her small economic empire, her pragmatism does not protect her or her female descendants from experiencing a chronic sense of cultural loss and displacement.

The bedspread resurfaces several times throughout the novel, primarily in Umbertina's reminiscences, but also in the preoccupation with the search for patterns, forms through which the characters try to frame and understand their actions. The material texture of Umbertina's bedspread, juxtaposed to Marguerite's self-destructive pursuit of the "last abstraction: the Love Affair" (258), marks the intergenerational and class differences among these women's lives as they search for, define, question, relinquish, and rethink their place in the world. In the year 1900, the 40-year-old Umbertina feels as if "a design, like the rich intricacy of the long-lost matrimonial spread, was complete. Her life's pattern was outlined and it was satisfying and beautiful to her" (102). Yet the pattern would disintegrate. Toward the end of her life, alone in her own family, Umbertina feels as if she is holding something that no longer exists because she has no one to whom to describe the intricate patterns of her story: "She had won, but who could she tell the story to?" (145). Clearly, for Barolini, telling one's story as well as one's ancestors' stories generates the impetus for writing *Umbertina* as well as putting together *The Dream Book*. Her shrewd understanding of the links between the silence surrounding her work and that of other Italian American women led her to embark on a project that would legitimize her voice as it legitimized the voices of other writers.

Umbertina's concern with providing the finest linen for her daughters' dowries captures her desire to endow her daughters with what, she believes, they need in order to achieve a comfortable life, but also her own entrapment within, and collusion with, a world that she has always understood and accepted as a man's world. Purchased with the money earned by Umbertina's labor, the linen that fills her daughters' hope chests fails to capture the significance and power of the lost bedspread. Wanting to teach her daughters about tradition, continuity, and survival, Umbertina recounts to them the story of the long-lost bedspread and reminds them that they must pass on to their daughters the linen she has given them. Having provided, through her resourcefulness, economic security for her family, but incapable of truly questioning the structures of patriarchy, Umbertina leaves everything else to her sons. Without financial and emotional strength, her daughters grow to be passive and acquiescent women who quickly surrender—if they ever develop—any ambition besides that of pursuing middle-class consumerism and fulfilling the traditional feminine role in marriage. Carla, Umbertina's daughter, is committed to "marriage, motherhood, and American-style domesticity," like many daughters of immigrants (Gabaccia, *From the Other Side* 120). And while Carla's daughter, Marguerite, and especially Marguerite's daughters, will manage to break away from this insidious, debilitating tradition, Marguerite cannot extricate herself from the entanglement of her own maternal heritage.

It is fitting that the lost bedspread appears to the dying Umbertina at the close of the section devoted to her:

> a sudden brightening came to her eyes as in a vision of light she saw the lost *coperta* of her matrimonial bed with all the intensity of its colors and bright twining of leaves and flowers and archaic designs in its patterns. "Ah!" she gasped at its beauty. (146)

The bedspread represents that "beauty" Umbertina had erroneously believed she could do without, but comes to crave at the end of her life's long journey. With seven living children, 27 grandchildren, having survived the death of three of her children and of her own husband, and having built a small economic empire, the almost 80-year-old Umbertina has come a long way from the Sila mountains where, barefoot, she herded her goats. Yet, on her deathbed, as the vision of the bedspread appears before her, she craves water from the spring of Castagna. There is no simplistic nostalgia about Umbertina's last craving, only the recognition of the deep scars that the trauma of poverty, geographical uprooting, and cultural and linguistic isolation and disconnection leave on immigrants.

If the first-generation immigrant craves, on her death bed, water from the spring of her village—an impossible homecoming—then for the following generations things become even more complicated. While the dying Umbertina's request for water from the spring in Castagna is not understood by her children, the feeling it expresses is passed on as an unspoken desire, a profound loss for which they have no words, no language. It is this sense of loss that cannot be adequately articulated into one language—English or Italian—that is at the heart of the creativity of so many Italian American women authors. *Umbertina* makes a powerful argument for the importance of cultural memory, without which one is doomed to experience an all-consuming displacement, as Marguerite does. "Poetry is not a luxury" (*Sister Outsider* 37), Audre Lorde has said, and the bedspread is a source of poetry—the poetry of the quotidian—and a figure for the hope that Umbertina cultivates like the plants she stubbornly grows in cans in the New York tenements. Umbertina's desire to keep the bedspread is rooted in the recognition of how the understanding of one's place in the world has a connection to where one comes from. As Mary Saracino puts it, "Where you are born has far less to do with who you are than whom you are born to" ("Sunday Rounds" 53). One's parents and ancestors serve as the connecting link to the place of one's origins. This is the lesson that Umbertina's descendants need to heed in order to understand the sense of chaos and powerlessness they so often experience. While such crisis is already evident in the lives of Umbertina and her daughters, it reaches its moment of highest tension with Marguerite, whose unwanted pregnancy and premature death suggest both the desire to create and the powerlessness to do so.

Marguerite's daughter, named after her great-grandmother, will begin to gather the scattered and broken threads of the stories of the women who came before her. At the same time, one must remember that the search begins with Marguerite, "an American transplant filled with fears and desires" (5), who likens herself to the Sicilian Persephone (16), the mythical maiden doomed to live between the luminous fields of Demeter and the shadowy kingdom of Hades. In the most well-known version of the myth, Persephone never becomes a woman, except as an embodiment of her mother.[12] Yet, she is the Queen of the Underworld—where Marguerite and Tina need to travel to pose yet unasked questions to Umbertina—and an adept traveler who learns to move between two radically different worlds. That is the skill that Marguerite lacks but tries to teach to her daughter.[13] The importance of the novel's intergenerational focus becomes evident as the life stories of the four generations reveal the interwoven design of familial and cultural history.

In her study, *Travelers, Immigrants, Inmates: Essays in Estrangement,* Frances Bartkowoski argues that "the phenomena of displacement and dislocation are inscribed in the history of the ethnic writer as the one who brings old tales to light, tales of world and family politics—politics of language, location, and identity" (85). Marguerite's unfulfilled search for artistic vocation emerges obliquely in her "restlessness" (181), her moving from place to place, and her inability—or unwillingness—to construct a permanent domestic space. Marguerite's houses are characterized by "this visible edge of impermanence, of things falling apart" (304). "I don't care where I live" (305), she used to say, but her daughter knows that "she did care. She cared enormously for place, and each one they came to and claimed, she worked at to make beautiful. And then moved on" (305). Her daughter Tina thinks how "curious" was her mother's attachment to "drawers and boxes and to the idea of having everything contained, in place; she who tore it all apart so readily, ready to move on, sending them winging like birds of passage on the flights of her inquietude" (306). Marguerite and Tina combine elements of the traveler, "dislocated by choice," and the immigrant, "dislocated by force"—in terms of Bartkowski's distinction (85).

After hearing of Marguerite's death, her mother wonders: "What did she want? What was she looking for? . . . All that moving around. All those homes she set up and then tore down. And moving those girls around so they had no normal life at all. . . . What was it all for? To punish us?" (286). Carla unself-consciously understands the painful gap between Marguerite's generation and her own, for it is Carla's silence and disconnection from her origins that underlie Marguerite's own sense of displacement. In *Umbertina,* Barolini fulfills the task of the ethnic writer as described by Bartkowski, because the interconnected stories of her four women characters reveal the intricacies of the immigrant inheritance.[14]

Marguerite's care for "place" articulates a search that is simultaneously geographical, cultural, intellectual, creative, and emotional, a search for a space "in the world" (182). Her tragic death captures Barolini's perception of the fragility of her position as an aspiring artist and emblematizes Italian American women authors' self-doubt and anxiety of authorship.[15] Similarly repressed in her artistic aspirations, Lily Bart, the protagonist of Edith Wharton's *The House of Mirth,* dwells on her unrealized aspiration to redecorate her aunt's drawing room, which would provide an ineffectual outlet for her creative talent.[16] While, like Lily, Marguerite is displaced, class and ethnicity underscore her displacement and mark the difference between the tragic heroine of Wharton's novel and one of the characters of the triad created by Barolini. Robert Viscusi has compared *Umbertina* to Henry James's *The*

Portrait of a Lady. Like James, Barolini lived in Rome as an expatriate, although obviously her ties to Italy are dramatically different. James was not haunted by the kind of class anxiety that justifiably haunts Barolini's characters, and James's orientalizing of the Italians is oddly paralleled by Marguerite's chronic sense of insecurity and displacement in relationship to the Italian bourgeoisie she now belongs to by marriage. Marguerite's ambivalent feelings toward the Roman bourgeoisie, in relationship to which she remains, ultimately, an outsider, bespeaks the complications of class identity and identification for writers of working-class background.

Marguerite's simultaneous attachment to and disregard for the domestic space articulates her conflicted relationship to a motherland that is never clearly identified, for Marguerite has an awareness of her Italian American identity at a time in which neither her family nor her native U.S. culture recognize it. A foreigner both in the United States and in Italy, Marguerite, like Barolini, learns Italian as a young adult, with neither the encouragement nor the approval of her family. In her essay "How I Learned to Speak Italian," included in *Chiaroscuro,* Barolini recalls that nothing in her immediate familial and cultural circle encouraged the interest in Italian language and culture that led her to seek Mr. de Mascoli, the teacher who guided her apprenticeship in the language of her origins, and later to travel to Italy on her own. Her own second-generation Italian American father described Italian as a useless language that would not help her "get further" (*Chiaroscuro* 31), like Spanish or Portuguese might. Yet, Italian was the only language spoken by her "monumental" grandmother (*Chiaroscuro* 28), who presided, much like Umbertina, over the annual family gathering. In Barolini's memory, this grandmother was mute, because she did not speak to her and the other grandchildren. For Barolini, Italian language and silence are thus intertwined with memories of her grandmother, even as she found, in this strangely familiar foreignness, the source of her creativity.

In what can be read as an oblique exploration of her own conflicted relationship to the American and Italian literary worlds, Barolini portrays Marguerite as muse, translator, spectator, and amateur artist striving to articulate a speech for which she finds no accurate words. Devoting her intellectual attention to her husband's professional and personal success (Tamburri, "Gender/Ethnic" 33)—she is his translator as well as his wife/caregiver—saps Marguerite's energies, though it does not represent the main obstacle to her artistic affirmation. Marguerite's displacement may figuratively reflect Barolini's own complicated position on the Italian literary scene, in which her husband, the poet Antonio Barolini, much like Marguerite's husband, felt perfectly comfortable.

That in Italy Barolini became a translator further complicates her relationship to language and, more specifically, to the ways in which Italian and

English shaped her sense of identity as a writer. Translating, moving back and forth between English and Italian, enabled this author to realize a deep-seated desire of many third-generation immigrants: to understand and speak the language of their ancestors. Unlike her grandmother, she became an adept linguistic and geographical traveler. Writing of a time when she had "receded into the shadowy recesses of translation and camouflaged . . . [her] voice with another's," Barolini recalls the fragility of her "hold" on her work and the fear of being pushed "into the morass of self-doubt" (*Chiaroscuro* 47–8). "For the ethnic," Bartkowski notes, "translation . . . will always be translation's into the master's language from the native/mother tongue" (86). Barolini's trajectory as an "ethnic" writer reflects the negotiation between languages and identities: The notion of a "native/mother tongue" is obviously rather complicated for third-generation ethnic writers such as Barolini, for whom the ancestors' mother tongue is simultaneously native and foreign, while "the master's language" has already become "native/mother tongue." Yet, the descendant of immigrants will always maintain in her language the cultural substratum of her ancestors' language.

By attempting to express the cultural dislocation from which both she and her mother suffer, Tina is able to save herself. Once she becomes pregnant, she decides to have an abortion and sells her mother's jewels to pay for it. Tina thus both discards Marguerite's inheritance and is empowered by it to move on without the encumbrance of an unwanted child. What separates Tina and Marguerite is a sharply different sense of class and national identity. Underneath the mask of the expatriate, Marguerite hides the face of the immigrant, and the sense of shame that the latter identity carries.[17] Tina, born and raised in a comfortable middle-class milieu, feels at greater ease with her dual cultural and national allegiance, although she, too, must come to terms with the Italian American identity she at first repudiates, as testified to by her revulsion at the idea of being somehow related to the Italian American tourists she meets in Rome. Tina's ambivalent attitude toward Italian culture—and specifically Southern Italian culture—also becomes apparent while she is traveling in Calabria, where she feels torn between being a tourist and being a traveler. The image of Tina as a "tourist" of her "heritage," a phrase Barolini uses to refer to herself in "Becoming a Literary Person Out of Context" (270), aptly describes Tina's first encounter with Calabria as well as that early stage of Italian American women writers' encounters with Italy. Tina, like these writers, must learn to reconnect with and reclaim her cultural heritage.[18]

Tina's search for her great-grandmother represents a quest for a poetical subject, although such a quest does not actualize into a life choice. By taking a Ph.D. in Italian, Tina begins to write *about* Italian authors, but she has not yet learned a language for her own particular cultural identity. The bedspread, an embodiment of the ethnic subject matter, remains in many ways inaccessible, displayed in the museum, not revivified in poetical language. Yet, if Tina does not become a poet, Barolini does become a writer.

Barolini's narrative of female development argues for the importance of ties between women and highlights the ways in which they can be sources of strength and resourcefulness for themselves and their daughters. But it also demonstrates the ways in which mothers can deplete their daughters' strength. While a feminist consciousness does not fully develop in Umbertina or in her granddaughter Marguerite, it begins to emerge in her great-granddaughters Tina and Weezy, although gender and class consciousness do not necessarily intersect in these characters. Although not a central figure, Weezy occupies an important place in the larger social fabric of the novel because of her more explicitly articulated feminist politics, which must be viewed in the context of the Italian feminist movement in the 1970s.[19] With her less conflicted national and ethnic identification, Weezy offers an important contrast to Tina, and thus highlights the different ways in which the threads of family and cultural inheritance can interweave in a family and, on a larger scale, in diverse communities.

Barolini's novel examines the interconnections between class and race that are central to the debate on the construction of whiteness. Referring to the racism suffered by the early Italian immigrants but also to their subsequent assimilation into "whiteness," *Umbertina* foregrounds the ties between race and class oppression, for example, when Marguerite reacts to her parents' racism by thinking that her "folks can't remember when their own folks were Negroes" (204).[20] In this way, *Umbertina* sheds light on class transition and the process of cultural assimilation that made it possible for the so-called white-ethnics, such as the Jews, the Irish, and the Italians to become "white" (Roediger 182).[21]

Umbertina belongs to the literary tradition that has produced such works as Dorothy Allison's *Bastard Out of Carolina*, Louise DeSalvo's *Vertigo*, Joanna Kadi's *Thinking Class*, Kim Chernin's *In My Mother's House*, and Sandra Cisneros's *The House on Mango Street*. These memoirs and autobiographical novels are, like *Umbertina*, overtly gendered narratives, informed by women's experiences. They are also, like *Umbertina*, shaped by working-class identity, concerned with working-class history, and thus constantly merge personal and cultural memory.[22] Working-class literature is, in general, less interested in the self-contained story of the solitary individual struggling against, and overcoming, adversity than in the sometimes subtle ways in which the stories of individuals are interwoven with the stories of communities and their cultures. Working-class writers such as Dorothy Allison, Tina De Rosa, Esmeralda Santiago, and Janet Zandy have written of the high price, in terms of cultural loss, that upward mobility requires of working-class people. "My parents, like most working-class parents, wanted a better life for their children," Zandy writes, "but, they did not wish a better life that extracted as its cost familial and historic memory" (*Liberating Memory* 1). *Umbertina* tells of the pains of class migration: It is a story of simultaneous acquisition and loss, pride and shame, mobility and paralysis, victory and defeat—a story that, while specifically Italian American, cuts across the ethnic divide in its concern with gender and class.

While *Umbertina* troubles the idea of romantic love, it does reach its closure within the parameters of traditional romantic narratives: Tina's marriage to Jason Jowers, her fiancée of Anglo-Saxon ancestry with a family house in Cape Cod, suggests that class and ethnic anxiety and a desire for assimilation have not lost their hold. Umbertina is utterly unsentimental—"She had no time in her life for romance or daydreams" (54)—but it is through the more problematic character of Marguerite that Barolini offers a critique of romantic love as that which women turn to when, incapacitated by familial, cultural, and societal circumstances, they search communities and relationships in which they can thrive. While Marguerite's marriage to the Italian poet Alberto Morosini is on the verge of dissolution, she vainly looks for solace in analysis, with a male psychoanalyst, exploring fantasies that never fully develop into tangible creative work. Finally, she becomes involved in a self-destructive affair with a narcissistic writer. In the tradition of *kunstlerromans* such as Kate Chopin's *The Awakening* and Charlotte Perkins Gillman's *The Yellow Wallpaper,* the Marguerite section of *Umbertina* explores the circumstances that hamper female creativity, in a middle-class context, when it is directed outside domestic bounds.[23] What underscores the narrative of the Marguerite section is the tension rooted in the lack of a discourse to articulate the consequences and implications of class transition.[24]

Cultural and social roots are devastatingly complicated for Marguerite, and her journey comes to a tragic halt. The reference to Marguerite as Persephone proves ominous for her, but auspicious for her daughter Tina, who will travel south, to Calabria—once the site of Greek cults, including a cult of Persephone—to search for her great-grandmother. Tina will come to understand that she must travel the geography of memory to map out a story that incorporates the past but must also not allow that past to stifle her.

While Barolini unravels the significance of the bedspread in the lives of the Longobardi women, it is not until the end of the book that she fully exposes the vital interconnections between personal memory and working-class history. The lost *coperta* reappears on Ellis Island as an immigrant artifact preserved in the Museum of Immigration. Tina's brief encounter with her great-grandmother's bedspread points not to resolution but to the possibilities open to working-class immigrant women, whose silenced voices can be heard only through the voices of their descendants:

> Tina stood entranced at the spectacle of a magnificent bright-hued glori-
> ously woven bedspread that bore the motifs of Calabrian design. . . . as she
> neared the glass of the case and read the card, it said: "Origin: Calabria.
> Owner unknown. Acquired by Anna Giordani in 1886." (407)

The silence that surrounds the "unknown" owner articulates the ways in
which the history of the poor is written: The exhibit honors the name of
the social worker, Anna Giordani, who never managed to "like" the immigrants, "but did her duty unflinchingly, as a kind of penance and discipline
for her soul" (66), and who clearly kept Umbertina's exquisite bedspread
for herself.

In what can be described as a blatant case of cultural robbery, the immigrants themselves are relegated to the silent condition of namelessness.
Tina cannot possibly recognize the bedspread as her great-grandmother's
since the story has not been passed down to her. While she regrets that
Umbertina did not bring a bedspread such as the one displayed at the Museum with her—"Then it would have been passed down to me, maybe"
(407)—an almost miraculous encounter with her dead ancestor occurs, as
the "woven designs of grapes and tendrils and fig leaves and flowers and
spreading acanthus" speak to her "of Italy and the past and keeping it all
together for the future" (408).

Tina's quest for selfhood, a quest that is intertwined with the understanding of one's cultural identity, remains, on the surface, only partially
successful since she herself does not become a writer, a storyteller who can
keep it "all together for the future." Tina instead becomes a Dante scholar,
thus connecting to an Italian tradition that is dramatically distant from the
story of the bedspread. Tina's journey, however, traces the development of
Italian American female identity. Tina, who at first rejects and is even
ashamed of the appellation "Italian American," comes to embrace "Italian-
American identity" (359) during her trip to Calabria. And while she feels
that Umbertina had "eluded her" (393), once back in the United States the
trip "flashes through her mind like glinting pieces of mosaic that she tried
to shape into a whole, a pattern of serious design" (392).[25]

At the close of the novel, as Tina pieces together the "fragments" (392)
of the memory of the trip to Calabria, Barolini ties two important strands
of Italian culture: Persephone, who is first referred to in the prologue, and
Dante, who appears prominently in the final section. Tina, who at times
sees herself as an incarnation of her Persephone-like mother, must learn to
trace her mother's steps in a symbolical descent into hell. This is a hell from
which she comes back, like Persephone, but also like Dante, the pilgrim of
the *Commedia* who returns from his journey to tell the story. In Barolini's
novel, Dante does not embody a literary tradition foreign to Italian Amer-

ican immigrants but, rather, represents one gate through which an Italian American woman can begin to explore and incorporate Italian mythologies and histories into Italian American cultural life.

Traveling, which for Tina at first signifies "a reprieve from all the choices . . . belonging nowhere and having no past, no future" (347), becomes the means by which she finds her place, a sense of multiple cultural "belonging," a connection to her past, and a key to her future. Through Tina we come to a better understanding of Marguerite's story, a story that her daughter can learn from the diaries she has left.

Like many Italian American women writers, Marguerite is the first college-educated woman in her family.[26] In this century, access to literacy has made it possible for Italian American women to write their stories and the stories of their female ancestors, those who first crossed the borders and first made the development of Italian American culture possible. *Umbertina* identifies some of the ways in which those who cross borders—geographical, cultural, social, chronological, ethnic—can learn to use their mutable identities as the rich soil for their creative and socially transformative work.

Umbertina's status as an Italian American classic is undisputed. To make a case for *Umbertina* as an American classic, however, is to make a case for Italian American literature—and particularly Italian American women's literature—as American literature.[27] Barolini's investment in being recognized as an "American" author—as opposed to an Italian American author—is one she shares with authors such as Tina De Rosa. Such an investment in the notion of "American" identity as articulated in the claim "I am an American writer" can be linked to the silence and isolation suffered by these authors in the early stages of Italian American women's literary emergence (1970s and 1980s—and, of course, earlier). It also seems to be born out of the resulting craving for widespread legitimacy and mainstream recognition.

Umbertina, Marguerite, and Tina constitute for Italian American women what Zora Neale Hurston's Janie Woods, Alice Walker's Celie, and Toni Morrison's Sethe have become for African American women, and Sandra Cisneros's Esperanza Cordero for Chicana women: not cut-out figures or models to emulate, but complicated characters who capture the conflicts, failings, and achievements of their cultures. As Italian American literature takes its place in the American canon, Italian American women writers' stories will continue to speak to larger constituencies of readers, for these stories are rooted in the cultural history of America, a history that Italian American women writers recount, challenge, and transform.

❈❈❈   ❈❈❈   ❈❈❈

Accent is a kind of chanting; all men have accent of their own, though they only notice that of others.

—*Thomas Carlyle*

❈❈❈   ❈❈❈   ❈❈❈

Chapter 3

"A Song From the Ghetto"

One day I'll own my own house, but I won't forget who I am or where I came from. Passing bums will ask, Can I come in? I'll offer them the attic, ask them to stay, because I know how it is to be without a house.

—*Sandra Cisneros,* The House on Mango Street

I have come home to something remembered and longed for though never seen before. . . . I am returning to a place I have never seen, to a childhood I have never known. What kind of memory is this? Do my Italian genes hold something like this scene, or does something Mama has said about her childhood in Italy match this?

—*Dorothy Calvetti Bryant,* Miss Giardino

A third-generation Italian American girl, her beautiful sister whose brain has been damaged, probably by encephalitis, her Italian American father and Lithuanian American mother, her paternal grandmother, an immigrant working-class neighborhood, primarily Italian, in Chicago, and all of these immersed in a mixture of history and fable, elegy and song, presented in exquisite prose that has the rhythms of poetry: This is what makes up the narrative world of what was for long an obscure novel by an Italian American unknown.

Few critics had ever heard of *Paper Fish* prior to its reprint in 1996. Only 1,000 copies were published in 1980 by the Wine Press, a now-defunct publishing house, and the book went out of print within months of its publication. Those few first readers, however, were struck by the novel's beauty and well understood its place in the emerging Italian American canon.[1] Jerre Mangione, the author of *Mount Allegro* and coauthor of

La Storia: Five Centuries of Italian American Experience, praised De Rosa's extraordinary literary debut as

> a first novel that breaks through the barriers of conventional fiction to achieve a dazzling union of narrative and poetry. . . . Hers is a delightfully fresh voice, filled with ancient wisdom which is new and probing, miraculously translating the most ineffable nuances of human existence in a language that is consistently beautiful and vital.[2]

Fred Gardaphé, who reviewed the book for the *American Italian Historical Association Newsletter,* argues that it was "Through writers like De Rosa, [that he] . . . learned that Italian-American culture was multi-dimensional and could never be simply categorized" ("Breaking and Entering" 12). Helen Barolini reprinted an excerpt from the novel in *The Dream Book,* while Mary Jo Bona analyzed its interweaving of issues of gender, ethnicity, and illness in an article published in *MELUS* in 1987. These scattered efforts, however, did not prevent *Paper Fish* and its author from disappearing into the shadows, as they did for 15 years. Neither could the fact that a handful of Italian American academics, myself included, occasionally taught the book by photocopying it. De facto, *Paper Fish* remained excluded from the annals of literary history.

Like other women's works published long after their composition, such as H.D.'s *HERmione* (1981), or that received late recognition through a reprint, such as Zora Neale Hurston's *Their Eyes Were Watching God* (1937), *Paper Fish*—like *Umbertina*—sheds light, through its publishing history, on the development of Italian American—and especially Italian American women's—literature.[3] It is, of course, ironic that debates about the ways in which the canon is impacted by gender, class, ethnicity, and race were burgeoning in the 1980s. While such debates certainly helped many books receive due attention, they did not, in any way, aid *Paper Fish.* The plight of De Rosa's now widely recognized Italian American classic is not unlike that of myriad books in a publishing world in which books have become disposable, ephemeral commodities. At the same time, the silence surrounding this book and, to a lesser extent, *Umbertina* in the early 1980s, must be examined in light of the fact that this was the same silence that shrouded virtually all books by Italian American women in that period. In truth, as I have argued earlier, for a long time these writers were not regarded by publishers as being of any interest to the academic and lay readership. Therefore, neither the authors nor their supporters had the credibility necessary to propel these books into an already arduous publishing and literary world. As is the case for Barolini's *Umbertina,* by paying attention to the history of *Paper Fish,* we can better understand the cultural forces that influence and shape the construction of Italian American women's literary history.[4]

Tina De Rosa was born in Chicago in the 1940s. Her maternal grand-parents were Lithuanian, but as a child De Rosa identified the maternal figure primarily with her paternal grandmother Della, whom she describes as the most influential person in her life. Born in Boscoreale, near Naples, probably in 1888, Della came to America when she was about 17 years old. Della died in 1963, when the author was 19 years old, leaving a void that De Rosa would try to fill through her writing. Her writing thus became a "home" in which the author could take refuge, a site of soothing memories in which even sorrow could become the source of a magical storytelling.

Until age 17 De Rosa lived with her family in the Taylor Street area on the West Side of Chicago. One of the few people in her neighborhood to go to college, she attended Mundelein College of Loyola, a Catholic school in Chicago. After working at various jobs and gaining some writing experience, she earned a Master's degree in English from the University of Illinois, where she studied under Michael Anania, who first read early drafts of *Paper Fish* and suggested that she cut and revise the manuscript. In 1977, Jim Ramholz of the Wine Press became interested in publishing the book.[5] In 1978, while trying to finish *Paper Fish,* holding two jobs, and struggling through economic hardship, De Rosa received a writer's residency from the Ragdale Foundation that enabled her to complete the book (Gardaphé, "Interview" 23). *Paper Fish* was thus written in stages: begun around the year 1975, it was completed in 1979, although the author put it away for over a year in between. To this day, *Paper Fish* remains De Rosa's only published book, with the exception of a biography of Bishop Scalabrini (1987), of mostly documentary value.

Although not central to the story, De Rosa's Lithuanian background emerges in fragments that shed light on the experience of cross-cultural identity, one that De Rosa also examines when she focuses on the predicament of third-generation Italian Americans like herself. Cross-cultural marriages such as that of De Rosa's parents, although not frequent among first- and second-generation immigrants, did occur in ethnically diverse Chicago. Different ethnic groups coexisted in the same neighborhood, as was the case on the West Side that, although regarded as primarily Italian by outsiders, included many ethnicities, such as "Irish, German, Mexican, Greek, Jewish, Polish, and Czech . . . among others" (Pacyga in Holli 606).[6] While growing up, and as she started writing, De Rosa defined her ethnicity as primarily Italian American, as testified to by her essay "An Italian-American Woman Speaks Out" (1980), and by her other published works, namely *Paper Fish,* the biography of Bishop Scalabrini mentioned earlier, a few essays she wrote in the 1980s, and a few poems published in 1996.[7]

De Rosa's silence about her Lithuanian ancestry depends not only on the central role played by her paternal grandmother keeping Italian culture alive in the family through her storytelling and her food rituals but also on the seeming reluctance of her maternal relatives to discuss their origins and the reasons for the family's emigration. In *Paper Fish,* unlike Grandma Doria, Carmolina's maternal grandmother remains a distant, unresponsive figure, one that thus expresses another layer of loss—the loss of history, of connection.

⁕⁕⁕   ⁕⁕⁕   ⁕⁕⁕

While it does privilege Italian culture, *Paper Fish* gives voice to the disorienting experience of a different kind of cultural dislocation, one that Sarah, Carmolina's mother, especially suffers from as she negotiates being an immigrant in the United States and being Lithuanian in an Italian American family. Once married, Sarah must leave behind "the small white houses of the south side of the city," with their "picket fences between the yards" (49), and move into the little coldwater flat on Taylor Street: "the guttural and minced Lithuanian in the throats of her family, her neighbors, was stilled" (49), while the "sweet" and "musical" Italian spoken by her husband's family "fell" "meaningless" to her ears (50). The contrast between the musicality of Italian and its meaninglessness to Sarah is especially poignant as it prompts a reflection on the multiple ways in which immigrants could view themselves and be viewed as foreigners in the United States. The pregnant Sarah's question as to "which language the baby would speak" (59), as she listens to the Italian language that remains incomprehensible to her, reminds us of the old Umbertina and the silence she is immersed in as her family members chatter among themselves in English. If Barolini incorporates, particularly through the characters of Marguerite and Tina, the repercussions of such a heritage of silence, De Rosa explores one more level of complexity as she dramatizes the interaction of two cultures within one family, while the English-speaking world appears as a pressing cultural force ready to wipe out such linguistic and cultural layers. At the same time, De Rosa, like Barolini, writes in English, a native language for both authors that nevertheless symbolically bears the traces of an Italian accent.

De Rosa's mother's family lore, which fascinated the young Tina De Rosa, remained vague, even mysterious. By contrast, she was exposed in her daily life to the Italian language and customs, both in her household and in the Little Italy in which she grew up. *Paper Fish* dramatizes the author's relationship to her dual heritage. Grandma Doria is the wise and benevolent, although also authoritarian, matriarch to whom everyone, including her "foreign" daughter-in-law Sarah, turns for guidance. De Rosa, who never traveled to Italy, reconstructs her ancestors' homeland through Grandma Doria as a phantasmal presence instead of the geographically and historically realistic portrayal of *Umbertina.* De Rosa's Italy is ethereal, even mythical. An emotional and cultural bridge with Italy, Grandma Doria constructs for Carmolina the story of a distant, fantastic "land that got lost across the sea, the land that was hidden on the other side of the world" (15). Through Grandma Doria's words, De Rosa captures the ancestral loss that haunts the characters in *Paper Fish,* branching out and reaching into the texture of their present lives.

In "My Father's Lesson," an autobiographical essay published in 1986, De Rosa reflects on the expectations that her family, especially her father, had about her future, and describes her philosophy of "work," a philosophy that is in harmony with her aesthetic vision. Unable to relish the work opportunities that her new status as the first educated member of her family who could now aspire to middle-class status and comfort, De Rosa turned to literature:

> For a long time, I believed my father's promise, and wondered why I kept changing jobs. I suppose that I was seeking perfect employment, the kind my father always said I would have. But I was also discovering that I am a writer, and that, for me, an indestructible distinction exists between my employment and my work. Always, I would be wanting to run home. (15)

Through the distinction she draws between "employment" and "work," De Rosa both rejects the paternal "promise" of success and pays tribute to the father who unwittingly taught her "how to be a writer" (15). Like her father, who "spent his whole life doing the sad and hidden work of society, then came home and hid his face in the little world" of his family, De Rosa finds refuge in her books, her "silent children" ("My Father's Lesson" 15).

De Rosa's aesthetics of work, rooted in her father's experience, can be usefully compared to Pietro di Donato's representations of the laborer's relationship to a demonized "Job," a powerful force that "loomed up, damp, shivery gray," "waiting" to swallow the workers with its "giant members" (8). In *Christ in Concrete* (1939), di Donato simultaneously illustrates the dehumanization of the workers—"The men were transformed into single, silent beasts" (9)—and infuses labor with the humanity of the workers themselves. Like other Italian American and working-class authors, di Donato "elevates the common worker to the status of a deity . . . as a way of dignifying the plight of the worker" (Gardaphé, "Continuity" 5). This longing for dignity and legitimacy is pervasive in De Rosa's literary work as well, although di Donato's is more clearly and unambiguously politicized and relies on a narrative more rooted in the tradition of the realist novel than *Paper Fish.*[8]

In "An Italian-American Woman Speaks Out" (1980), De Rosa articulates her political concerns as she ponders the devastating impact of capi-

talist ethics on members of small immigrant communities, on neighborhoods swallowed whole by economic greed:

> What happens to a person who is raised in this environment full of color,
> loud music, loud voices, and genuine crying at funerals and then finds her-
> self in a world where the highest emotional charge comes from the falling
> of the Dow Jones average, or yet another rise in the price of gold? (38)

To fight alienation, De Rosa imagines a utopian, uncontaminated space, a
"home" where *her* "work" becomes possible, where she can put to good
use her father's "lesson." In a self-conscious manner, De Rosa acknowledges the worker's necessity to sell her labor, and yet manages to conceive
of a space that is, as much as possible, sheltered from the ill effects of capitalist exploitation. De Rosa thus envisions her "home" as separate from the
alienating world of the modern laborer.

In addition to "My Father's Lesson" and "An Italian-American Woman
Speaks Out," published during the 1980s, De Rosa turns to the essay in a
meditation on the homeless, in which she indirectly continues to explore
her own concern with a home that is both real and imaginary, rooted in
history and myth. In "Silent Night, Homeless Night," De Rosa returns to
the theme of home, which takes on a poignant quality as she looks at the
faces of the homeless who flock to the Chicago shelter where she volun-
teers. De Rosa's essays document the writer's journey toward authorial
self-fashioning, one that often requires negotiation between Italy and
America, between the myth of the tightly knit family and the myth of the
individual, between the American dream and the dream of Italy.[9] The myth
of a self-contained and self-sufficient individual distinctive of Anglo-
American culture is at odds with the central place of the family in the pre-
capitalist, predominantly agrarian culture of late-nineteenth-century
Southern Italy. It was this Italian cultural heritage, caught in a time capsule
and transformed into myth, that the immigrants passed on to new generations of Italian Americans, who were thus torn between the familial culture and capitalist America, with its ruthless individualism.[10] From this
perspective, *Paper Fish* develops De Rosa's autobiographical narrative in a
fictional text that, while documenting the disappearance of the world of
the author's childhood, testifies to the struggle between conflicting cultural
values sustained by Italian immigrant women as they engaged in the
process of becoming cultural as well as legal citizens of the United States.[11]

"I no longer belong to the Italian-American working class," De Rosa
wrote in 1980, "My parents were successful in moving me out of it. After
I moved far enough, *I* wanted to leave, and went as far as I could. But
sometimes I try to go home, and that is where the heartache lies. You find

out that you really can't go home again, no matter how much you might want to" ("An Italian-American Woman" 39). *Paper Fish* represents De Rosa's attempt to "go home again" and soothe "the heartache." "Bella-Casa," the last name of the family in *Paper Fish,* means "beautiful home." An analogy can be drawn between the separation experienced by the immigrant, and the separation from the family that moving into the middle class entails for working-class people. Like many other working-class writers, De Rosa views the family as a homeland that can be revisited only through writing.[12] The idea of home is intertwined with the drama of homelessness, a homelessness that De Rosa does not view simply as a metaphor, but as an integrating part of her social reality.[13]

Another Italian American writer, Carole Maso, writes in the autobiographical essay "The Shelter of the Alphabet": "I am a wandering soul, but not an aimless one." She announces her need "to imagine a home that might be moveable . . . a home that can be conjured within . . . [Home is] Where language trembles and burns" (*Break Every Rule* 16). This trembling, this burning, seems to occur in the space where one's languages and identities meet and conflate momentarily, without discord. Maso's lyrical meditation thus articulates the relationship between language and home and the idea of writing as a refuge, an idea central to her work and pervasive in De Rosa's novel.[14]

For Maso, the alphabet itself provides shelter from the anguish of living: "When I write sentences, I am at home. . . . When I am not, I am damned, doomed, homeless. . . . In the gloating, enormous strangeness and solitude of the real world, where I am so often inconsolable, marooned, utterly dizzied— all I need to do is pick up a pen and begin to write—safe in the shelter of the alphabet, and I am taken home" (*Break Every Rule* 19). Writing, for De Rosa and Maso, is a ritual, a prayer that offers solace and safety from the disorienting sense of displacement that pervades both these writers' work. Both authors articulate a condition that is personal and cultural, weaving connections that go beyond the mythical loss, connections that are historical and political: "This country is not a home to me," she writes, indicting an America less and less concerned with the plight of its weakest children. "I have had it for good this time with the Republicans" (*Break Every Rule* 12).

Written after the deaths of De Rosa's grandmother and father, *Paper Fish* represents an attempt to capture a lost world: "I wanted them to be eternal," she writes, remembering her family: "I wanted the brief, daily lives they lived never to end" ("Career" 9). Struggling with her sorrow over the loss, in a brief period of time, of most of her family, the author kept trying to tell her family's story, but overwhelmed by the intensity of her memories and loss, De Rosa would temporarily abandon the writing to start again, later, with a new section. As she wrote, her family members "would die over and over again," as she puts it, to be reborn in her fiction.[15] The result is a prismatic text whose pieces cohere in a fragmentary narrative reminiscent of the fiction of high modernism:

> *Night. Blink. An eye moving. Whose eye? A twist of the hand, fingers grip the dark, the dark has the hands of a skeleton.* (92)

This passage from the chapter that describes Carmolina's wanderings through the streets of Chicago captures that sense of fear and danger that looms underneath the radiant narrative of Carmolina's idyllic relationship with Grandma Doria. Not even the matriarch seems to have the power to shelter Carmolina from the hands of skeletons lurking in the dark.

De Rosa's "poetry" and "stories" create "scenes" realistically familiar to the Italian Americans from Chicago (Gardaphé, "Breaking" 12). Yet her impressionistic style construes an almost surreal world: The characters, painted with light, unfinished strokes, evoke a feeling more than they present realistically detailed figures. The story of Carmolina BellaCasa, a third-generation Italian American child, unfolds as a series of overlapping layers in which past, present, and future interweave in a temporal dimension that disregards linearity and follows the rhythms of a mythical time, yet one that is interwoven with the complexities of immigrant history. It is in this mythical time rooted in history that the author frames the tiny moments of the lives of Carmolina and her family with the scrupulous precision of a realist writer.

The structure of *Paper Fish* aptly portrays—as it emerges out of—the overwhelming grief that triggered the author's creative process. De Rosa's modernist strategy becomes the means by which she captures her memories and translates them into poetry:

> She [Grandma Doria] watches Carmolina singing in her small broken Italian; she is growing up with the music tooled inside her brain. The sound of Carmolina's growing is filled with music in her head, of the laughter and quick tears of her large family around her. The sound of Doria's time was quiet, was patient, the sound of her growing up was slow and deliberate. (19)

De Rosa foregrounds the immigrant author's sensitivity to the sound and texture of language, of a life lived between languages, while the experimental narrative calls to mind the prose of expatriate modernist authors, for example H.D., as possible literary antecedents.[16] H.D.'s experimental fiction, however, with its fragmentary style, its fractured selves, its mythical texture, was published posthumously (after 1980), and thus could have not served as an influence.[17]

The eight parts that form the book's rigorous structure—including a prelude and an epilogue—fit together in a shape that keeps undoing itself as its boundaries blur.[18] The opening words of the first section, "This is my mother," which appear under the word "Prelude" (1), stand almost as a footnote to the prelude, suggesting that the writing itself is the "mother," the locus of creativity that resurrects the past, incorporating it in a continuum in which it blends with present and future in the time of memory. The clash of tenses soothes the sorrow of many losses, and the unobtrusive authorial voice offers the fragmented memories as an elegiac chorus of voices: Grandma Doria's grieving and acceptance of ancient and recent losses of her mother, her sister, her husband, her homeland; Sarah's silently carrying the burden of the loss of her family and language; Sarah, Marco, and Doria all cradling the grief that is Doriana; while Carmolina is simultaneously observer and filter of the narrative voice and fully involved participant in the family's sorrow.

The prelude plunges the reader into a timeless dimension as it opens with the vision of the unborn, not yet even conceived Carmolina, observing her mother and father:

> My mother's skin brushes strawberries, her skin will brush my father's, that night their skin will make me, but I know none of this. I am less than the strawberries, I am less than the carving my father is making with his hands, less than the brown intent of his eyes over wood, less. (2)

This "less" than life possesses a sight and a voice that seep through the walls of houses, through the consciousness of each character; this "less" than life recounts these intimate moments through the creative power of an ancient and imaginative storytelling.

If De Rosa wrote without knowledge of literary foremothers and sisters, her character, Carmolina, finds sustenance in the voice of her grandmother. A vehicle of cultural transmission and source of emotional nourishment, Grandma Doria provides Carmolina with the material out of which the author forges the book's poetry.

In her essay "Career Choices Come From Listening to the Heart," De Rosa writes:

> In our cold water flat, my father, who was a policeman, constantly played classical music, and operas. My grandmother, an immigrant from Bosca Royale [*sic*] near Naples, sang all the time. She sang while she cooked, while she cleaned, while she made the beds. I listened to their music. I could see that the lives they were living were simple, ordinary lives, lives that no one would ever notice, but that there was a beauty there that must be understood in the eyes of God. (9)

Paper Fish expresses the author's understanding of the fragility of immigrant, working-class memory and history. Asked by Gardaphé about the title of her book, De Rosa said that she had chosen it because "the people in the book were as beautiful and as fragile as a Japanese kite" ("Interview" 23). But the fish carries other associations, too. A few pages into the book, the fish emerges through the nauseating "smell of dead fish burning," unbearable to Sarah who, pregnant with Carmolina, screens herself with her hand from the smell while "the smoke rested outside the window like a serpent; it stared out of its white eyes" (10). The sleeping Doriana, "stuffed in under all the sheets and blankets," is compared to a "dead fish" (73). The skin of Sarah's hand is described as "puckered and scaly like a fish flat and dead on a beach where the ocean tossed it away" (53). Throughout the book, death and birth intertwine in the fish imagery, replete with analogous associations in Christian symbolism, according to which the fish stands for Jesus and the serpent for Satan. This is one more instance in which opposites intertwine in the novel: good and evil, safety and danger, loss and affirmation, elegy and celebration are two faces of the same coin.

Water imagery is endowed with similarly contradictory associations. In the opening pages, the encounter between Marco and Sarah is described as a falling "into the sea":

> He fell beneath the surface of the sea. He floated into the blue water, his head showing like a rose that has a face, like a silent animal filled with anguish, filled with joy, and his heart, his life, was liquid, fluid like a fine fish, and he fell far beneath the sea. He was a marionette without strings, the sea was his string, his ribbon, holding him gently. His life dallied below him, below the water, his life was magnificent and his smile was small, above the liquid line of the sea. He was a doll, floating, with a marvelous secret just under the water. (4–5)

The language of this passage exemplifies De Rosa's style: Her prose is dense, sensual, musical, and evocative of surrealistic images and sounds. The ambivalence of the fish (both beautiful and revolting, delicate and offensive) and the water (nurturing and threatening, liberating and suffocating) establish from the very beginning a clash of images and themes sustained throughout the book, consistent with the novel's function as both celebratory song and dirge.

Accordingly, Carmolina's beautiful sister, Doriana, is afflicted by a mysterious illness: She is a "swan, a black swan that flew into the incorrect night, followed the wrong moon," leaving her family "with glass eyes" (2). "Broken" early in her life, Doriana is the child so beautiful that she "frightened" her own mother (2). She represents the unknown, the mystery that the author never tries to solve, only contemplates in awe, resigned to the fact that "it is all leaves, leaves falling out of a tree, with no hands to catch them" (2). Doriana's origin remains a mystery even to Grandmother Doria, although she is the one who weaves the tale that makes the unfathomable accessible, describing Doriana as "lost in the forest":

> In the forest the birds are. Ah, such beautiful birds. White birds. Blue and pink. Doriana she go into the forest to' look at the birds. The birds they sing in the trees, they sing, they turn into leaves. Doriana she have a key to the forest. It a secret. Only Doriana know where she keep the key. One day Doriana go into the forest. She forget the key. She get lost in the forest. She get scared. Her face it turn hot like a little peach and she scream and try to get out of the forest. . . . She try to come home. From the forest. She no find her way. (100)

De Rosa's exquisite language turns "broken" English into poetry. *Paper Fish* thus confers literary dignity on the speech of those first-generation immigrants who struggled to express themselves in a language that often felt hostile and unconquerable.

Writers such as Diana Cavallo and Maria Mazziotti Gillan have articulated the linguistic tribulations of immigrants. The speaker of "Public School No. 18/Paterson, New Jersey," contrasts her "words smooth" in her "mouth" "at home," where she "chatter[s]" and is "proud," to her silence in school, where she "grope[s] for the right English/word," fearing "the Italian word/will sprout from . . . [her] mouth like a rose" (Gillan 12). The protagonist of *A Bridge of Leaves* describes his grandmother "stammering the brittle sounds of a new tongue that flushed waves of Mediterranean homesickness through her with each rough syllable" (Cavallo 14). In her memoir *Were You Always an Italian?*, Maria Laurino writes eloquently of the language her family fabricated to keep connected with their Italian side and to adapt to the new country: "We spoke only English at home, but my parents kept alive an assortment of southern Italian dialect words that signaled a quiet intimacy or set off the alarms of subterfuge" (101). Italian words do not prevail in De Rosa's text, but the texture of spoken language, of oral culture—and of its beauty and artistry—pervades *Paper Fish* as she fashions her own particular kind of accented writing. Legitimizing orality—and *Paper Fish* is indeed a "speakerly" text with its own distinct accents[19]—the novel stands as a tribute to the unrecorded beauty and poetry of the voices of women immigrants exemplified by Grandmother Doria.[20]

Like Grandma Doria, Doriana is instrumental in what Gardaphé calls Carmolina's "lyrical self-awakening" (*Italian Signs* 131). Doriana's consciousness represents a hidden self to which the narrative longs to gain access, although her direct perspective emerges only briefly. Throughout the novel, Doriana and Carmolina mirror each other. From the very first encounter between the baby Carmolina and the "small person," they recognize a mysterious sameness as they look into "each other's eyes" (11). Frightened after overhearing her family discuss the possibility of institutionalizing Doriana, Carmolina runs away and disappears in the streets of Chicago.[21] Thus, Carmolina replicates her sister's dislocation: completely disoriented, she cannot find her way home. De Rosa plunges the reader into the mental and emotional universe of the young girl and, in doing so, endows the grim urban landscape with fantastic traits and a poetic aura that are diametrically opposed to the restaurant scene in the opening of the novel.[22] "Streetlamps are blue eyes, beating. . . . The sky is black fabric, the devil will roll it away. . . . A dog barks. It is no one's dog. It is the devil's dog. It will swallow you and you will live in the devil's belly" (92). Carmolina wanders for three days through this frightening world that "someone turned" "upside down," having "nowhere to go" (92). Her journey and subsequent illness bring all the conflicts of the novel into focus. If Doriana cannot heal, Carmolina will recover from her illness to develop an identity outside the symbiotic relationship with her sister.

Unlike Doriana, Carmolina finds the "key" to exploring the forest and, after three days, in a symbolic resurrection, comes back "home"—both to the home of the past and to a new home that she will construct for herself. Carmolina warning her father of her intention to leave when she grows up—that she will go away forever—parallels the predicament of Esperanza, the protagonist of Sandra Cisneros's *The House on Mango Street* (published in 1984, four years after *Paper Fish*), who wants to leave behind Mango Street and its poverty. Esperanza leaves "to come back. For the ones . . . [she] left behind. For the ones who cannot out" (110). Esperanza embodies the author's need and willingness to leave and come back—through writing. That is the function of Carmolina as well, although De Rosa's "return" is, as we shall see, quite problematic. Analyzing the final scene in which Carmolina, as a young woman, faces her own mirror image, Bona argues that

> The fact that Carmolina's own face is reflected in the mirror (without the shadow of Doriana or the reflection of her grandmother, who had stood next to her) reinforces Carmolina's acceptance of death and her role as a young, ethnic, American woman who will keep the fire inside of her, however difficult and demanding that may be for her. ("Broken Images" 103)

While both Doriana and Carmolina represent sacrificial, Christ-like figures, Grandma Doria's symbolic system empowers Carmolina to save herself.

Doriana's instability reflects the dislocation of the Italian family in America: She appears to be always on the edge, removed from the world she inhabits, moving toward another world. Linking the displacement of immigration and mental illness, Bona argues that, like other Italian American women writers, De Rosa "uses the topic of illness both as a realistic comment on the prevalence of sickness in underprivileged communities and as a metaphor for the immigrant experience of living in a world that does not readily welcome outsiders" (94).[23] This lack of stability, reminiscent of Marguerite's restlessness in *Umbertina,* articulates the perennial sense of homelessness experienced by many immigrants.[24]

> Grandma Doria employs the dichotomy of home and forest to explain to Carmolina both Doriana's beauty and her illness:
> "Where is the forest, Grandma?"
> "Behind her eyes," Grandma whispered. She turned to Carmolina. "Doriana, she have a beautiful face, no?"
> "Yes, Grandma."
> "Her face, why you think it so beautiful?"
> Something squeezed tight inside Carmolina. It was made of glass; it could break.
> "I don't know, Grandma. Why?"
> "Her face, she so beautiful," Grandma swiped at the tears, she was angry at them, "because Doriana fight so hard to come home. She look out her eyes every day and try to come home. When you fight to come home, you beautiful." (100)

Doriana's incapacity "to come home" figuratively expresses the impossibility of homecoming so deeply rooted in immigrant identity. Grandma Doria holds the "city" responsible for the illness that consumes Doriana. The city is "like a spider sucking the blood of the wonderful child," and "the child bled out her brains, her smiles, her own words into the empty grey light of the city and there was nothing to feed her" (64). Like a "giant" (49), the city destroys the little family, and its "buildings" are described as "bones crushing against little Doriana" (64). Through the use of body imagery, De Rosa represents the urban monster as driven by a deliberate and ineluctable force, greedily devouring the fragile Doriana, reducing the family to "little pieces" (63). De Rosa thus explores the trauma of the transition from agrarian to urban culture experienced by Southern Italian immigrants who abandoned their homeland because of disastrous economic conditions, yet cannot help longing for the land they left behind, as is the case even for the pragmatic protagonist of *Umbertina.*[25] But if the city crushes the immigrants "like a giant," De Rosa defies its destructive power by composing the "little pieces" (63) into one redemptive vision.

Paper Fish depicts a world few readers have encountered before in fiction or in film versions of Italian American lives. Chicago's Little Italy constitutes the setting in which Carmolina witnesses the disintegration of her ethnicity. In De Rosa's *bildungsroman,* Carmolina's growth is juxtaposed to the vanishing of the community from which she derives cultural nourishment.[26] Berrywood Street disappears "as though it were a picture someone wiped away":

> The city said the Italian ghetto should go, and before the people could drop their forks next to their plates and say, pardon me?, the streets were cleared.
> The houses of the families with their tongues of rugs sticking out were smashed down, the houses filled with soup pots and quick anger, filled with forks and knives and recipes written in the heads of the women, were struck in their sides with the ball of the wrecking crane and the knives and bedclothes and plaster spilled out. (*Paper Fish* 120)[27]

The demolition of the Italian ghetto resembles a carnage, and *Paper Fish* becomes the means by which the author attempts to rescue the memory of what has been wiped out.

The choral narrative created by De Rosa takes on the characteristics that Zandy identifies as typical of working-class literature:

> . . . although it relies heavily on autobiography as a genre, its subject is rarely isolated or romanticized individualism. Rather, its *raison d'être* is to recall the fragile filaments and necessary bonds of human relationships, as well as to critique those economic and societal forces that blunt or block human development. (*Working-Class* 5)

While De Rosa painstakingly recovers a history that otherwise would be lost, the nostalgia that pervades *Paper Fish* never becomes a pathetic longing for the stereotypical tokens of a stultified, one-dimensional Italian American culture. The imaginative and deeply personal story of Carmolina remains rooted in the collective history of Italian immigrants in Chicago, although, as Zandy writes, "Liberating this kind of [working-class] memory involves the reconstruction of a set of relationships, not the exactitude of specific events" (*Liberating* 3). De Rosa's book stands as an elegy drenched with the sounds, colors, and smells of the quotidian life of a working-class Italian American family living in a coldwater flat on the West Side of Chicago in the late 1940s and 1950s.

While the first Italians arrived in Chicago a century earlier, in the 1850s, from Northern Italy, the largest migration of Southern Italians occurred between 1880 and 1914 (Candeloro in Holli 229). The Italian population in Chicago never reached the numerical proportions of that in New York, and settled in several ethnically diverse Little Italies rather than in a large all-Italian neighborhood. If in the first half of this century Italians were not fully accepted or integrated members of the community, with the rise of Mussolini to power and the outbreak of World War II, things worsened for Italians in the United States—regardless of their political beliefs. *Paper Fish,* set in the aftermath of the war, illustrates the sometimes subtle prejudice suffered by Italian Americans in the United States. Introducing Marco at the very opening of "The Memory," the narrative describes Carmolina's father as "a young man, tall and thin, still not comfortable in his policeman's uniform. . . . He was, in the eyes of the department, still a rookie, Italian and stupid. He was treated politely, but with little respect" (4). Rather than indicating trouble-free assimilation, Marco's position in the low ranks of the police department may reflect, historically speaking, the attempt of local authorities to send ethnic policemen back into their own neighborhoods to deal with the "locals." But it is when Carmolina is ostracized for being a "dago kid" (89) that one recognizes De Rosa's awareness of cultural tensions and her condemnation of bigotry, specifically against Italian immigrants. *Paper Fish* forces one to contend with an American culture that simultaneously celebrated Shirley Temple and Dorothy of *The Wizard of Oz,* and ghettoized children of working-class and ethnic minorities.

Popular cultural representations of Italians in Chicago have focused on the mafia wars and such notorious figures as Al Capone who—much like Mario Puzo's and Francis Ford Coppola's Don Vito Corleone—appeal to the fantastic vision of Italians that mainstream America has cultivated. After all, the gangster is an American hero: Defiant of the law, he is a warped descendant of the American colonist, with whom he shares the fearless determination to expand his territory.[28] De Rosa defies stereotypical representations of Chicago Italian Americans as mobsters by portraying the very neighborhood ruled by Al Capone in a completely different light: "It was Al Capone's neighborhood," she recalls, "we were always in fear of that. . . . We were so denigrated. People were afraid to come to my neighborhood." Thus, she turned to writing to show what was "beautiful" about the world she grew up in: "I wanted to tell people that they couldn't trash us like that."[29] The Italian Americans in Chicago, De Rosa demonstrates, have other stories to tell, like the lyrical and moving story of Carmolina and her family.[30]

◈◈◈   ◈◈◈   ◈◈◈

After a brief spurt of local attention on its publication in Chicago, *Paper Fish* vanished into the shadows of cultural invisibility. This novel stands as an important text in Italian American and multicultural literatures because it emerged out of a "void" that remained a void for 15 years, until its reprint by The Feminist Press in 1996. The author's own description of the novel as "a song from the ghetto" articulates the links between literary isolation and urban marginalization.[31] De Rosa's "individual talent" surfaced without a tradition to support and facilitate its emergence. The author's claim that her novel has more in common with a book like Anne Frank's *The Diary of a Young Girl* (1952) than with an Italian American tradition sheds light on the writer's preoccupation with the power of human creativity to survive and emerge in the direst of circumstances but also with the consequences of racial hatred. The link with *Anne Frank* also clarifies the multiple links that *Paper Fish* maintains with the traditions of autobiography and *bildungsroman,* and minority literatures.[32] In focusing on the struggle of a working-class Italian American girl to come of age in the Chicago of the 1940s, *Paper Fish* obliquely retraces the steps of an author whose work can be fully understood and appreciated only in the context of the burgeoning of multicultural literature in the last two decades of the twentieth century, in which works that carry the visible signs of one's cultural and familial history are finally making their way into the U.S. literary canon.

In a compelling essay on ethnic discrimination, Rose Romano denounces the silencing of Italian American voices and asserts that "censorship doesn't always have to be censorship in order to be effective" ("Where is Nella Sorellanza" 152). Since its reprint in 1996, which has put an end to 15 years of "effective" censorship, *Paper Fish* has claimed a place in American literary history and, in doing so, it has also contributed to legitimizing Italian American women's literature as a whole. Yet, such a victory does not come easy. Explaining that "the immigrant genre presents readers with the repeated coalescence of wonder and shame in relation to one's place in a given culture," Frances Bartkowski argues that

> What speaks to the victory of wonder over shame is the ethnoautobiographical text itself as a document of having claimed a place, culturally speaking. Yet the narratives of this coming-into-place are replete with the brutal lessons of shame, even as they recount the exultation of instants of shamelessness. (88)

The history of *Paper Fish* is the history of a journey toward cultural recognition. Recognizing the shame that lies at the core of her writing, De Rosa affirms the power of "wonder" to transcend shame. "Though I grew up in what the world would call a ghetto," she writes, "I was surrounded constantly by beauty" ("Career" 9). Overcoming the isolation of both urban *and* literary ghettoes, *Paper Fish* transforms "the disempowered experience of an unshared tongue" (Bartkowski 86) into a poetic feast of words.

☌ ☌ ☌

With works such as *Paper Fish,* why has Italian American women's literature struggled so much to come into its own? The lack of recognition and the many other external circumstances that have hindered for so long the successful emergence of De Rosa, Barolini, and other Italian American women authors has placed them in a position that parallels that in which authors of other minority groups, at times with a harsher history of discrimination—as is certainly the case for African Americans, Native Americans, Asian Americans, and Latinos—have found themselves. The complications of white ethnicity play their part, but so does the fact that it has taken Italian American women writers longer than other groups to organize themselves, to sustain each other's work, and to become spokespersons for their literature and culture while also avoiding simplistic, quasi-patriotic celebration of that culture. De Rosa's work could in many ways be regarded as the Italian American equivalent of Zora Neale Hurston's *Their Eyes Were Watching God*. But should De Rosa be compared to Zora Neale Hurston? The politics are dramatically different, for De Rosa has chosen not to offer any kind of public recognition of her being an Italian American author, at least following the reprint of *Paper Fish* in 1996.

De Rosa has firmly repudiated, in a number of published interviews, the appellation of Italian American writer, embracing that safe universal of "I'm a writer" (Meyer 64). In addition, De Rosa has been dismissive of the very feminist project that has made the rebirth of her novel possible: "I'm not a feminist. I'm not an Italian American writer" (Lauerman 3), she has repeatedly claimed since 1997.[33] Without dismissing the importance of self-definition, which makes one feel he or she is a "real" writer, De Rosa's comments cannot be easily ignored, for they perpetuate, in a manner of speaking, the silence surrounding Italian American women writers that De Rosa herself has suffered. If even the author of *Paper Fish* and "An Italian American Woman Speaks Out" (1980) feels the necessity to deny her identity as an Italian American woman writer, how can we speak of Italian American women's literature? Yet we can, not only because the books do exist and speak for themselves—at times even against their authors' voices—but because other writers have bravely embraced the appellation of "Italian American author," and in doing so have contributed to giving visibility, legitimacy, and recognition to the literature itself. Literary people well understand the power of language to confer existence to that which has been forgotten, lost, denied. Is this not, after all, the very power underscoring De Rosa's elegy to her lost Italian American world?

Accent . . . is a word which, in its popular use, carries a stigma: speaking without an accent is considered preferable to speaking with an accent. . . . The popular, pejorative, use of the word begs an important question by its assumption that an accent is something which is added to, or in some other way distorts, an accepted norm.

—D. Abercrombie

Chapter 4

Speaking Through Silences, Writing Against Silence

there was something about his Sicilian features,
his accent,
his whole goddamned hard-luck story the just
gnawed on me so,

—*Lucia Perillo,*
The Oldest Map with the Name America

Where is my country?
Where does it lie?

—*Nellie Wong, "Where is My Country?"*

My mother does not need to utter a word when she is angry. As my older sister claims, her silence is more eloquent than a press conference. Her disapproval translates into a stone-dead silence that we, her children, have learned to read quickly. It is a special brand of silence; it is the silence of words that remain unspoken but hang in the air, thick and substantial, drenched with meaning. It is a silence patiently cultivated within Southern Italian culture, the inheritance of subjugation and oppression.

In the United States, a country of immigrants, being an immigrant ironically still often means to stand as a silent outsider in relationship to both the culture of origins and U.S. culture. Waiting for my turn at the Italian Consulate in Newark, New Jersey, I observe a family of four: husband, wife, two children. I hear the parents exchanging words in thick Sicilian

dialect. I am comforted by its sounds. My husband notices how close, almost huddled together they are. I tell him that these people feel they are
outsiders both in Italy and the United States. "How do you know?" he
asks. "I know," I answer, "I am Sicilian. I know."

⊗⊗⊗   ⊗⊗⊗   ⊗⊗⊗

The dialectics of speech and silence lie at the core of this chapter, in which
I explore how the signs of ethnicity are inscribed in writings that one
could describe as palimpsestic. Whether it is the self-silencing induced by
cultural assimilation, or the result of rewriting and rethinking the modes
of existence and articulation of ethnic identity, a reading of such dialectics
reveals a rich body of creative work that both expands and redefines the
Italian American canon, and particularly the body of literature produced
by Italian American women.

In contemporary politics and thought, ethnicity evokes the elusively
defined borders of transnationality, migrancy, and homelessness. Being
eradicated from one culture leads to a life divided between the ghostly
yet palpable memories of the country of origin and the new, contradictory attachment to the country of emigration that Giuliana Miuccio so
well describes in "Apolide." The social forces of acculturation and assimilation pressure authors from cultural minorities to express themselves in
the language of the dominant culture, to adhere to its aesthetics, to mold
their art within its parameters, and to reject the fruitful possibilities of
moving between languages and cultures. To argue that emigration "forces
a disintegration of self, culture, and society," and to posit an integration
of such elements prior to emigration, would mean to ignore the factors
that often trigger departure from the country of origin (Ostendorf 577).[1]
The terms fatherland and motherland, when used in reference to the experience of immigrants, invoke abandonment, refusal, something that
must be examined from perspectives that vary depending on different
historical circumstances. The marginality of immigrants preexists emigration and in many cases prompts it. To become an immigrant, then,
means to relinquish a position of marginality, only to find oneself in a
different context and yet in a comparably marginal position. The immigrant's understanding of the historical and psychological circumstances
and repercussions of emigration serves as the catalyst that forges identity
out of these positions.[2]

Whether immigration is the result of economic or political reasons—
and even these vary dramatically if one compares late-nineteenth-century
Italian immigrants to late-twentieth-century ones—a fracture, a separation, and a complicated longing for connection, defines the identity of the
immigrant. If loss and separation preexist emigration, immigration, rather

than healing the fracture between self and culture, reenacts the drama of separation and marginalization. Various forms of economic, social, and political oppression suffered in the country of origin constitute the baggage that immigrants carry with them to the new country, where the very conditions they escaped from are often replicated. The literature produced by immigrants and their children articulates their struggle to extricate themselves from the constraints of such conditions, which often survive the achievement of economic emancipation, as is the case for some sections of the Italian American population.[3]

Commenting on the lack of recognition for Italian American authors, Fred Gardaphé rightly refers to them as "cultural immigrants" on "the American literary scene" ("Third Generation" 72). Much Italian American literature articulates the struggle of a culture caught between assimilation and exclusion.[4] On the one hand, the self-silencing that acculturation entails resonates in language, seemingly purging it of ethnic ties, at least on the surface; on the other hand, for those who maintain the signs of ethnic identity in their language, lack of recognition generates a perception of cultural invisibility. As Rose Romano admonishes in her poems, it is easy for Italian Americans to hide (*Wop* 35), by camouflaging, and even rejecting ethnic identity, to submerge themselves in the whiteness of mainstream U.S. culture; however, this is achieved at the cost of loss of cultural identity and even self-hatred. "Were you always an Italian?" asked former New York governor Mario Cuomo to the journalist Maria Laurino during an interview, hinting at the self-hatred that can lead Italian Americans, in Maria Mazziotti Gillan's words, to "deny that booted country" (*Where I Come From* 12). In "Scents," the opening chapter of *Were You Always an Italian?* Laurino interweaves the story of shame and self-hatred she associated as an adolescent with her ethnicity into the story of the resulting self-silencing of ethnic identity, which she connects with a revealing story of suppression of smells. The search for an aseptic self, free of the charge of ethnic identity, is importantly linked by Laurino with the desire to escape "the class boundaries" (29) of her youth. Her memoir reverses the trajectory of the escape of her youth as she considers "what it would be like to uncover a voice that could tell the stories of . . . [her] past" (29).

Contemporary Italian American women have consistently reconsidered the ways in which to tell and construct the history of their culture. The literature of many of these women simultaneously verbalizes and silences ethnicity. This kind of writing, in which a thinly disguised accent reveals ethnic identity, dramatizes the cultural conflicts at the heart of the experience of hyphenation.[5] In an essay published in an Italian American paper, *Attenzione,* Tina De Rosa laments the sense of isolation she experienced as

a result of an internalized perception of her working-class culture of origin as an aberration from the standard of the North American middle class.
Appropriately, the essay is entitled "An Italian American Woman Speaks
Out." Ironically, she would later disavow, as we have seen, the very ideas
that sustain her work. In *Vertigo,* Louise DeSalvo continues the exploration
of Italian American female identity she had begun with the essay "Portrait
of the Puttana as a Middle-Aged Woolf Scholar" and the novel *Casting Off.*
While the former contains a preliminary reflection that would later ma-
ture in her book-length memoir, *Casting Off* defied pious images of Italian American womanhood but also encoded Italian American ethnicity in
the Irish surnames of both her characters.

Many Italian American women writers root their self-exploration in a
relentless analysis of the place occupied by their ethnicity in U.S. culture.
In a review essay of Rose Romano's *The Wop Factor* (1994), Mary Jo Bona
argues that "the poet who talks back . . . compels the reader to recognize
the potential cultural genocide inherent in . . . passing." She quotes Romano: "Most Italians escape by hiding,/don't teach the children Italian,/use Italian to tell the old stories,/and never complain./Now most
Italians pass/and don't know it" (165).[6] Several Italian American women
authors have explored the reasons for and implications of passing. The
critic Camille Cauti, for example, draws an interesting analogy between
food and language as she analyzes the practice of "culinary passing," which
she describes as the attempt "to gain acceptance among an ethnic group to
which one does not belong via the preparation and eating of certain
foods" (Giunta and Patti 10). Kym Ragusa examines passing from a multiplicity of perspectives in her video *Passing,* a dramatic monologue in the
voice of her African American maternal grandmother who retells her own
experience of passing when she found herself in the South in the 1950s.[7]
Forced to "pass" as "white" in her own Italian American family and Bronx
neighborhood as a child, Ragusa quickly learnt how the dynamics of class,
ethnicity, and race operate in social as well as familial contexts. Her maternal grandmother's recollection indirectly mirrors Ragusa's own experience
of passing as she, too, faces the question of origins and belonging. In a later
prose memoir, "Ritorni," Ragusa recounts the complexities of shame in
turn associated, through her history, with African American and Italian
American identity. After acquiring her Italian American father's name, in
the 1980s, in the climate of ethnic and racial hatred and violence in which
the murder of Yusef Hawkins in Bensonhurst took place, Ragusa found
herself wanting to rid herself of that name.[8]

The poet and feminist scholar Sandra Mortola Gilbert began using
her Italian last name only later in her career, although her poetry is
drenched with the sounds, the smells, and the stories of Italian Ameri-

can culture. In the early 1980s, Gilbert wrote to Barolini: "I am really Sandra Mortola Gilbert . . . and my mother's name was Caruso, so I always feel oddly falsified with this Waspish-sounding American name, which I adopted as a 20-year-old bride who had never considered the implications of her actions!" (Barolini, *The Dream Book* 22). Gilbert's Italian American voice emerged in her poetry, which at first she seemed to consider a largely unrecognized, somewhat clandestine writing: "As for my poetry . . . I don't feel myself to be a tremendously established poet. In fact, I'm always interested when people even know that I write poetry" (Hongo 99). Gilbert's comment establishes a revealing connection between women's writings, Italian American ethnicity, and lack of recognition.

In *Crossing Ocean Parkway: Readings by an Italian American Daughter* (1994), the cultural critic Marianna De Marco Torgovnick considers her marriage to a Jewish man, which enabled her to "cross," as epitomizing the self-silencing of the *"paesani"* (countrymen/fellow Italians) who "often sport last names that aren't Italian" (viii). Ironically, Torgovnick herself "sports" her Italian last name, De Marco, specifically in *Crossing Ocean Parkway,* only to relinquish it in later.[9] Cris Mazza, whose provocative experimental fiction places her among the most intriguing contemporary avant garde authors, creates a character in *Your Name Here_____* who is in search of her identity, having no secure knowledge even of her name. And while the novel does not address in any explicit way ethnic themes, as Ted Pelton suggests, its "prominent theme of naming and self-naming resonates for students of ethnicity in American culture" (286). The protagonist of Renée Manfredi's "Running Away with Frannie," when asked by her traveling companion, "Who are you again?" answers: "I'm not sure." One of the protagonists of Dalia Pagani's striking novel *Mercy Road* embarks on a dark voyage into the Vermont winter, and sheds name, identity, and, literally, pieces of her body.[10] This concern with the implications of naming is not unique to Italian American women writers. Sandra Cisneros's Esperanza Cordero undertakes a symbolic journey in which her rejection of her name and its significance in English and Spanish bespeaks her awareness of the links between language and social marginalization in U.S. society as well as her conflicted relationship with the predominantly patriarchal Chicano culture.

Janet Zandy's poem "My Children's Names" articulates the relationship between class and ethnicity in U.S. culture through the juxtaposition of the speaker's children's names—"Old world names/Names reeking of steamer ships,/close quarters, and shadows," names redolent of immigrant and working-class history—and the names they desire—"Diaphanous names/Clear pools, clubs, and right-school names. . . . /American names." Zandy's poem beautifully captures the self-silencing of one's ethnic identity, which is the result of the social pressure to assimilate and often translates into an insidious form of self-denial and even hatred. The link between ethnicity and silence is at the core of *Continents Apart,* an autobiographical video by Franca Barchiesi, an actress and filmmaker who moved to the United States as a child, following her parents who had emigrated years earlier. The lack of dialogue in the video—there is only music—expresses the filmmaker's understanding of the condition of the child immigrant who lives in a world of silence, broken by incomprehensible sounds, but it also articulates the power of silence to signify, to speak, so to say.

Italian American women writers have variously and creatively articulated, in oblique ways, the visceral attachment to an idea of home linked to ethnic origins and the urge to leave that home behind. Often they end up plunging in a space in-between, in a virtual condition of homelessness. Carole Maso's novel *The American Woman in the Chinese Hat,* for example, is centered around multiple forms of displacement, from geographical, to linguistic, to psychological. The protagonist, an American woman in France living her own particular form of contemporary American expatriation, is absorbed by a search for ways to bridge past and present, worlds, cultures, sexualities, identities, languages, joie de vivre, and grief. She is one of those who lives "at the limit of things" (159). Literally embodying displacement, Maso's character speaks English "like a foreign language" (102), and slips "easily back and forth in time"—and place—"Like someone who refuses to give up anything" (34).[11] Incapable of translating herself to herself (or to others) either in French or English, she remains trapped, beautiful, and elusive like the language that depicts (and fails to depict) her.[12] *The American Woman in the Chinese Hat* is a book about memory and loss—both themes favored by Maso—and about the attempt to salvage what one has lost by naming it in writing: Writing combats the annihilation of silence.

The experience of Maso's character could be described as utterly removed from the experiences of nineteenth- and early-twentieth-century Italian immigrants. Yet, a kinship exists between what Maso depicts—she acknowledges that *The American Woman in the Chinese Hat* is an autobiographical novel—and the experience of emigration, in spite of the dramatically different historical, geographical, social, and economic circumstances. For example, Denise Giardina describes the longing of her Sicilian immigrant character Rosa Angelelli: "My hair is still black. I catch it with a net, like black lace. I make it myself. I watch for the butterflies to return. Then I will leave this place" (*Storming Heaven 51*). Acutely aware of language, Maso's character speaks in fragments; her speech is reminiscent of the broken tongue of immigrants like Angelelli: In both cases, a lyrical and elegiac language serves to articulate the position of writers who, like Maso and Giardina, inscribe ethnicity in texts that also evade it.

For these characters *and* their authors, ethnic identity, reflected in names, cannot be traded for the promise of an American narrative of success; at the same time, the nostalgic evocation of the motherland no longer represents an option, particularly for third- and fourth-generation writers. While the sense of displacement and the longing for something undefinable—an unreachable "home" one has never seen or lived in—that characterizes, for example, *The American Woman in the Chinese Hat,* are quite different from what early immigrants might have experienced, they effectively describe what these immigrants' descendants might face. Culturally disoriented, these authors continue to grapple with questions of cultural origin and identity. As the contemporary transnational movement calls into question and dissolves traditional notions of ethnic identity, these writers enact a shift away from the traditional immigrant narrative. It thus becomes necessary, when including these writers in Italian American literary history, to challenge the categories that define such a history.

The Case of Agnes Rossi

The work of Agnes Rossi, a writer of Italian and Irish ancestry, can be regarded, particularly if read vis-à-vis the work of other Italian American women as well as the writers of other minority groups, as an example of the kind of negotiations between cultural/ethnic identities undertaken by Italian American women at the end of a century in which global economy is promoted, but the voices of all the localities—geographical, ethnic/racial, socioeconomic, sexual, and so forth—that make up U.S. culture are not truly heard in the political arena.

Agnes Rossi was born in 1959 in Paterson, New Jersey, of Italian and Irish parents. This dual heritage would later play out in her novels and stories. Her paternal grandfather had come to the United States from Gubbio, in the Italian region of Umbria, in Northern Italy, in 1911. He worked as a coal miner in Scranton, Pennsylvania, and died, 35 years later, of black lung disease.[13] Rossi's parents, as was the case for many second-generation Italian Americans, moved quickly into the middle class, although the family maintained a clear, albeit not openly discussed, sense of working-class identity.[14] Rossi studied at Rutgers University and then went on to receive the M.A. in English from New York University.

Rossi's ambivalent, evasive representation of her Italian background in her fiction contrasts with her more direct, although by no means uncomplicated, approach to her Irish ancestry in her two novels *Split Skirt* and *The House-guest*. Rossi's works bear directly on questions of ethnic self-representation and identity politics, especially in a late-twentieth-century context, in which representations of ethnicity eschew static demarcations.

Rossi's authorial development epitomizes the simultaneous acceptance and denial of Italian American identity, suggesting an ongoing conflict that underlies her creative process. While the protagonist of "The Quick" (1992), Marie Russo—whose last name strikingly resembles the author's— is identified through her name as Italian American, the younger protagonist of *Split Skirt* (1994), Rita, is, like the author, Irish and Italian, but the only explicitly mention of her ethnicity "didn't survive the final edit."[15] The editing process that unwittingly cancels the signs of ethnicity can be read as an involuntary, albeit effective, self-censorship, one that creates an apparently accent-free story and speaker. One must not forget that accent is a function of two or more positions, simultaneously articulated.[16]

Ethnic boundaries intersect in a world struggling to create viable methods for cultural identification and connection. Accordingly, Agnes Rossi's characters suffer from cultural displacement that leads to a form of emotional detachment. In "The Quick," Rossi resorts to the detached first-person voice of Marie. Marie's narrative articulates a disjunction between story and self, which in turn mirrors a fracture between self and community. Rossi thus obliquely inscribes some of her own conflicts and issues in the fragmented identity and choices of her character. While Rossi publishes her work in the early 1990s, when stereotypical and folkloric representations of her ethnicity still prevail, she also must confront the hostility that her own Italian American milieu has for female artistry. Like many other Italian American women writers, Rossi writes with virtually no knowledge of other Italian American women's voices, which might enable her to place herself, with confidence, in the realm of an already existing literary tradition.

In addition, her dual Irish and Italian background, more than two decades after the white ethnic revival, and many more decades after the assimilation of both groups into American whiteness, prompts her to engage both ethnicities in a dance in which two worlds that jar against each other now cross and blend.[17] Rossi tries to establish in her fiction the subject position from which she writes, but also to avoid the entrapment that speaking solely from that position would entail. As we shall see, her accents are multiple.

Relying on a memoiristic approach, "The Quick" strives to tell an Italian American story through a plot in which, ironically, ethnicity goes unnamed. Scattered, fragmented traces, however, do surface. Marie's seeming lack of awareness of, or interest in, her Italian ancestry parallels the absence of any sense of politicized class identity. That Marie Russo is a working-class Italian American from Paterson, New Jersey, is a fact that emerges unobtrusively, as if neither the author nor the narrator give it much importance or are fully aware of it. Rejecting linear narrative and relying instead on the associative narrative more characteristic of the contemporary memoir, Rossi inserts an accent in the interstices between the fragmentary memories that make up "The Quick," an accent that is ever so slight, yet unquestionably present.

Marie, like other second-generation Italian Americans—for example, Carla in *Umbertina*—does not maintain any overt tie to her ancestral country. "Chris and I," she reflects, "never considered ourselves related to my parents' relatives, especially the ones we never saw, the ones who were just blue airmail letters that lay around the house for a while and then were gone" (85). The memory of the relatives, metonymically identified first with the vase and then with the blue airmail letters, represents a vestige of Italy, a memory that has been destroyed by the family, like the vase, or has simply vanished, like the letters. Marie has internalized the invisibility of her ethnicity. Her inability to connect with it may lie at the core of her emotional and cultural displacement, the core around which "The Quick" revolves.

In almost Pirandellian fashion, Marie enacts the conflict between character and actor. The parts she plays seem to take over, and while at first she surrenders to their power, eventually she rejects them all. In all her relationships, with the exception of her friendship with Phyllis, an older fellow worker, Marie experiences a discomfort that makes her acutely aware of the contrived quality of her roles as daughter, sister, girlfriend, college graduate, teacher, wife, and mother. Marie's silence and passivity—the subject of her own retrospective narrative—are colored by an inherited acceptance of gender roles. At the end of the novella, her move into an empty and "shabby" apartment (57) signals her claim of a blank space, devoid of cultural scripts, within which, having surrendered all roles, she can plunge into her past, begin to remember, and tell. Like contemporary memoirs, "The Quick" does not strive to achieve resolution nor does it attempt to fashion a chronologically cohesive narrative. Marie Russo's storytelling acknowledges loss and despair with utter honesty, and asserts the need for this Italian American narrator to connect with her past in order to find the words for a newly forged language, one that encapsulates the predicament of those who live between cultures.

Rossi confers unity on the disjointed events of "The Quick" through the monotonous, seemingly removed voice of its narrator, part protagonist, part witness. The story opens in the present and then unfolds into a spiral of memories that the narrator weaves in and out of the present.

Rossi's reliance on memory and life story place "The Quick" within the tradition of memoiristic fiction as well as the *bildungsroman* and the *kunstlerroman* (much like Tina De Rosa's *Paper Fish* and Barolini's *Umbertina*). Rossi, like other feminist writers, tells a story of failed artistic emergence—and, thus, failed development. Marie Rossi is no Stephen Dedalus: Her gender, in conjunction with her ethnicity and class background, stifle whatever creative genius she might have. Rejecting a linear narrative, "The Quick" recapitulates Marie's life, a life punctuated by mild attempts at self-assertion and forcible attempts at self-erasure: She recalls that she could have "made a life" for herself, but "she didn't want to." (70). Ultimately, Marie's life story expresses a fracture between narrator and narrative: She disclaims any connection with her narrative subject, just as she disclaims any connection with her Italian relatives. By consolidating the intricate and seemingly disjointed narrative of "The Quick" around loss—loss of people, hope, opportunities, memory—Rossi obliquely describes the impact of loss of ethnic identity on her characters.

Cultural displacement is articulated through Marie's longing for a place that might feel like home. This very longing leads her to return to the parental home after quitting her job: "I'd been away long enough to dream up a romantic notion of home as a safe place where I'd be able to get my bearings" (29). Marie's homecoming, a disillusioning experience, well describes Italian American women's relationship to their "home" culture, a culture that they yearn for in spite of the complications involved in their homecomings. Lesbian writers such as Mary Cappello and Janet Capone have written on such complicated homecomings. Capone writes of the pain of craving home in the social isolation that she experiences as an Italian American lesbian, particularly when home is associated with the "homophobia and ignorance" within her family (Tamburri, *FUORI* 39). For Marie, the search for a home begins when, as a 12-year-old, she glues a lock on the door of her room, but the glue gives out "with no fight at all" (63) when her father pushes it open, completely unaware of his violation. Marie's realization that her father "would always crash through, without even meaning to, and, worse, without even knowing he'd crashed through" (64) further describes the modes of female oppression within the patriarchal family as well as the pressure toward unquestioned unity, even when it involves the denial of individual boundaries.

The search for a home, a safe home, takes Marie to disparate places, such as Woolworth's, her friend Phyllis's home, the burned house of the Metuchens, the house of her marriage to Ralph, and finally the empty apartment in which her storytelling begins. This search expresses Marie's attempt to negotiate between self-definition and cultural/familial definition. Rejecting romanticized notions of home, Rossi does not resolve

Marie's conflicts nor does she offer miraculous epiphanies that will transform her characters. The world she depicts is utterly anti-romantic and anti-heroic.

Social outcasts like those who inhabit the world of "The Quick" also populate *Athletes and Artists* (1987) and the other stories in *The Quick:* lonesome truck drivers, waitresses, failed artists, ex-drug addicts, jobless men and women. These figures live on fragile borders and lead their lives at such a distance from mainstream culture that its myths do not even appeal to them. Yet, they are not sustained by any alternative cultural sources: They are drifters grieving unnamed losses. Marie's inability to name and thus mourn the loss of her ethnicity is linked with the fact that she identifies Italian culture with the patriarchal ideology ruling her household. Her relentless remembering and interpellation of her audience—"I want to tell you some of things Phyllis told me that summer but I don't want to have to go on and one [*sic*] about what color blouse she was wearing when she said a particular thing" (58)—radically contrast her with her mother, who lives in silent expectation of her husband's explosions.

Rossi is one of a handful of writers who have explored the father-daughter relationship in Italian American culture. In Josephine Gattuso Hendin's *The Right Thing To Do,* Gina realizes that she is "everything" to her father and that "he could only deal with losing her by controlling her life, so that whatever happened to her would show his mark" (32). The novel's focus on the father-daughter relationship is underscored by references to Persephone, a mythical figure of daughter/wife—but also traveler and immigrant—who appears in the works of many Italian American women writers, such as Gioia Timpanelli, Phyllis Capello, Rita Signorelli-Pappas, Susan Caperna Lloyd, and Diane di Prima.[18] It is this paternal mark that Marie tries to escape, often to no avail. The voicelessness and passivity of Italian American maternal figures, however, pose a more pernicious threat to the daughter's self-definition than does the father's overt abuse. Marie, like Hendin's Gina and Barolini's Marguerite, must confront an inheritance of female subordination and passivity that stifles one's voice and one's life.

The Italian Canadian writer Gianna Patriarca depicts the burdensome inheritance of maternal silence in poems such as "Italian Women," "My Birth," and "Daughter." The speakers of these poems must face the haunting image of women who "serve their own hearts/in a meal they never share" (9). There's no conviviality here, no partaking, no breaking bread, no communal table. These are women whose lives are typically entwined and emotionally enmeshed with those of their children. Women writers of Italian descent have to fight both the culture that silences their ethnicity and the ethnicity that silences their gender. If Marie is, on the one hand, capable of rejecting the model of femininity offered by her mother, on the other, she lacks the tools to fashion or seek new models for herself. Marie's need to reconcile her desire for "a conventional life" with her wish to be "eccentric within that life" (69) parallels her struggle to bridge the gap between two cultures. While she surrenders to the seductiveness of the American dream—she dreams of a "Cape Cod house" (70)—she later realizes its inadequacy when she thinks that the shabby apartment she moves into after her divorce feels "more like home than the house with three bathrooms did" (57). Ethnicity is envisioned by many writers as an imaginary "home," a soothing place where one might be at peace, at home. Yet, writers like Rossi reject such a nostalgic view and propose that home is ultimately unattainable. Her relationship to Italian American culture is confused, repressed both in Marie's life and in Rossi's account, emerging occasionally, but never enough to provide the opportunity for any kind of insightful self-examination. Embodied in lost airmail letters or broken china, Marie's—and her author's—ethnicity is represented as a ghost culture that the narrative vainly tries to conjure up.

The vanishing of ethnicity is rendered through abrupt narrative shifts, textual fractures and gaps, lack of cohesion and closure as well as the sense of cultural displacement and disconnection that pervades "The Quick." Marie's account of her life as a mosaic of scattered and seemingly incongruous episodes resembles her depiction of her ethnicity as a preposterous accumulation of tokens. A scene centering on a violent argument between Marie and her father ends with the shattering of her mother's china and Marie dwelling on the objects that inhabited her mother's cabinet, specifically a flowered vase, a gift that her father's relatives had sent from Italy. Italy is evoked through a dwarfed "six-inch bust of Verdi" and a plate with the grotesque face of the "sixties pope," John XXIII, "the one with the little round head that looked like a newborn baby" (85). These parodically reductive images reify and infantilize Marie's cultural heritage, broken to pieces much like the china from her mother's cabinet. "I never heard a louder noise inside" (82), Marie thinks as she recalls the shattering of her mother's heirlooms. The absence of a clear referent for "inside" creates a syntactical ambiguity that collapses the house, the china cabinet, and Marie's precarious sense of selfhood.

With its souvenirs and its seldom-used dishes, the cabinet symbolically functions as a dusty repository for the family's ethnicity, inaccessible and now hopelessly broken. The souvenirs, grotesque and commodified embodiments of Italian culture, parallel the phony cultural role available to Marie. Both Italian and American culture are depicted, through their association with certain artifacts, as sterile and stifling. While walking up and down the aisles of Woolworth's, where she spends "a good part" of her Saturday afternoons "wandering amidst water pistols and perspiration shields and brands of cold cream nobody ever heard of" (53), Marie meets a friend who introduces her to Ralph, who later becomes her husband. As a synecdoche for a culturally impoverished society, the store that provides Marie with a husband represents the American alternative to the Italian souvenirs, capsules of a culture that neither Marie nor her parents have experienced directly.

At Woolworth's, Marie "feels at home" and can even meditate (53). This image of meditation is akin to the image of the "house with a supermarket-style door" (17) that Marie describes at the beginning of the novella as she is about to plunge into her past. Her cultural landscape is an assemblage of odds and ends from both Italian and American mythologies, all of which stifle her emerging sense of selfhood. And yet, it is out of these odds and ends that she must mold that selfhood. Only by identifying the sources of her dissociation can Marie experience her story and speech as her own. Shaping her memories of loneliness, loss, death, and defeat into a story serves as a self-created rite of passage for a woman who "felt like an impostor" (57) in the conventional life she had accepted.

Helen Barolini writes that both of her parents, children of immigrants, passed on to their children conflicted feelings about their origins.

> In striving to get past the old generation they severed themselves too drastically from it; their lives became all in the foreground, without depth or ties to the past, all a surface of American success. ("Becoming a Literary Person" 263)

Marie's father's vaguely defined dreams of success that he hopes to attain vicariously through his daughter's education are juxtaposed to Marie's rejection of any form of socially acceptable recognition. Although Marie does not share her father's aspirations, she cannot fully free herself from various cultural constraints, affected as she is by her mother's silent acquiescence and her father's expectations of success and dread of social failure. She also inherits from her parents a longing that can never be satisfied, a sense of emptiness that can never be filled. If the broken china is not mended, Marie does at least start, by the end of the novella, piecing together the fragments of her life. While her storytelling signals her emergence as a narrator, as a character she can not fashion her story or her part. Being a first-person narrator, however, Marie becomes a producer of discourse and thus reverses her positions as a woman within Italian American culture and as an Italian American within American culture.[19] Rossi legitimizes Italian American culture by creating it as a literary experience. Not only does her novella express a search for cultural legitimation, it also questions the forces that legitimize (or delegitimize) cultural experiences.

In "The Quick" Rossi explored dialogic possibilities through Marie's semiconfessional dramatic monologue. Rossi's implied audience in "The Quick" differs greatly from the silent patriarchal "God" addressed in the first part of Celie's epistolary narrative in Alice Walker's *The Color Purple.* Marie wills into existence this elusive reader/listener, recognizing the necessity of an other who will listen. At the same time, the text of "The Quick" never produces a responsive voice such as that of Nettie in Walker's novel. Phyllis, the older woman with whom Marie establishes a relationship that defies the norms prescribed by Marie's social and cultural milieu, never plays a role as active as Phoeby's, Janie's friend and sympathetic audience in Zora Neale Hurston's *Their Eyes Were Watching God,* Walker's acknowledged model. Walker's and Hurston's engagement in a literary exchange in which they act as each other's audience, but also as precursor/mother/sister/discoverer, translates into the epistolary relationship between Celie and Nettie, anticipated by the relationship between Janie and Phoeby. In contrast, the absence of a female interlocutor in "The Quick" reflects Rossi's lack of a literary community. If, as Barolini argues, Italian American women authors "write out of the void" ("Becoming a Literary Person" 263), with no community to nurture their voices and no space to legitimize their stories, then Rossi's fiction articulates the search for a community of women to validate authorial speech.

Such a search prompts the narrative structure of *Split Skirt,* Rossi's first novel (1994), in which Rossi draws on and yet departs from the tradition of dialogic, communal ethnic narratives exemplified by works such as Alice Walker's *The Color Purple,* Cristina Garcia's *Dreaming in Cuban,* and Amy Tan's *The Joy Luck Club* and *The Kitchen God's Wife,* in which the ethnicity of the author legitimizes the credibility of the narrative and establishes a relationship between character and author based on ethnic identity.[20] In her novel *Casting Off,* Louise DeSalvo also relies on alternating sections in which each of the two female characters speaks, in monologues of sorts, although the friendship between the two women constitutes an important undercurrent of these solitary voices. *Split Skirt* centers around the encounter between Rita and Mrs. Tyler, both married, respectively of Italian/Irish and Irish descent. The two meet in the grim setting of the Bergen County jail in New Jersey, in which they spend three days, Rita for drunk driving and possession of cocaine, and Mrs. Tyler for one of her escapades as a kleptomaniac. While the narrative of *Split Skirt* overtly recognizes Mrs. Tyler's Irishness, it withholds Rita's Italian background. The names by which the characters refer to and address each other, Mrs. Tyler and Rita, act as age and class markers: Rita is a lower-middle-class, street-smart 27-year old, while Mrs. Tyler is a sophisticated upper-middle-class woman in her 50s who nevertheless retrieves her working-class origins through her confessional narrative. Thus, we see her questioning her class identity as she slips "in" and "out" (98) of the expensive clothes her mother-in-law purchases for her.

Mrs. Tyler's ethnic self-revelation is instrumental in her self-presentation and in shaping Rita's perception of her. Mrs. Tyler generously informs Rita, and the reader, that she has no doubts about her origins—like her mother, she is Irish, a "Brennan" (157)—but Rita never mentions her own last name, thus preventing direct ethnic identification. William Boelhower argues that "by discovering the self implicit in the surname, one produces an ethnic seeing and understands himself as a social, an ethnic, subject" (81). As we have seen, the issue of naming has been of particular relevance to many Italian American women writers who, resorting to anglicizing their name or assuming a husband's name, have surrendered the most immediate sign of ethnic identification.

The exposure or self-exposure of one's Italian ancestry has recently become more widespread. In a lecture entitled "Cryptoethnicity," given at the 1995 Modern Language Association (MLA) Conference in Chicago, Linda (Bortalotti) Hutcheon thus "outed" Sandra Mortola Gilbert, Marianna De Marco Torgovnick, and Cathy (Notari) Davidson, noting that for the men, "Frank Lentricchia, Dominick La Capra, John Paul Russo, Joseph Pivato, there is no cryptonym, no social cryptography" (Ciongoli and Parini 248).[21] Scholars of Italian American literature are familiar with Sandra Mortola Gilbert, the poet and memoirist (as well as acclaimed feminist scholar and former president of the MLA) who has, through most of her career, written and published poetry that, although until a few years ago less well known than her criticism, clearly revealed her Italian American identity. Torgovnick, another well-known scholar, has become familiar as an Italian American author to readers and critics of Italian American literature only after the publication of the collection of essays, *Crossing Ocean Parkway: Readings by an Italian American Daughter* (1994), for which she used her maiden name, De Marco. Yet another case is Davidson, who, as far as I know, has not shown a specific concern with elaborating on her Italian ethnicity in published work, with the exception of references in her memoir, *36 Views of Mount Fuji* (1993).[22]

The effort to articulate one's ethnic voice and to construct narratives that claim a position of agency for members of immigrant communities is further complicated when an author must transcend the culturally imposed limitations on gender and sexual identity. She may translate her multiple foreignness into a language that is acquiescent and rebellious at once. The speaker of Maria Mazziotti Gillan's "Public School No. 18/Paterson, New Jersey," contrasts her "words smooth" in her "mouth" "at home," where she "chatter[s]" and is "proud," to her silence in school, where she "grope[s] for the right English/word" (*Where I Come From* 12). Such dynamics between speech and silence, Italian and English, family and school, also pervade poems such as "Growing Up Italian," in which English is likened to hail that hits the speaker hard, while Italian dances on her tongue and is silenced by the hostile school environment (*Where I Come From* 54). In her first book of poems, a chapbook entitled *Taking Back My Name*, Gillan turns self-silencing into the subject matter of her poetry. An interrogation of American culture's intolerance for Italian Americans—even as the tokens of Italian American culture have become in the last decade successful commodities—underscores the works of many contemporary Italian American women authors who feel compelled to reverse their history of cultural silencing. Not unlike Frances Winwar's anglicization of her name, the speaker of Gillan's "Public School No. 18, Paterson, New Jersey" resorts to self-silencing because she is afraid that "the Italian word/will sprout from . . . [her]/mouth like a rose" (*Where I Come From* 12). For contemporary Italian American women writers, the Italian word often is doomed to remain unspoken. The characters in Rita Ciresi's first work, *Mother Rocket,* a collection of short stories, represent a wide ethnic spectrum because, as Joshua Fausty argues, the author "infuses her ambivalent sense of her cultural identity into her characters, linking her quest for authorial/ethnic self-definition to their multicultural identities" (204).[23] Her narrative reveals a delicate negotiation between the impulse to cancel traces of ethnic identity and the impulse toward writing with an accent.

In *Split Skirt,* the absence of Rita's name, then, "produces" ethnic invisibility. Italian American ethnicity surfaces, though, when Mrs. Tyler tells Rita about Judy Gennaro, her long-lost "best" friend, the only one she ever had (159). She quotes the reaction of her husband, John, after hearing screams coming from the Gennaros' house, where Judy is repeatedly the victim of her husband's abuse: "Goddamn Italians" (159). John's comment, which reproduces the common stereotype of Italian American men as wifebeaters, represents the only direct reference to Italians in the book. When she first refers to Judy, Mrs. Tyler mentions only obliquely her background: she is "Mediterranean" (157). She never specifies her ethnicity. Moreover, John's remark does not elicit further elaboration on Mrs. Tyler's part or a response from Rita: Mrs. Tyler acts as if she is unaware of Rita's ethnic background, which is not surprising, since Rita herself seems to have erased ethnic memory. Nevertheless, it is noteworthy that in *Split Skirt* the two women who act as Mrs. Tyler's confidantes are both Italian. The receptacle of their friends' secrets and their author's ethnic identity, these characters serve as alter egos of sort. Rossi thus inscribes her ethnic autobiographical narrative in a text that does not advertise itself as an Italian American novel.

If Mrs. Tyler sees "secrecy" as the only means by which to maintain "her two separate realities" (122)—she sees herself as a "double agent" (120)—the narrative of *Split Skirt* self-consciously dramatizes Rossi's own "separate realities," her ethnic "split," by developing into a series of alternating sections in which the two characters take turns telling their stories, playing the parts of both author and audience. Destabilizing authorial power, the dual narrative of *Split Skirt* enables each character to recount her story as an autobiographical oral narrative, a genre characteristic of the early stages of ethnic literature, which typically presents the speaker as an authorized witness.[24]

In her study of ethnic writers, Bonnie Tusmith argues that the "specific motivation behind" the use of such strategies as vernacular speech patterns is the "artistic validation of one's ethnic culture and value system against a hegemonic European American standard in literature" (25).[25] Rossi's narrative does not rely on the vernacular in the overt way in which other texts do, yet it does emphasize the oral aspect of storytelling. Thus, the author questions the "validation" of the ethnic experience by shifting the focus onto the individual and away from the group experience, and connects authenticity with self- instead of group-authorization. Throughout the novel, Rossi struggles to forge a viable relationship between self and other, rejecting notions of community based solely on loyalty to the ethnic group, and thus articulating her position as a writer who draws on her ethnic experience by rewriting its stories and rethinking ideas of authenticity and tradition. While both Mrs. Tyler and Rita commit themselves to speaking the "truth" (23), to going back to the origins, they soon realize that they are so enmeshed in roles and plots they did not fabricate for themselves that the "truths" they tell are always provisional and require scrutiny and questioning on their part. These narrators therefore engage in a process of continuous reauthorization, which also includes reevaluating their positions in old plots and even self-consciously questioning the plots they envision for themselves.

What has distinguished Italian American women writers from their male counterparts has been a greater willingness to expose the flaws of their culture, despite the ostracism that oftentimes follows from such a choice. The historian Donna Gabaccia argues that oral histories of immigrant families diverge along gender lines; women characteristically "more willingly discussed family problems than men, who more typically presented sanitized or romanticized memories" (Gabaccia, "Italian American

Women" 43). This greater willingness to give voice to family secrets, to break the silence, is evident in the works of Mary Cappello, Louise De-Salvo, Mary Saracino, Daniela Gioseffi, Kym Ragusa, Susanne Antonetta, and Maria Laurino; these women all have addressed historically unspeakable subjects, such as physical violence within the family, incest, racism and prejudice, working-class shame, mental illness, and adultery. Kym Ragusa's video *fuori/outside* explores the interconnections between family secrets and one's sense of identity, within the family and within the culture. The silence and secrecy within her Italian American father's family over her African American origins is, in turn, connected to the silence surrounding her Italian American grandmother's and great-grandmother's history, as well as the history of violence against women and of discrimination against Italian Americans.

Writing about working-class identity and history, Janet Zandy has repeatedly emphasized that becoming part of the middle class represents, in certain respects, a sign of the success of working-class families who want to push their children out and beyond the constraints of their working-class living conditions, but it also represents a painful separation and migration from one's home. Typically, this separation is geographical as well as social and economic: It involves leaving the neighborhood to move into the suburbs. It takes the form of a migration that is reminiscent of the other migration, also motivated by the desire for social and economic improvement. Leaving "home" means leaving a community, with all the concomitant manifestations and consequences.

Like other multicultural writers, Rossi rejects the notion of an exclusive narratorial power in favor of a decentered narrative that allows a multivoiced narratorial situation. In the last section of *Split Skirt,* Rossi resorts to a third-person narrative: Acting as a removed camera eye that privileges Rita's perspective, the narrative records the two protagonists' reunion outside the county jail. The seemingly omniscient narrative gaze does not come across as an all-powerful, all-controlling device but, rather, as enacting a shift toward yet another subject position, one from which the authorial voice brings together different perspectives.

In a multicultural society, John Brenkman argues, it is necessary that everyone become "fluent enough in *one another's* vocabularies and histories to share the forum of political deliberation on an equal footing," and that everyone engage "others' contingent vocabularies" (89) as well as one's own. *Split Skirt* illustrates such an engagement with "others' contingent vocabularies," through its inclusion of the voice of Luz, the Hispanic teenage prostitute who speaks in the first person in the penultimate section. Luz's connection to Rita and her role as a "sister" (127), another sister, enables her to participate in the narrative space Rita and Mrs. Tyler have been forging together. Appropriately, Rossi dedicates the novel to her own "sisters." Typically, multivoiced narratives by "ethnic" authors create a space that, in privileging certain voices, also excludes nonmembers, for example Amy Tan's intergenerational novels, Cristina Garcia's *Dreaming in Cuban*, Alice Walker's *The Color Purple*. In *Split Skirt*, Rossi experiments with a different kind of narrative perspective. If Rossi employs the dialogue between her two characters as the means by which to establish a conversation between her own Irish and Italian ethnicities, the inclusion of Luz signals an effort—albeit a problematic one—to open up the ethnic space and to create a narrative that emphasizes not sameness and consensus but difference and possibilities for communication, even as her choice poses the question of what is involved in presuming to speak on behalf of an-other.[26]

Yet, clearly defined boundaries in Rossi's narrative prevent the other from being subsumed into the narrating selves. Rita and Mrs. Tyler cannot see Luz and her cellmate Madeline. Separated by the walls of their cells, they can only hear each other's voices. Of course, one may find Rossi's use of prison as a setting troubling. Although there are realistic elements in her representations, one might argue that her novel does not pay adequate attention to social and racial issues. Nevertheless, her characters' words generate both self-centered monologues and self-less conversations, directed inward and outward, asserting both uniqueness—difference—and connection. Rossi's multivoiced narrative maintains the specificity of Italian American, Irish American, and Latina characters, but it also explores possibilities for a broader dialogue that recognizes the creative potential of intersections and opens the borders of the ethnic/authorial space.

Discussing what he calls a "third generation renaissance" of Italian American writers, Gardaphé explains:

> When we examine later writers, those who are grandchildren of immigrants, we enter a period in which the immigrant past is recreated, not through self-reflection, but through a more distant historical perspective, a perspective gained by removal from the ethnic experience and resulting in the recreation of the immigrant experience in America through more distinctively fictional forms. ("Italian American Fiction" 71)

Mrs. Tyler's recollection of her fear of being mistaken for an "immigrant" (49)—the only reference to the journey that brought her family to America—epitomizes in its singularity the status of ethnic memory for writers like Rossi. The recovery of memory and the claiming of cultural identity constitute two related strategies adopted by Italian American women as well as women from other ethnic minorities. Rossi's work articulates an effort not so much to recover that memory but to reinvent it, which is what she does in her novel *The Houseguest,* loosely based on her family history, as the author herself informs the reader.[27]

Other authors explore the place of memory without necessarily linking it directly to ethnic experience. Carole Maso opens her novel *Defiance* with the provocative claim: "It's a memory, so you can change it" (3). Yet, emigration complicates and deepens one's relationship to memory, possibly because of the gap between different versions of stories heard within the family and the geography that framed and shaped stories and the people who inhabited them; places and people can be known in immigrant history only through what is remembered and passed on. If the past, as Salman Rushdie writes, is "a country from which we have all emigrated . . . [and] its loss is part of our common humanity" (12), Rita, Mrs. Tyler, and Luz transcend the specificity of their experiences by sharing their memories and participating in each other's sense of loss and displacement, their "common humanity" in Rushdie's sense.[28]

Demonstrating the specificity of the cultural displacement experienced by Italian American women, Rossi compels the reader to define and question the kind of recognition sought by Italian Americans and members of other culturally unrecognized ethnicities. The inadequacy of prevailing representations of Italian American culture in the United States prompts authors like Rossi to narrate different and untold aspects of the ethnic experience—and Rossi is not alone. For example, Rose Romano rejects the label of "ethnic" that reduces cultural identity to a series of tokens, devoid of referential ties to the diversity of Italian American social reality. In "Mutt Bitch," she claims: "If I have no culture/I can say nothing;/therefore, if I say nothing,/I have no culture" (*Vendetta* 37). Romano, like Rossi, rejects the notion of a quintessential Italian American identity. These and other Italian American women writers establish themselves as intellectual voices that move beyond nostalgic and blindly celebratory views of their ethnicity. In doing so, they demonstrate the power of literary texts to explore, interrogate, and offer forceful alternatives to current social and political realities. As Romano indicates, one has no choice but to speak if one wants to have a culture. Italian American women's writings negotiate and trouble categories of the personal and the public, exposing how the lives and voices of individuals in the minority are products of dominant discourses of identity, even as they show how such people can become effective agents of resistance and change. These works challenge the mainstream imagination and its stereotyping; they present alternative visions of ethnicity that both include an awareness of the hostile powers working against its expression and dare to imagine a future—and to create a present—in which such forces would cease to have relevance.

The signs of Italian American culture have become so stultified that for Italian American women it is imperative to reclaim those signs, and to reinscribe new meanings in them. Rossi and other writers capture the problematic status of Italian American culture by simultaneously articulating and suppressing the signs of its presence, and they require a reader willing to learn how to read the almost-silent signs, how to hear the voices that speak with an accent that wants to be heard.

❀ ❀ ❀

A beautiful Mediterranean credenza cabinet with double speakers, a perfect accent to any room decor.

—*State (Columbia, S. Carolina),*
Oxford English Dictionary

❀ ❀ ❀

Chapter 5

"Spills of Mysterious Substances"

I wonder if those feasts were a kind of ritual performed by people who had lived too long in the shadows of want and hunger, a way of telling themselves that at least on certain days the good life was theirs.

—*Michael Parenti*, Dirty Truths

. . . after my mother's death, I inherited a large portion of my grandmother's "collections." These included bundles of fabric tied by her hand, dating from the early 1900's, as well as family household objects handmade in Italy, decorative pieces, family books and writings from the 1800's. The sculptures and installations of the last years have incorporated many of these objects, some exquisitely beautiful, some the stuff of everyday.

—*B. Amore*, Lifeline—filo della vita:
An Italian American Odyssey 1901–2001

Though she didn't know how to read or write, when it came to cooking she knew everything there was to know.

—*Laura Esquivel*, Like Water for Chocolate

M y daughter had just begun kindergarten at the Immaculate Conception Elementary School in Schenectady, in upstate New York. Apart from the small icon of the Madonna delle Lacrime of Syracuse (Sicily, not New York) hanging above her bed that my mother had given her, this was Emily's first formal encounter with the mysteries of Catholicism. A few weeks into the school year, visible signs of devotion began to emerge, especially at dinnertime, when Emily would solemnly cross herself before

eating and recite: "In the name of the Father, the Son, and the Mother."
Pleasantly surprised to learn that the Catholic Church had finally made
room for the Mother in the divine hierarchy, I did not question her; I sim-
ply smiled at this welcome change in the prayer imprinted in my child-
hood memories. A few weeks later, though, I was disabused of my illusion.
Emily switched to the orthodox formula: "In the name of the Father, the
Son, and the Holy Spirit." When I asked her, "Whatever happened to the
Mother?" her sour answer was: "Oh, mommy, she was a mistake!"

This anecdote captures the predicament of Italian American women,
particularly those of Southern Italian descent, as they find themselves negotiating a relationship fraught with contradictions to a patriarchal culture
in which women are simultaneously marginalized and placed at the center of worship, religious and familial. Mothers and grandmothers can be
the objects of a secular veneration that might lead one to argue that a kind
of matriarchate exists in Southern Italy, where each village has its own variety of Madonnas—such as the Madonna of Alemanna of Gela and the
Black Madonna of Tindari[1]—and women saints, such as Santa Lucia, who
died in the fourth century A.D. during the persecution of Diocletian and
who is worshiped as patron saint of Syracuse and—her eyes on a platter—
of the visually impaired; or Sant'Agata, celebrated in Catania on 5 February in a lavish feast with an elaborate procession during which the statue
of the saint is carried through the old city, including up the steep Via San
Giuliano that the *portatori* (bearers) ascend without hesitation, despite the
massive burden on their shoulders.[2] During the feast, people eat pastries
called *minne d'a santa,* "the saint's tits," to commemorate her mutilated
breasts, in honor of the virgin saint who refused to give in to the lascivi-
ous desire of the Roman consul Quintinian. These gory images of mar-
tyrdom, which often take on cannibalistic overtones consistent with
Catholic dogma and stories, are by no means infrequent in the iconography of Mediterranean Catholicism—and thus in Southern Italian and Italian American culture.[3]

Italian American women transcribe in their works modified versions of
the prayers and recipes, customs and icons, rituals and legends that populate the cultural landscape of their ancestors. In Louise DeSalvo's novel
Casting Off, the cookbook is portrayed as a palimpsestic autobiographical
text. Helen, one of the two protagonists, thinks of how "one could read the
progress of her life in the spills of mysterious substances that now nearly
obliterated her favorite recipes. . . . this dripping and this dribbling had
been Helen's way of making history, and she had been reluctant to give it
up in favor of the pristine page with no splotches and no spills. . . . Sometimes she wondered why she always remembered events in terms of the
things that she had eaten" (28–30). The phrase "mysterious substances" can

be used to describe those elements of material culture that are transplanted from one soil into another, to develop and blossom into simultaneously new and unfamiliar entities.[4] This chapter examines some of the ways in which Italian American women authors incorporate representations of material culture into their works and use these cultural productions as the signs through which to articulate ethnicity but also as the markers of difference, as accents that signal these authors' distinct uses of the cultural materials of their ethnic origins. These accents are traces of cultural memory that has undergone the trauma of emigration, with its devastating but also creative and culturally productive results.

The study of material culture takes on a progressive politicized significance when combined with the study of the cultures of ethnic minorities, women, and working-class people—in other words, those groups that, through a process of systematic oppression, have been excluded from public discourse. Such an exclusion has in turn denied them cultural dignity. Indeed, it is specifically within a class context that we must consider the relevance of material culture to a group's sense of identity and history. Feminist writers, artists, and scholars have argued for the recovery of material culture as part of a process of cultural reclamation without which marginalized people would be doomed to remain silenced. Alice Walker, for example, writes of the quilts and gardens of poor African American women whom she describes as both her forebears and her artistic models. These "anonymous" women were, in Walker's words, "artist[s] who left their mark in the only material [they] . . . could afford and in the only medium their position in society allowed them to use" (239). Joanna Kadi entitles her collection of writings by Arab-American and Arab-Canadian feminists, *Food for Our Grandmothers.* It is not accidental that, as Kadi notes, "the theme of food is woven through the book. A common Arabic theme is used to embody the themes connecting each section, and a recipe using that common food accompanies each section" (xx). Her anthology thus stands as an "offering" to the grandmothers and the community (xx).

Feminist scholarship has emphasized the importance of women's domestic work in relation to women's creativity and aesthetics: "For women, the meaning of sewing and knitting is 'connecting'—connecting the parts of one's life, and connecting to other women—creating a sense of community and wholeness" (Hammond, quoted in Hedges 5).[5] Yet, one cannot forget that while needlework carries the signature of female artistry, garment work has historically been the source of exploitative, underpaid female work in the Old World as well as the New.[6] An important item of material culture, the bedspread that appears in Helen Barolini's *Umbertina* (discussed in Chapter 2), helps us understand much about immigrant culture and history: It embodies Umbertina's hope for economic success and social ascent and it also constitutes a physical token of the ties to her culture of origins, to her native village that she longs for on her deathbed. The study of material culture, *Umbertina* suggests, is imperative for women and working-class people, for their history is to be found in the history of objects such as that bedspread.[7] Like other Italian American women authors, Barolini foregrounds the importance of material culture and the very real consequences that the loss of artifacts can have on the members of a cultural group.

For many authors who understand their work as both literary and political, poetry and politics are not merely theoretical acts: they cannot be separated from—in fact, they must be articulated through—the language of material culture. As Italian American, especially working-class academics and intellectuals as well as writers, artists, and filmmakers, have become increasingly concerned with describing and interpreting themselves—as opposed to being described and interpreted by others—they have inevitably engaged in the recovery and analysis of their material culture. Louise DeSalvo, Sandra M. Gilbert, Mary Cappello, Maria Mazziotti Gillan, Nancy Savoca, Mariarosy Calleri, Kym Ragusa, Nancy Azara, Helen De Michiel, B. Amore, Susan Caperna Lloyd, Rosette Capotorto, JoAnne Mattera, and Penny Arcade—to mention just a few—are among those who have actively engaged in reconnecting with and recreating the languages and stories of their communities and cultures.

Material culture both epitomizes the material circumstances of the lives of the economically and socially disenfranchised and bespeaks the resistance that they have courageously offered to the forces and institutions that would crush them, as in the story of Mary Cappello's grandfather, a cobbler who inscribed poems and journal entries on the scraps of his labor: Cappello in turn incorporates his writings into her memoir *Night Bloom* (1998). Often at odds with a culture they simultaneously embrace and reject, Italian American women—and, in a heightened way, gay and lesbian writers—seek to transform core values and rituals of their culture along the terms of the lives they have chosen. Thus they generate narratives that defamiliarize the familiar and familiarize the unfamiliar in distinctly Italian American contexts such as the church, the kitchen, the dinner table, the pizza parlor, the garden, and the shoe repair shop.

Religious iconography and food provide some of the most significant and provocative manifestations of Italian American culture in literature, film, and art, possibly because they have been, more than other elements of material culture, frequently subjected to stultified representations by the media. In the works of many Italian American women writers and artists, they surface under a new guise, shedding light on and telling anew old stories and histories.[8]

In the Name of the Mother

In an essay entitled *"La famiglia:* An Ethno-Class Experience," included in *Dirty Truths,* Michael Parenti weaves personal memory and cultural analysis, and comments that, among early Italian immigrant communities in the United States, religion was the domain of women:

> The immigrant males might feel some sort of attachment to the saints and the church but few attended mass regularly and some openly disliked priests. In the literal sense of the word, they were "anticlerical," suspicious of clergymen who did not work for a living but lived off other people's labor and who did not marry but spent all their time around women and children in church. (258)

According to Italian American men, then, women experienced religion as distinctly feminine. Yet, one must not forget the markedly patriarchal structures and strictures of Catholicism that these women had to negotiate as they lived their religion—and spirituality—as daily experiences, rooted in the quotidian, as opposed to the extraordinary.

For years, Italian American women have been reinventing and creatively incorporating the religious experiences of their mothers and female ancestors, infusing their complicated sense of Italian American identity and history in these "rewritings."

"Spirit House of the Mother," "Tree Altar," "Dwelling," "Goddess Wall": monumental sculptures, characteristically carved in wood, reminiscent, with their shimmering gold and deep blood red, of the lavish religious processions in Southern Italy. These works by the sculptor Nancy Azara recall the mixture of primitive and baroque, beautiful and ugly, grotesque and holy, the violence and healing of Southern Italian Catholicism. Much like the processions, in which the human and the divine meet on an egalitarian level, Nancy Azara's sculptures appropriate the divine and pay tribute to a woman-made religion. Thus, Azara explores in her work the problematic power of female creativity within the domestic space. In an essay on Azara, the art critic Flavia Rando writes:

> The construction of monumental environmental sculptures has a particular significance in the context of a feminist [art] movement that recognizes both women's responsibility for the making of home (for others) and women's difficulty in finding a sanctuary for the self. (17)

Like Azara, many Italian American women writers and artists question the place of women in their intrinsically Catholic culture and, in remaking old mythologies, they mold new ones.

Azara's work is mythical and political in a contemporary way. Her wood
sculptures, for example, evoke "the sacred connection between women and
trees" (Turner 65). Azara's work emerges within the context of a cultural
and artistic movement centered on women's spirituality, a movement that
maintains important links with ecofeminism.[9] Azara's art, with its recovery
and gorgeous transformation of discarded natural materials, thus expresses a
clear—even as it is artistically evocative—stance against ecological devastation. "The whole point of earth-based spiritual traditions . . . is that there is
no dichotomy between the material and the spiritual world. . . . the whole
subversive character of this tradition is based in the idea that the material
world is the ground of the sacred" (Adler in Turner 65). The spirituality of
Azara's sculptures sinks its roots in ancient Southern Italian myths, but it also
sends out a powerful message that reverberates for the contemporary world.

Southern Italy, because of the lasting influence of ancient Greek culture, was slow to convert to Christianity. When the conversion did finally
occur, it took place through a peculiar blending of Christian and pagan elements, in Sicily more acutely than elsewhere in Italy. Churches were built
using the columns and stones of Greek temples, for example, Santa Maria
dei Greci in Agrigento, the Cathedral of Santa Lucia in Siracusa, and the
Cathedral of the Madonna dell'Alemanna in Gela. The new cults combined with the old, which thus survived, albeit in a veiled manner. The
many religious festivals that mark the passing of the year are often rooted
in the cults of ancient goddesses. It is especially during the religious feasts
that the clash—or blend—of Christian and pre-Christian elements becomes most evident. While the Church seemingly oversees these celebrations, it is typically various popular organizations, often descendants of the
medieval guilds, which are actually in charge. The religious frenzy that
characterizes so many of these celebrations is more reminiscent of ancient
Greek and pre-Greek rituals of worship, or medieval mysticism, than the
structured and controlled rituals of the modernized Catholic Church.

Susan Caperna Lloyd, photographer, filmmaker, and writer, recounts
her fascinating search for the roots of the matriarchal cult of Demeter and
Persephone in Sicily in her travel memoir *No Pictures in My Grave: A Spiritual Journey in Sicily* (1992). Unlike her earlier video *Processione,* in which
a male narrator traces the history of the Easter Procession in Trapani, high-
lighting its deeply felt place in the local culture of the Trapanesi, *No Pictures in My Grave* is unquestionably a woman-centered book. This memoir
is about multiple journeys and discoveries, rooted in the geographical and
the spiritual, in history and myth. The story of the Italian American woman
traveling to Sicily and negotiating an ambivalent relationship with a community that is at once protective and suffocating is interwoven with the
compelling description of the preparations for the Easter procession and

the entire town's involvement and, ultimately, with the insights that Lloyd achieves, insights that are personal and cultural, historical and mythical.

Following the Easter Procession in Trapani, and traveling throughout Sicily, she becomes aware of the subversive aspects of Catholic rituals practiced by the people under the censoring eyes of an all-controlling Church. While embracing the subversive and anti-authoritarian Catholicism of the Trapanesi, the author must struggle to find a place within the patriarchal hierarchy that governs the unfolding of the procession, from which the women are excluded, having been assigned the role of mournful spectators. Yet, as she feels the need to turn the cultural story into a personal one, she poses a question that then motivates the entire Sicilian journey and the narrative that grows out of it:

> I recognized something of my grandmother in this powerful though sorrowful Madonna, and I became determined to understand the long-suffering nature of Italian women's lives. How was it that in Sicily the focus of the whole town was not on the dying son but on the grief-struck mother? (6)

Her travel through the island becomes a "spiritual journey" during which her encounters and "readings" of the rituals, the icons, and the artifacts of Sicilian religion and culture lead her to identify the survival of woman-centered religious practices that Lloyd believes sink their roots in the ancient cult of pre-Christian goddesses. In her reading—one that is given credibility by the archeological and architectural history of the island—[10]Demeter becomes the Mater Dolorosa while Persephone, the child lost to the underworld, becomes Christ. Thus, the author connects Easter with pre-Christian fertility rituals that took place in the Spring and were associated with the cult of the goddess of the harvest and the goddess of the underworld.

By the end of her journey, the author is able to participate actively in the Easter procession—as a *portatore,* a bearer of the platforms and statues—and is thus able to find "the lost part" of herself (188), which she simultaneously equates with the Black Madonna, Cybele, *l'Addolorata,* and "the thankful Demeter having found her daughter again" (188). Through her autobiographical narrative, Lloyd documents the blending of Christian and pre-Christian elements in the Sicilian Easter procession. Searching for the matriarchal roots of the procession, the author paints a portrait of a popular and subversive Catholicism that, while seemingly bowing down to the Church, maintains its own integrity and a distinctly anti-authoritarian quality.

It is this peculiar kind of Catholicism that one recognizes in the pages of Tina De Rosa's *Paper Fish.* The appreciation for the small objects of creation that prevails in Grandma Doria's fables and throughout the narrative draws on a Catholicism linked to the people and to the earth, reminiscent of Franciscan mysticism and its rejection of the authoritarian practices of the Church. The poetry of the book lies in its capacity to uncover, through language, the sacred in mundane objects and rituals. It is significant that the working title of *Paper Fish* was "Saintmakers": In De Rosa's eyes, the "faces" of her family members and "the tiny, ordinary lives they had led" are indeed "holy, and of great value" ("Career" 9). This holiness maintains a physical and mundane quality; it is not an abstract entity. In *Paper Fish,* "Doriana's face was the ivory-white face of the Virgin Mother. . . . Grandma Doria watched the sleeping face of the child on the pillow. The eyelids closed perfectly, like the lines in a saint's statue; the eyelids seemed carved by the hands of a saint-maker" (*Paper Fish* 63). The sacredness of the quotidian is revealed especially in the descriptions of Grandma Doria's work and stories: Her "shabby old fingers" perform miracles (21); while "breaking the red peppers" for the sausages that will make Carmolina laugh as she eats them, Doria is simultaneously "making the world" for her granddaughter (15).[11] The domestic detail takes on a mystical aura as the storyteller's touch discovers the spiritual in the most mundane objects and details. Thus, Carmolina's reversed writing on a bakery bag suggests her "access to literary creativity in the midst of everyday reality" (Bona, "Broken Images" 98). Indeed, it is this "everyday reality"—the reality within which material culture is to be found—that provides the poetic subject matter of the book.

De Rosa's pantheistic vision endows her surroundings, people, places, and objects, with spirituality. The rugs that hung out of the houses resembled "great tongues" that "dry in the sun" and that "panted out of the clutter of the tight rooms into the sunshine above the head of the horse who watched the children" (34). In the description of the first encounter between Carmolina's parents, Sarah and Marco, which takes place in her father's restaurant, where Sarah works as a waitress, a spiritual aura equally envelopes Sarah *and* the pots in the kitchen: As "the sunlight through the windows banged the pots hard and metallic, the silver light bounced off them and into her eyes" (4). The kitchen glows with the light of Sarah and Marco's newly born love and the reader is transported into a universe in which the ecstasy of love is a miracle that happens inside the small restaurant, filled "with light," to the delight of God and the children looking on the scene (5).

The spiritual aura that pervades the narrative draws on Doria's Southern Italian roots and the distinct brand of Catholicism practiced in Southern Italy. Blending folklore and Christian beliefs, Doria manufactures tales that explain the world to Carmolina and teach her about sorrow and joy, life and death:

There is a mountain in Italy filled with candles. . . . Each person has his own
candle. When he is born the candle is lit; when the candle goes out, he dies.
You can see this mountain, Carmolina, only in your dreams, but God will not
let you see your own candle, even in a dream. If there is a mistake, and you
see your own candle, you will die. This is how people die in their sleep. (24)

Doria's God is not infallible. The story of the mountain of candles, like all
of Doria's fables, draws on a mythology rooted in the storytelling of peasants who, while timorous of God and intimidated into subjection by a
Church complicitous with the landlords, were undaunted in their transformation of Christian dogmas.[12]

In his discussion of Part VI of the novel, Fred Gardaphé points out that
Grandma Doria "is carried on a chair up to Carmolina's room in a scene
that recreates the traditional procession of the Madonna" to see her granddaughter dressed as a bride:[13]

> Carmolina achieves her adult identity, not by attaching herself to a man, but
> by taking it from her grandmother who acknowledges it through the bless-
> ing she gives her granddaughter.
>   In preparation for the visit Grandma Doria dons her blue dress. . . . Blue
> is the color traditionally associated with the Madonna, and it is fitting that
> the blue-eyed matriarch of the BellaCasa family wears it as she is carried up
> to see her granddaughter. (Gardaphé, *Italian Signs* 137)[14]

Unmistakably, the unorthodox religion of the book has its origin in
Grandmother Doria, who is repeatedly associated with "God" in the novel.
This humanizing of religion—a recognition of the divine in the human—
which, after all, is intrinsic to the origins of Christian theology, is creatively
incorporated into this and other domestic rituals of the BellaCasa family.
    De Rosa's poetry continues the reimagining of the stories and icons of
Italian Catholicism, which is an integrating part of the narrative fabric of
Paper Fish. Discussing the conceptions of her poems "Therese" and "Mary
of Magdala," De Rosa describes the poetical moment as a mystical one, in
which one poem comes to her visually, the other audibly. In both poems,
the connection with Jesus is central, and the two speakers are portrayed as
female Christ figures. Like Lloyd, who sees Christ as a Christian transformation of Persephone, De Rosa is interested in exploring the feminine aspect of Jesus. In "Mary of Magdala," Mary, the speaker of the poem,
juxtaposes Jesus to the violent men who want to kill her, and to the elders
who spied on Suzannah during her bath, "brutally" sundering her "pri-
vacy"(Giunta, *VIA* 237).[15] "Therese" also evokes Jesus, although in quite
different tones. The speaker is St. Therese of Lisieux, the Little Flower to
whom Jesus appears "like a simple shadow" (Giunta, *VIA* 235) among the

Carmelites. Mystical and sensual at once, the poem depicts an experience of Catholicism that is distant from the official dictates and practices of the Catholic Church. The visionary experience takes place in the modest pantry of the convent, where the communion between Therese's and Jesus' bleeding palms occurs. De Rosa's choice of Therese and her mysticism rooted in the quotidian connects the spiritual with the objects and gestures of domestic life.

Therese of Lisieux provides a model for the protagonist of Nancy Savoca's film *Household Saints* (1993), based on Francine Prose's novel, in which the saint stands for a mysticism of the mundane and the quotidian. Engulfed in the strange mysticism she has inherited from her grandmother—a mixture of food recipes, icons of saints, prayers, and superstition—Teresa Santangelo sees herself as a reincarnation of the Little Flower and attempts to follow her example of joyous self-sacrifice. Through a mix of mysticism and superstition, comedy and poetry, Savoca evokes a world in which the domestic simultaneously engenders a feminine/feminist spirituality and a critique of Catholicism and domesticity. While the scene of the miracle of the shirts in Savoca's film offers a critique of domesticity, there is, in the vision of this filmmaker, something unmistakably holy about Teresa's madness and her compulsive domesticity: Her chores become prayers. In critiquing that which oppresses women, Savoca also creates a poetical evocation of the power of women to create and endow with poetical significance the monotonous and dulling work of domestic life.[16] Like De Rosa's poetry, *Household Saints* intertwines the objects of religion and sexuality in ways that are unpredictable and not easily decipherable. Teresa surrenders her virginity as a gift to God, another "flower" she offers to her Jesus. In a striking scene, after she has lost her virginity, she lies on the ground in her sparsely furnished, convent-like room: Her arms are outstretched as if on a cross.

Catholic icons and sex also commingle in Louise DeSalvo's *Vertigo*, in which she writes of the nights during which, as a child, she would be awakened by her sister's nightmares and the "stifled moans" of her parents' lovemaking. "To distract herself," she would "concentrate on the holy picture of the Sacred Heart of Jesus tucked into the corner of . . . [her] mother's mirror," dimly lit by a nightlight at the foot of her own bed, placed in the same room as her parents. The child observes, with perverse fascination, Jesus "holding his bleeding heart in front of him on an outstretched plate" (72). This gory Catholicism has much in common with Latin American Catholicism, especially as it is experienced and revisited by women, as evident in the paintings of Frida Kahlo.[17] The mingling of the "sounds and smells and movements" of her parents having sex and the graphic picture of the Sacred Heart does not solely offer an example of the striking pictorialism of the Catholic iconography of DeSalvo's childhood world—and that of so many Italian Americans; it also serves as the means by which DeSalvo sheds light on childhood trauma. *Vertigo,* which also deals with the sexual abuse that the author suffered as a child at the hands of a female caregiver, and with her sexual precocity as an adolescent, uses religion to explain the tangled ways in which sexuality emerges in a child's life. DeSalvo's description focuses on the physicality of the experience of witnessing her parents' sex. The extreme, almost obscene, image of the heart bleeding on the plate, is all the more significant in light of the author's refusal of her mother's food, which I will discuss later in this chapter.[18]

Kym Ragusa's video *fuori/outside* offers another insightful and provocative representation of religion. The cultural recovery of the Procession of the Madonna of Mount Carmel in the Bronx—which is included in her memoiristic video *fuori/outside* through archival footage—is linked to the filmmaker's attempt to help her aging grandmother, who suffers from Alzheimer's disease, to recover her lost memory. Although no miracle occurs, this attempt serves as the springboard for other kinds of recovery and discovery, as Ragusa unveils family secrets for the first time. The delivery of these secrets by the grandmother to the granddaughter proves vital to the latter's self-understanding and to the reconstructive work of family and cultural history in which Ragusa has engaged. In some strange way, a miracle does happen.

Italian American women deal with Catholicism through the lens of gender and ethnicity but also grapple with gender and ethnicity through the lens of Catholicism. Unlike Italians of Italy, Italian Americans have historically experienced their Catholicism as marginal, in opposition to Anglo American protestantism and, even more so, to Irish Catholicism. Elaine Romaine describes her view of the relationship of Italian immigrants to the Irish church in a provocative poem, "you were always irish, god," that addresses this Irish god in a church in which the speaker "confessed/to being Italian" (Barolini, *The Dream Book* 306).[19] The women authors participating in the current Italian American literary and artistic renaissance also confess to being Italian, thus using confession, one of the most self-deprecating rituals of Catholicism, as a vehicle for ethnic and authorial assertion.

Contemporary Italian American women especially maintain a relationship to Catholicism that is much more complicated than that entertained by earlier authors such as Sister Blandina Segale or Rosa Cassettari, for whom devotion to God and the Madonna is a much simpler affair. The authors of these early autobiographical narratives do not intend to underscore their texts with the kind of multifaceted questioning of the place of religion in Italian American culture that we find in their literary descendants. The latter feel the urge to extricate themselves from but also to incorporate Catholicism into their works and lives. The objects, prayers, rituals, and fables of Catholicism are rewritten, with different accents, in the works of Italian American women, both affirming and deflecting the power of the religion they represent.

Italian American women authors thus recognize the necessity to confront the Catholic religion that many of them have repudiated at some point in their lives. In their works, they assert their power to rewrite Catholicism and, blending it with old and new mythologies, employ it as a vehicle for self-exploration and artistic affirmation. Catholicism enters the literature of Italian American women through the front door, but it is never treated obsequiously. Capturing and recreating the complexities of Southern Italian Catholicism and its blending of Christian and pre-Christian elements through its stories and material embodiment, women of Southern Italian ancestry especially regard the patriarchal practices—and theories—of Catholicism as an oppressive, yet rich, tradition—one to be both denied and appropriated, in order to disclaim, and reclaim, their ethnic identity.

Making Food

"Eating dinner alone feels like a symbol of my capitulation to American culture and my complete assimilation as an Italian American" (Tamburri, *FUORI* 31). Giovanna (Janet) Capone thus captures the experience of connection and disconnection common to many Italian American women who cling to the ritualistic quality of meals, and for whom eating is sacramental.

Food as a literary subject matter has long been a staple of Italian American literature. Male writers such as Pietro di Donato, Jerre Mangione, John Fante, Toni Ardizzone, Jay Parini, Peter Covino, and Anthony Valerio have illustrated in their works the multifarious ways in which food represents a central, never simple, element in Italian American culture. Tom Perrotta, for example, shows the links between the emotional desolation in the lives of his characters and the food they eat in the story "The Wiener Man."[20] Peter Covino's riveting poems "Box of Broken Things" and "Rice" offer terrifying descriptions of the connections between food, violence, and family politics: In these poems, the dinner table is a site of unspeakable violence, the altar on which women and children are sacrificed.[21]

The quality and intensity of this kind of poetical exploration of food emerges over and over again in the writings of Italian American women authors who, because of their gender, maintain an even more complex relationship with food and food rituals.[22] Cooking and eating—but also the processes by which and material conditions in which recipes are transmitted, foods prepared, conserved, offered, or refused—are central to the work of Italian American women authors.[23] For them, food dramatically articulates both a perception of the domestic space as oppressive and an awareness of the ways in which women empower themselves within that traditionally oppressive space.

Writers such as Louise DeSalvo, Rose Romano, Tina De Rosa, Sandra M. Gilbert, Mary Cappello, Anne Calcagno, Rosette Capotorto, Helen Barolini, Diane Raptosh, Nancy Caronia, Maria Laurino, Loryn Lipari, Kim Addonizio, Lucia Perillo, Mary Saracino, and Kathy Freeperson, among others, but also filmmakers such as Nancy Savoca, Kym Ragusa, Franca Barchiesi, Cara DeVito, Mariarosy Calleri, Rose Spinelli, Jeanette Vuocolo, and Liliana Fasanella, have variously turned to food as a tool through which to subvert popular views of Italian American ethnicity. Performance poet Annie Lanzillotto uses food as the springboard for controversial reflections on the links between gender, class, and sexuality, for example, in her monologue "Confessions of a Bronx Tomboy." Mary Cappello delves deep into the ambiguities of Italian food as a central cultural icon, writing, for example, of her father's refusal of his Sicilian family's food. While these writers—with the exception of Barolini—have not turned to the cookbook as a genre, they are all concerned with the interconnectedness of food-writing and life-writing, with recipes as narratives.[24] For a number of Italian American women, recipes—and the stories that surround them—represent literary occasions through which to explore their relationship to the cultural forces shaping their creative visions.

Criticizing Scorsese's *Italianamerican* (1974), Barolini argues that this autobiographical documentary offers yet another stereotypical representation of Italian Americans since it opens with Scorsese's parents sitting "at the food-laden table, eating," then cuts to the director's mother showing him how to make tomato sauce. "Doing the sauce, of course, is *the* metaphor for being an Italian American woman," remarks Barolini with sarcasm ("Becoming a Literary Person" 272). Barolini rejects this oversimplified view of Italian Americans, alert to the fact that such a view is deeply ingrained in American culture.[25] Yet, in 1988 she published *Festa,* a book of recipes that presents her as *the* Italian American woman "doing the sauce" rather than attempting to become a literary person. The title of one of her autobiographical essays, "Becoming a Literary Person Out of Context" (1986), clarifies the literary and autobiographical nature of *Festa.* With an awareness of the lack of context out of which her own work, as well as the work of other Italian American women, has emerged—and of the reasons behind such a lack—Barolini utilizes diverse spheres, even traditionally nonliterary ones, as occasions to become an author, an author "out of context."[26]

But contexts have, fortunately, changed. A shift has been occurring, even as predictable and culturally impoverished representations of Italian Americans continue to inhabit the world of media and advertising. Italian American women have, aggressively and creatively, questioned and rewritten the narratives that relegated them into unimaginative kitchens. Whether it is through films like Nancy Savoca's *True Love* and *Household Saints* or Kym Ragusa's *fuori/outside* and Mariarosy Calleri's *Hidden Island/L'isola sommersa,* or an unequivocal cookbook like Barolini's *Festa,* Italian American women have turned to food as a subject matter to contend with in their work.[27] The dinner table becomes a highly politicized site, as in Nancy Caronia's essay, "Setting the Table," in Giovanna (Janet) Capone's essay "A Divided Life: Being a Lesbian in an Italian American Family," in Louise DeSalvo's memoir "Anorexia," and in Rosette Capotorto's poem "The Oven." These authors variously address issues of homophobia, class identity, mental illness, drug addiction, abuse, and familial power dynamics within the context of the convivial gathering.

In the early 1990s, Rose Romano represented, as Fred Gardaphé puts it, "the avant-garde of an Italian American cultural consciousness . . . ready to explode" (*Dagoes Read* 196). And the explosion takes place among the flavors of Italian American cuisine. Defying stereotypes, Romano responds to the cultural cooptation of food—the most popular Italian American commodity alongside the mafia—and reappropriates the "signs" of Italian culture that, as Gardaphé indicates in his book, fill "American streets." Romano stuffs her poetry with food, as in the poem "To Show Respect," that opens with the lines, "Imagine a room full of Italian-American/Lesbians" (*Vendetta* 22). While the images of food convey a familiar abundance, Romano's *tavola* is undeniably not a traditional one, for gay and lesbian Italian Americans have not quite negotiated their seat at the Italian American table.

"'Italian,'" writes Mary Cappello in "Nothing to Confess: A Lesbian in Italian America," "'is the essence that I fear betraying in the exposition of lesbian desire'" (93). In poems such as "Ethnic Woman," "Confirmation (AKA The Sauce Poem)," "Italian Bread," "And She Laughs," "That We Eat," "Grandmother Cooking," "Vendetta," "Native Language 101," "Only the Americans," and "A Little Spaghetti," Romano constructs, largely relying on food imagery, the autobiographical narrative of a Sicilian Neapolitan American lesbian *contadina contessa* poet from Brooklyn, who lived for about a year in the small town of Alcamo, Sicily. Her work challenges the dictates of what she describes as an Italophobic, misogynist, and homophobic American culture.[28] "I'm tired of being stirred around/in a melting pot as though/I'm not a human being,/but a plum tomato," she writes in "Vendetta" (*Vendetta* 41). Although she juxtaposes Italy and America,

Romano refuses to romanticize the bounty of a nurturing motherland; instead she finds out for herself that Italy can be so culturally stifling—and perhaps even more misogynist and homophobic than the United States—that you can choke on Italian food.

Sandra Mortola Gilbert is another author who, in her representations of food, juggles convention, stereotype, evocative memory, and cultural critique. The descriptions of food in her poetry can be saturated with violence—more or less covert—as evidenced in "Mafioso." The poet addresses some notorious Italian Americans:

> Frank Costello eating spaghetti in a cell at San Quentin
> Lucky Luciano mixing up a mess of bullets and
> calling for parmesan cheese
> Al Capone baking a sawed-off shot gun into a
> huge lasagna—
>   are you my uncles, my
> only uncles? (*Kissing the Bread* 302)

While this poem expresses Gilbert's response to the popular representations of Italian Americans as mafiosi and spaghetti-eaters, her poetical reworking of tired stereotypes liberates them from the constraints to which they have been subjected by their commodification. Like Romano's poetry, Gilbert's is both rooted in and defiant of tradition. The image of the mafiosi transported from Sicily "in barrels/like pure olive oil/across the Atlantic" (302) possesses a quality that evades Puzo's, Coppola's, and Scorsese's analogous intertwining of food and violence.[29] The interjection, after the first stanza, of the lines "are you my uncles, my/only uncles?" offers a critique of the stereotype that these authors and filmmakers have accepted, and perpetuated unquestioningly, even as they have worked them into compelling cinematic images.

In the two epigraphs to her book of poems, *Emily's Bread* (1984), Gilbert establishes a connection with the Anglo-American tradition on which she has written extensively, especially with Susan Gubar in *The Madwoman in the Attic* and the three volumes of *No Man's Land,* by invoking Emily Brontë and Emily Dickinson, nineteenth-century recluse poets, as breadmakers. Yet many of the poems in this book speak of another seclusion: they speak of the hidden stories of other women, "the immigrant aunts . . . [the poet] visited/in the suburbs of . . . [her] childhood," who "told" her "stories" and who appear in a poem entitled "For the Muses" (17–18), where they serve a function analogous to, yet contrasting with, that of the two Emilies. Gilbert thus artfully kneads together the two cultural breads of her poetical

narrative: the English and American literary imagination and the immigrant, Italian American imagination.

In her most recent book, *Kissing the Bread,* the image of bread emerges
centrally again, although this time it is unequivocally associated with the
ancient Sicilian custom of kissing the bread before discarding it. "Still Life:
Woman Cooking," another poem in *Emily's Bread,* opens with the image
of spaghetti that

> . . . spins in its cauldron, a tangle of roots,
> moon white, writhing under bubbles. (65)

The writing emerges from the "cauldron" of the poet's memory, the
kitchens of her ancestors, those marginal yet powerful places refashioned
by her imagination. Ebullient memories, "writhing under bubbles," push
to come out, even though the price is high: the boiling spaghetti is "a tan-
gle of roots," both life-giving and suffocating, while the aromas of this
process of recovery can be "as sharp as needles" (65).

Gilbert draws an analogy between the cooking process—dividing, mea-
suring, pouring, sifting, straining—and the poetical process that requires a
searching, painful digging that prompts tears, "onions filling . . . [her] eyes"
(65). While "Every night is the feast of tongues," the poet wonders, "sometimes,"

> what is that white disturbance—
> like foam, like hissing—
>
> in the flour bin? (65)

Here as elsewhere, Gilbert endows her poetry with a certain eeriness, particularly forceful in the depictions of food. "Dark pots of jam" and "pale
cold eggs" in "The Kitchen Dream" (101) leave the reader "wondering,"
just like the speaker of "Still Life: Woman Cooking," who asks, at the close
of that poem, "What is that song the brook trout sing/as they crackle in
the pan?" (65).

The questioning mode and the dream-like aura so pervasive in Gilbert's
poetry invest the things of quotidian life with an elusive and ancient quality. In an essay entitled "Mysteries of the Hyphen: Poetry, Pasta, and Identity Politics," Gilbert writes that in her poetry she has turned to Italy "as a
country and a concept, as a lost land and a sometimes lost, sometimes
found history"; her poetry dwells on "the mysteries of Italy as they appear
to an outsider who is also, in a vexed and vexing sense, an insider"
(Ciongoli and Parini 52). Her poetry, she claims, has been "literally and fig-

uratively fed" by these mysteries. Food and mysticism mingle in Gilbert's reflections on her creative work: "The moony roots of spaghetti writhing in a pot, baby zucchini sliced into green-cold coins on a butcher block, mystical minglings of basil and rosemary and garlic—all these are culinary talismans for me" (Ciongoli and Parini 52).

Susan Leonardi argues that in a literary text a recipe can function as "embedded discourse" and "narrative strategy" (340): "Like a narrative, a recipe is reproducible, and, further, its hearers-readers-receivers are *encouraged* to reproduce it and, in reproducing it, to revise it and make it their own" (344). A recipe indeed works as "an apt metaphor for the reproduction of culture from generation to generation" and "the act of passing down recipes from mother to daughter works as well to figure a familial space within which self-articulation can begin to take place" (Goldman 172).

A "feast of tongues" is at the center of Gilbert's poem "Still Life: Woman Cooking" (*Emily's Bread* 65). Even in the title, Gilbert reverses the paralyzing implications of the domestic space by turning it into art—"a still life"—but she also revises the creative paralysis caused by the rhythms of domestic life. Discussing the possibility of defining a female poetic, Jane Marcus focuses on a "model of art, with repetition and dailiness at the heart of it, with the teaching of other women the patient craft of one's cultural heritage as the object of it" ("Still Practice" 84). Marcus argues that this is "a female poetic which women live and accept. Penelope's art is work, as women cook food that is eaten, weave cloth that is worn, clean houses that are dirtied. Transformation, rather than permanence, is at the heart of this aesthetic" (84).

For Gilbert, as for other Italian American writers, Italian—and especially Sicilian—was her family's secret language, the language she, as the youngest child in her family, could not understand, and which, as a poet, she attempts to recover. In "The Grandmother's Dream," the Sicilian dialect spoken by her grandmother in a dream is "slippery and cold" "like dark fish" (Barolini, *The Dream Book* 350), and yet Gilbert's poems draw on that elusive language, its silences, and its accents, as sources for poetical sustenance.

Not only does food provide Italian American women authors with a language and images through which to express the ambivalent relationship they, as women, maintain with the domestic space and material culture, but it also becomes a vehicle by which Italian American women can articulate the complexities of ethnic identity. In Louise DeSalvo's novel, *Casting Off* (1987), the Italian background of the overtly Irish Helen MacIntyre, for example, emerges solely through the lavish descriptions of food and in the use of the recipe as an autobiographical text of sorts.

In "Anorexia," a chapter of *Vertigo*, DeSalvo offers an original depiction of food by an Italian American author, one that reverses the narrative of sustenance. DeSalvo was not, technically speaking, anorexic (although one of her collegemates mentioned in *Vertigo* was, and would die of starvation years later). With another college roommate, she shares stories about "nearly lethal meals . . . [they] have eaten," stories that center on the idea: "if food could kill, and it can" (206). Early in "Anorexia," DeSalvo prefaces a list of seemingly preposterous foods with this matter-of-fact statement: "These are the things that my mother cooked that I couldn't eat, or wouldn't eat, or that I objected to for one reason or another" (201). The author then proceeds to give a long, systematic list, accompanied by hilarious parenthetical comments, of such items as heart, snails, squab, tongue, tripe, pig's feet, kidneys, and blood sausage. "Anorexia" desecrates every myth about Italian food. Here is one Italian American who prefers to reminisce about the all-American beef and mashed potatoes eaten at a friend's house rather than anything cooked by her mother at home. In DeSalvo's household, food was inedible, according to the author who would become a gourmet cook.

Eating disorders, according to Lilian R. Furst, coeditor of *Disorderly Eaters: Texts in Self-Empowerment,* can embody a "capacity for self-expression . . . through the mute action of eating choice," regardless of whether the outcome is "positively triumphant or negatively destructive" (6). Caterina Schiavon explores the link between identity and what one does not eat, and argues that anorexia and bulimia enact "a scandalous transgression of natural as well as social codes" (my trans., Brugo 65). In a book about survival, about the need and search for intellectual and emotional nourishment, the title "Anorexia" resonates powerfully. But while the first part of "Anorexia" relies on humor, a number of tragic narratives are inscribed in the author's account of her refusal to eat her mother's food.

This refusal is especially significant if one thinks of the place of food in immigrant culture and memory. In *We Are What We Eat: Ethnic Food and the Making of Americans* (1998), the historian Donna Gabaccia argues that "comfort foods are usually heavily associated with women as food preparers and organizers of the family's emotional life," and that "immigrants and their children glorified their mothers as 'feast makers' and culinary artists, in words that emphasized the warm sensuality that linked food to maternal love" (180). If the cultural expectation for DeSalvo's mother was to be the one to orchestrate the family's emotional life, to be the feast maker, the culinary artist, the fact that she did not fulfill these expectations must have been absolutely devastating, for her as well as for her family.

"Anorexia" sheds light on the complex relationship between the author and her mother who, because of her depression—a depression that would ultimately kill her—failed to provide her daughter with the food she needed, literally and symbolically. Significantly, as she comes to understand her mother's depression, she sees that "food was a problem" (218) for her mother. The adolescent DeSalvo's refusal to eat the foods her mother cooks bespeaks her hunger for life and her determination to fight against the debilitating, lethal power of depression. "Life, I have always believed, is too short to have even one bad meal" (4), DeSalvo writes in *Vertigo*. This motto captures the gist of DeSalvo's relationship to life as a survivor: a survivor of abuse, incest, and depression; a survivor of economic, social, cultural, and ethnic circumstances; a woman who turns to reading and writing as that which makes survival possible. It is this position that underscores the hunger for life that lies at the heart of *Vertigo*, even in the face of tragic events such as her father's violence, her sister's suicide, her mother's hospitalization, and her own struggle against depression. Life must be cherished in the single moments of its daily unfolding: Thus, the author regards eating as a ritual, a feast, a celebration of being alive, although somehow the awareness of impending tragedy—"life is too *short*" after all (emphasis mine)—underlies even celebratory moments.

Like Gilbert, DeSalvo links food and violence as she reflects on what prevented her mother from preparing meals as luscious as the one she eventually prepared for her future son-in-law: She remembers her mother's fear "of knives, of fire, how she was always cutting herself, or burning herself by accident, and how that would make cutting, chopping, cooking so hard for her" (*Vertigo* 217–18). In a poignant reversal of traditional representations of Italian American women and food, DeSalvo explores the ambiguity of women's relationship to food, pointing out how disabling cooking could be for this woman, her mother.

It is only appropriate that the personal effects from which the last chapter of *Vertigo* takes its title are DeSalvo's mother's and sister's kitchen utensils, "powerful totems" she "can't part with" (263). As she makes room for them in her drawers and cupboards, they "mingle" together (263), signaling the author's newly achieved understanding and acceptance of her mother's story. "By writing about her," she writes, "I have begun to know her, and to love her, as I could not when she was alive. What I have learned alters my memories of her, transforms the past, transforms her. But it changes my past, and it changes me, as well" (262).

The power of writing to reconcile, to recover, and to reconnect with the past is one Tina De Rosa knows well. Within the mythological narrative of *Paper Fish,* De Rosa inserts lyrical, strikingly pictorial images of food such as the unforgettable description of her grandmother's red peppers. Through these images, the author captures the memory of the material world of her childhood. This, too, is a book about the recovery of memories—a recovery that in turn makes survival possible. Carmolina is especially at risk: Her depressed mother, fully absorbed by Doriana's illness, does not fully give to her daughter. Carmolina must "steal" the blood her mother does not give as a "free gift": "I will steal it from the thin skins of her cells and inside her body," the Prelude reads, and "I will survive" (2). Grandmother Doria, by contrast, is portrayed as the generous magician who manipulates with equal skill the ingredients of tomato sauce and the words of the stories she tells Carmolina.

Depictions of food can be disturbing in *Paper Fish* as well, such as the image of the "headless chicken" jumping "off the block, its neck pumping red blood like a fountain straight upwards into a summer's white hair" (58). Its head, described "like a doll with eyes of glass" (58) bears a disturbing resemblance to Doriana, also described as glass-eyed. Doriana, as we have seen, is compared to a dead fish. The fish that gives the book its title also appears as something troubling, even nauseating: "Carmolina saw the sun glint silver on the fish heads, smelled the dead fish flesh. Fish tails and in-nards landed on the bricks of the alleyway, small circles of blood formed around them, the flies darted blue and black over them" (65). The ambiguity in De Rosa's depictions of food articulates both the nostalgia and the fear that remembering entails.

In "An Italian-American Woman Speaks Out" (1980), De Rosa writes that the "ghost of one's grandmother" is "as real as the food on one's plate" (38). The landscape of the past is sprinkled with the irresistible aromas of Grandmother Doria's foods, and yet *Paper Fish* also contains images of food that do not quite fit the narrative of nostalgia, so that De Rosa's lyrical reminiscences refuse simply to mythologize the world of her childhood. Uprooting, destruction, death, and unspeakable violence cast a shadow on the remembrance of that world, a world that is always painful to revisit not only because every return is a reminder that it no longer exists, but also because there are sites of memory that can never be revisited, although they haunt the writing ceaselessly.

Rosette Capotorto's poetry delves into the themes of family and conviviality so common to representations of Italian Americans in popular culture. Capotorto twists familiar narratives and turns the idyllic image of the Italian American table à la *Moonstruck* upside down; she offers, instead, the struggle for survival of working-class people. In "The Oven," Capotorto reworks the traditional image of the Italian family sharing a meal at a festive table. The setting is a family-owned pizza parlor in which the children work next to the adults:

> and then your little brother will be old
> enough to make the dough
> test his strength against
> the stain-less arm of the mixer

having been forewarned of its dangers
the little sister
the last one born
will make tiny pizzas
and there will be a photograph
to remember this by
a little girl rolling pizza dough
which the family
will eat
in six
tiny
slices. (Ciatu, DiLeo, and Micallef 99–100)

Capotorto's emphasis on how children can be at risk in contexts linked to food is comparable to DeSalvo's treatment of the theme of food in "Anorexia." By interjecting questions of class, ethnicity, and power within this poetical description of an Italian food so often subjected to emptily celebratory representations, Capotorto takes a stance against the olive-oil-and-pasta-commercial story that has stultified this complex and multifaceted element of Italian American culture.[30]

In "Broke," the culinary narrative takes on another poignant nuance, as the emotional devastation experienced by the speaker is reflected in the emptiness of her kitchen cupboard, where a solitary can of corn sits side by side with "some/kinda pasta you don't remember buying" (78). The notorious abundance of the Italian table here is replaced by a keen concern with the lack of food, as Capotorto draws the important, yet often avoided, connection between class politics and the politics of food. The defiant humor of "Dealing with Broccoli Rabe" reveals Capotorto's refusal to take herself too seriously—"three women in one week/told me my broccoli rabe had/changed their lives"—while also lingering on the sensual pleasure offered by the spectacle of "twelve pounds of broccoli rabe" (Caronia, *girlSpeak journals* 17). Here, as in the other poems, Capotorto questions conventional representations of Italian Americans and food while also maintaining and celebrating the vitality of food rituals.

☣☣☣ ☣☣☣ ☣☣☣

In the last several years, like many Italian American women, I have become concerned with trying to understand the place of Catholicism in my life and work. It is only after embracing my new identity as an immigrant and a first-generation Italian American that I have felt this calling. As a feminist, I had rejected Catholicism altogether in the mid-1970s, although a distinctly Southern Italian mix of mysticism and superstition would surface in my thinking, attitudes, and beliefs. I am not a practicing Catholic—although

I christened my daughter—and consider myself neither a believer nor the aggressive agnostic I became in my late teens and early twenties. Although I take issue with the principles and dogmas of Catholicism, I have begun to feel, a few years after emigrating to the United States, the powerful appeal of the stories and icons of Catholicism—such as the christening medal and small cross I will occasionally wear. Neither the icons nor the stories hold a referential value for me, and yet I value them, as the contemporary Italian American women authors I have discussed here value—and use—the objects of material culture.

Food holds a similar appeal, yet another powerful aspect of material culture that, like religion, gets read and rewritten in the signs of a language that, while strikingly connected to Italian American culture, has a way of challenging its norms in the hands of Italian American women writers: The literary practices of these writers serve both to critique and construct, as they conserve—and transform—the traces of material culture. The spills, the blotches, the dribbling on the pristine page that DeSalvo refers to in *Casting Off* serve as effective images to convey the fragmentary yet deeply evocative methods used by these authors to maintain their relationship with the material culture of their community of origin.

Far from wanting to sentimentalize the harsh circumstances of the lives of working-class Italian immigrants or to look at cultural tradition through the lens of a too-convenient nostalgia, the authors whose work I have discussed here shed light on the way in which Italian American culture cannot be fully understood without a careful consideration of the place and importance of material culture and of the ways in which recovery, rereading, and recreating that culture is vital to this group. These are necessary acts for Italian Americans if we are to free ourselves of the effects of the commodification to which our culture has been subjected and if we want to begin to trace and establish a sense of cultural legitimacy and dignity for ourselves.

The narratives of Italian American women are imbued with a fascination for the recovery and creation of stories in which material culture occupies a central place. As a result, they are variously linked to the history of Italian Americans in the United States. For women writers, this work of recovery, this assertion of the need for recognition of their cultural heritage, is fraught with ambiguities and difficulties. What if the very act of emerging as a writer means to escape from, even deny, that very culture for which one is now trying to become a spokesperson? The celebratory, nostalgic mode is one that very few Italian American women can blindly embrace: The risk would be to lose what one has gained—personal and political integrity, participation in different communities—in order to regain what, in fact, one never fully owned within the community of origin—unambiguous acceptance, safety, awareness of self. Recovery of stories requires defiance and transformation as well as the embracing of tradition. The process of making a history involves the encounter with a world one loves and hates, a world one must come to understand and cherish on completely new terms. Writing has the power to accomplish that.

For second- and third-generation Italian Americans, silence, Sandra Mortola Gilbert writes, is a "silence about our language, our food, our selves" ("Piacere Conoscerla" 116). In her poem "Ethnic Woman," Rose Romano rejects the view of "ethnicity" as "something" she "drag[s] out/of the closet to celebrate quaint holidays," and she eloquently explains the connection between self and ethnicity: "I could write my life / story with different shapes in / various sizes in limitless patterns of / pasta laid out to dry on a thick, white / tablecloth on my bed." She asks her imaginary interlocutor, "Must I teach you / to read?" (*Wop* 57). In "Ethnic Woman," Romano makes a claim for what "Italian food" is to her: not "ethnic food," but "food." Choosing the ingredients of ethnic identity leads to the poet's self-definition. Yet if the implied audience of the poem must learn to read and understand the intricate "patterns of pasta" of the poet's "life," the process leading to authorial self-creation is one that requires the ethnic to "teach" *herself* how to "read" the signs of her ethnicity, how to understand them, and how to rewrite them.

❈   ❈   ❈

Underbred contradictory people with accents and most preposterous views.

—*H.G. Wells*

❈   ❈   ❈

Chapter 6

Forging Public Voices:
Memory, Writing, Power

And of course I am afraid, because the transformation of silence into language and action is an act of self-revelation, and that always seems fraught with danger.

—Audre Lorde, "The Transformation of
Silence Into Language and Action"

Giving your experience a body, putting it down on paper, stakes out your little piece of reality, plants your flag on your territory of human experience.

—Anuradha Sankaran-Lazarre, Writing the
Memoir Workshop, New Jersey City University, 1999

What is not remembered is forgotten.

—B. Amore, Lifeline—filo della vita:
An Italian American Odyssey 1901–2001

In the early evening of March 8, 2001—International Women's Day—women, men, and children gathered in New York City at the corner of Green Street and Washington Place in front of the Asche Building to listen to the poet and singer Phyllis Capello and the storyteller Gioia Timpanelli. Small cards with a reproduction of Nancy Azara's collage "Fire" and inscribed names and ages of victims were passed around the crowd. Ninety years earlier, this had been the site of the Triangle Shirtwaist Factory Fire. In this same space in which people listened, held hands, embraced a friend, a child, a horrified crowd had witnessed women workers jumping to their death from the ninth floor in a desperate attempt to escape the fire that burned three floors—eighth, ninth, and tenth—of the building. On March 25, 1911, 146 workers, mostly young women—the average age was 19—died in that fire. Most of the victims were Jewish women immigrants. About one-third were Italian women immigrants.

This gathering, cosponsored by the Collective of Italian American Women and Casa Italiana Zerilli Marimò at New York University, was created to remember. To remember the women, like 17-year-old Isabella Tortorella and 23-year-old Meyer Utal, or Serafina, Tessie and Sara Saracino, ages 25, 20, and unknown, respectively. Almost a century after their death, their names surfaced in the memory and in the voices of the crowd.

For the Italian American women who organized this event, the Commemoration was an occasion, a most important one, to connect themselves with the radical history of Italian Americans and to claim solidarity with those supporting the search for legal, political, and social equality and justice. Appropriately, the event continued at the Auditorium of Casa Italiana with the Italian American historian Jennifer Guglielmo and the Jewish American women's studies scholar Annelise Orleck, who spoke about the history of the Triangle Fire to an audience brought together by political rather than ethnic solidarity. The collective memory of the Triangle tragedy has served—and will continue to serve—as a rallying point for the building of community and of the political awareness that social activism is so often, truly, a matter of life and death.

Claiming the Fire as an episode of Italian American history represents, for Italian American women, a gesture of vital political and cultural assertion, one that establishes unequivocally the importance of historical memory. Jennifer Guglielmo explains that,

> in the decades that preceded the fire, many Italian women in the U.S. fought the exploitation and dehumanization of industrial capitalism by devising methods of resistance in which they built revolutionary culture. . . . formally or informally.
> . . . after the fire, many garment workers dealt with their grief and outrage by building new alliances across lines of religion, ethnicity and language. And in many ways, the fire came to represent the beginning of a new era of collaboration between Jewish and Italian immigrant women. It's also important to remember that these new alliances were not immediately easy; they had to be continually negotiated as feelings of prejudice and mistrust were worked out and confronted day-to-day. ("Seamstresses")

It is vital for an Italian American women's organization to be involved in this kind of political and historical recovery at a time in which Italian American women recognize and strive to build multicultural alliances: It is a gesture both of reclamation and reinvention of solidarity and activism.

Such events as the Commemoration of the Triangle Fire are meant to help Italian American women remember their history. If these are women who do not want to forget that they are Italian American, they also are women who want to continue to ask questions about what that means, who do not identify themselves and their politics within the bounds of a narrowly conceived ethnic stance. That's one of the reasons why they write, paint, sculpt, photograph, make movies, research and search for answers—but, most important, they ask questions, sometimes dangerous questions, questions that destabilize the significance of the term "Italian American." And they propose views that might be seen as preposterous because they so deeply challenge pervasive cultural and political expectations of Italian American womanhood.

In this chapter, I bring together different threads of Italian American women authors' work. In focusing more closely on what makes a literary (or artistic, or cinematic) work political—in a progressive sense—I will explore what being a public intellectual and an activist has come to mean for a number of Italian American women writers. The parameters to use to contextualize this literature in political terms are necessarily different from those utilized when looking at groups with different political and social histories. We must understand, to adapt the title of Maria Mazziotti Gillan's book of poems, where these authors come from. It is important, for example, to recognize that Italian American women—but men as well—are characteristically disconnected from the progressive history that scholars such as Jennifer Guglielmo, Donna Gabaccia, Phil Cannistraro, and Sal Salerno are engaged in recovering. As Guglielmo's search for early twentieth-century records of Italian American women workers' activism testifies, one must not look in predictable places. Sometimes, as Guglielmo pointedly indicates, the kitchen can be the radical site for the search for a forgotten history.[1] In this chapter, I turn to the work that Italian American women have done in the last decade as memoirists, teachers, and cultural workers, to point to some of the strategies that these authors rely on as they act as spokespersons for—and also sustainers of—historically disenfranchised communities.

※※※　　※※※　　※※※

The contemporary memoir speaks of and to a collective cultural and political consciousness and seeks to recount stories that, while filtered through the voice of one individual, partake in the lives and voices of a community.[2] Memory often represents the inaccessible, the unspeakable. The work of the memoirist thus entails more than gathering the fragments of one's life into a unified, cohesive narrative of accomplishment and personal realization. I see the latter more as the work of the autobiographer, who is confident and secure in his place in culture and history. The genre of the memoir has emerged forcefully over the last two decades on the U.S. literary scene in conjunction with the literature of women and minorities, working-class studies, the literature of witness, and the groundbreaking work done on trauma theory by scholars such as Judith Herman, Shoshana Felman, and Dori Laub. This is work that opens venues, that creates a place for what has not been spoken: the place of memory. This is work that requires exploring the interstices of memory, the crevices of time, to dig out what should not be forgotten.

Janet Zandy writes that the raison d'être of working-class histories and literatures is "to recall the fragile filaments and necessary bond of human relationships, as well as to critique those economic and social forces that blunt or block human development" (*Working Class* 5). Zandy thus highlights the political importance of the work of memory, a work that is closely tied to one's social and political engagement with the present and the future. Can one make meaning out of a past that sometimes is too horrifying even to be contemplated? One can and one must, to honor the memory of victims, and to honor the pain of the witnesses who have carried traumatic memories within them. Strikingly clear images and sounds have haunted these witnesses, and now almost mystically haunt also those who were not there, the writers, like Maria Terrone, or the historians, like Jennifer Guglielmo, who feel compelled to speak the truth about atrocities and injustice. Memory has enormous political importance in the contemporary context because it creates or helps sharpen a much needed political awareness of social issues, from the violation of workers' rights—especially in sweatshops that replicate the working conditions that led to the Triangle Fire—to environmental racism and abuse. Activism around this kind of issues provides a vital mode for community building and grassroots organizing.

Appropriating memory is a crucial step for those who have been marginalized and denied access to public forums because of their gender, race, ethnicity, nationality, language, religion, sexuality, or class. Challenging the idea of the isolated writer's life, contemporary memoirs by U.S. authors such as Maya Angelou, Maxine Hong Kingston, Joanna Kadi, Suheir Hammad, Estella Conwill Majozo, and many others have provided important accounts of the untold histories of their cultures and communities. These memoirs fulfill an important cultural function through their focus on those life stories that have been excluded from public and historically sanctioned narratives.

The literature produced by Italian American women grapples with issues that, while specific to their Italian American history, also concern the histories of other communities: issues such as ethnic stereotyping, cultural assimilation, gender, race, sex and class oppression, domestic violence, mental illness, environmental abuse, and public health.[3] In breaching the boundary between traditionally private and public spaces, authors such as Louise DeSalvo, Mary Cappello, Nancy Caronia, Rosette Capotorto, Maria Mazziotti Gillan, Rose Romano, Sandra M. Gilbert, Daniela Gioseffi, Maria Laurino, Renata Gangemi, Kym Ragusa, and Susanne Antonetta have begun to transform "silence" into "language and action" (Lorde, *Sister*).[4] In an essay entitled "Taking Risks: The Creation of Feminist Literature," Judith McDaniel writes that "the risk we experience when we tell our stories truly is the risk of change: the risk that we will be changed by the telling and the risk our audience similarly experiences, that they will be changed by the hearing. In some traditions, this kind of truth is called witnessing" (Albrecht and Brewer 126–7). Italian American women authors also question traditional American narratives of individual emergence and success in favor of stories that question the power and social effectiveness of those narratives and affirm the strength of communities.

An exploration and reworking of the significance of community is central to the work of contemporary Italian American women authors, who are intent on remaking the very communities they have defied and escaped. As Audre Lorde knew well, there is danger involved in this act: the danger of becoming unpopular, of becoming the betrayer, the outcast, the exile. And yet, as Lorde puts it, "what is important . . . must be spoken, made verbal and shared, even at the risk of having it bruised or misunderstood" (*Sister* 40).

Autobiographical fiction and poetry, personal essays, videos, and full-length prose memoirs by contemporary Italian American women demonstrate that, like other members of minority groups, these writers are intent on creating personal narratives that explore the multiple links between individual and community. In speaking on behalf of their communities, however, Italian American women embrace a position fraught with contradictions. Memoirs such as Louise DeSalvo's *Vertigo* (1996), Mary Cappello's *Night Bloom* (1998), and Maria Laurino's *Were You Always an Italian? Ancestors and Other Icons of Italian America* (2000), videos like Kym Ragusa's *fuori/outside* (1997), Susan Caperna Lloyd's *The Baggage* (2001), and Renata Gangemi's *Talking Back* (1992), novels like Mary Saracino's *No Matter What* (1993) and Beverly D'Onofrio's *Riding in Cars with Boys* (1990), poetry like Rosette Capotorto's *Bronx Italian,* and performances like Penny Arcade's *La Miseria* (1991), recollect, celebrate, and record Italian American histories, but they also expose that which families and communities would often rather leave unsaid. The words of Italian American women authors have shattered the quasi-mythological status of the Italian family as a locus

of nurturance and safety. Mingling attack and tribute, they may depict the
family home as the setting for horrifying violence—as in Nancy Caronia's
"Go to Hell"—or, in less brutal though no less insidious ways, in Mary
Saracino's autobiographical novel *No Matter What*. Questioning the nostalgia and allegiance that often characterize Italian American literature, Italian American women write with great candor of the contradictions of a
culture in which—like in other cultures—love and violence, allegiance
and exclusion, go hand in hand, especially when it comes to women.

In *The Prison Notebooks*, Antonio Gramsci writes that "All men are intellectuals . . . but not all men have in society the function of intellectuals"
(9). Gramsci's statement sheds light on the work of Italian American women
authors as public intellectuals. His concept of the "intellectual function" underscores the point that intellectuals are not, at least inherently, all that different from the rest of us: Everyone has got it to some extent; what counts
is what one does with it. It is this intellectual potential that books such as
Mazziotti Gillan's *Where I Come From*, DeSalvo's *Vertigo* and *Breathless*, and
Cappello's *Night Bloom* not only recognize but also nurture and bring out—
in their authors and in their readers. In making certain words (and worlds)
public, writers can pursue the kind of social and political transformation
that is at the heart of the task of the public intellectual. In doing so, writers
call into question commonsense understandings of the disjunction between
public and private. The function of the public intellectual is to be a
spokesperson for the community—and especially for the silenced and disenfranchised who, paradoxically, are often marginalized by the same community on whose behalf these women speak.

A central question faced by a writer who envisions herself as a public
intellectual is the relationship to the dominant culture in terms of its chan-
nels of communication as well as the recognition it grants writers. Helen
Barolini identifies the ways in which Italian American voices are excluded
from national public forums in an essay entitled "Writing to a Brick Wall,"
which appears in her collection *Chiaroscuro*. The *New York Times*, she notes,
has been deaf and indifferent to Italian American authors, with the exception of a few, such as Mario Puzo, Gay Talese, and Francis Ford Coppola,
who cater to conventional and often ridiculing images of Italian Americans (Barolini, *Chiaroscuro* 98–101). Those authors who challenge such prevailing views—and women fall in great numbers into this
category—typically do not get their books reviewed, Barolini laments, or
their letters published in national venues. As Rose Romano reminds us,
censorship "doesn't always have to be censorship in order to be effective"
("Nella sorellanza" 152). But then, as Edward Said has pointed out, to be
a public intellectual one must be ready to be on the outside, to be an exile,
both literally and metaphorically: "The exile . . . exists in a median state,"

he suggests, "neither completely at one with the new setting nor fully disencumbered of the old. Beset with half-involvements and half-detachments, nostalgic and sentimental on one level, an adept mimic or a secret outcast on another" (49).

Said's description aptly illustrates the predicament of authors such as DeSalvo and Mazziotti Gillan, but also Flavia Alaya, Nancy Caronia, Rosette Capotorto, Mary Cappello, Joanna Clapps Herman, Rose Romano, Susanne Antonetta, and Mary Saracino, and filmmakers such as Renata Gangemi, Luisa Pretolani, Kym Ragusa, and Nancy Savoca. These authors constantly negotiate an ambivalent relationship to the community of origins as well as to the communities they are involved with through marriage (Herman), sexual and political identification (Cappello, Romano, and Saracino), or multiple ethnic/racial origins (Antonetta, Caronia, Ragusa, Gangemi, and Savoca). Existing in a "median state" means traveling back and forth between different communities and identities, juggling a self-conscious mimicry and a sense of outsidership that is simultaneously feared and proudly asserted, potentially stifling and powerfully enabling of creative achievement.

The work of many Italian American women writers wavers between the desire for home and the necessity to reject it. These authors can be described in terms of Said's definition of the exile, as "constantly being unsettled, and unsettling others." As Said puts it, "You cannot go back to some earlier and perhaps more stable condition of being at home; and, alas, you can never fully arrive, be at one with your new home or situation" (53). For these writers, specifically those who engage in the kind of radical work that questions the cultural dictates of the family, a state of permanent homelessness becomes a choice and necessity. Gay and lesbian writers such as Mary Cappello, Peter Covino, Vittoria repetto, and Mary Saracino experience the ambivalence of home in an especially acute manner as they negotiate the weight of homophobia within their Italian American families and communities, as Covino does in poems such as "The Poverty of Language." Italian American authors recognize the cultural marginalization of their ethnic group;[5] at the same time, they strongly and painfully recognize that they cannot fully embrace their community, that they must understand the ways in which it constrains and silences its members, and that they must act on such an understanding. The relationship with the community is, for these writers, as problematic as the definition of this politically ambivalent concept.[6] The community of origins often represents the very space they must evade, even as they confront, challenge, and reinvent it in their works and lives.

Cultural or political homelessness is a condition that is never easy or conflict-free, for it does not imply a disregard for home but, rather, a troubled and constant longing for a place that can still be evoked in writing and recreated in communities that selectively incorporate elements of the home of origins.[7] Permanent homelessness is the condition that Rosette Capotorto describes in her poem "Red Wagon": "I have no party/ affiliation I am/a one woman band/see my red wagon./I pull/it along piled with/paper and pasta." For authors such as Capotorto, a safe home is always—and only—a process, never a place of arrival.

Some of the most compelling contemporary Italian American memoirs are those that, shaped by working-class consciousness, best historically contextualize the stories they tell. These authors are concerned with understanding and responding to the ways in which race, ethnicity, gender, class, and sexuality intersect in American society. Although not explicitly concerned with examining Italian American identity, Sandra M. Gilbert's *Wrongful Death* (1994) interweaves an intimate personal narrative and a discussion of public health issues. In *Breathless: An Asthma Journal* (1997), Louise DeSalvo similarly combines a personal account of her illness and her political reflections on the asthma crisis that plagues American inner cities. These memoirs assert the power of Italian American writers as public intellectuals. It is through memoirs that politicize ethnicity that Italian American women authors are shaping a cultural movement that seeks to understand the place of Italian Americans in a multicultural context. In this chapter, I identify the feminist practices pursued through writing by a number of Italian American women. While this scope underscores the entire book, I wish to outline here with greater precision its methods and implications, particularly in relationship to the classroom, used as a favorite site for political activism through writing by a number of Italian American women, specifically Louise DeSalvo, Mary Cappello, Maria Mazziotti Gillan, Rosette Capotorto, and Kym Ragusa.

To become a public intellectual requires, at times, erasing the markers of ethnicity. This erasure can be a necessary stage in the negotiation between one's understanding of one's ethnic and cultural roots, and the uncomfortable position one comes to occupy as an Italian American intellectual in an American culture that stigmatizes Italian Americans—especially women—as anti-intellectual. For Italian American women, to become a public intellectual defies historical definitions and perceptions of both their gender and ethnicity, both within and outside the Italian American community—even as, I would argue, there is no such a thing as "Italian America," understood as some homogenous or unified social reality or monolithic community.

One example of this attempt to come to terms with the contradictions inherent in such a negotiation is DeSalvo's autobiographical essay, "A Portrait of the Puttana as a Middle-Aged Woolf Scholar," written in the late

1970s, first published in *Between Women: Biographers, Novelists, Critics, Teachers and Artists Write About Their Work on Women* (1984), and reprinted in Helen Barolini's *The Dream Book* (1985). The clash between "Italian" and "intellectual" is articulated through the seemingly paradoxical juxtaposition of the title words "puttana"—Italian for whore—and "Woolf scholar." In this essay, DeSalvo expresses her ambivalence about identifying herself as an Italian American. She views that identification as encumbering the process of intellectual growth she has pursued as a scholar of Virginia Woolf. This was her first attempt at memoir writing: At this point, DeSalvo had not clearly conceptualized her Italian American identity, although the essay provided cultural validation for many Italian American women who saw it as voicing key contradictions and struggles faced by Italian American women.

These readers welcomed DeSalvo's defiant embrace of the shameful term *puttana,* through which she reveals how she is constantly at odds with her ethnic origins. A decade later, DeSalvo includes that essay, significantly revised, in *Vertigo* (1996), a memoir in which, far from shying away from her Italian roots, she claims and embraces those roots, even as she relentlessly indicts the patriarchal modes of oppression within Italian American familial and cultural structures. Understanding the repercussions of cultural isolation, DeSalvo places herself within a large and ever-growing movement of Italian American women authors, a gesture that enables her to gain access to other unspoken personal narratives.

A self-awareness of the ways in which women have not been allowed full use of their voices underscores the memoirs of Italian American women. What shapes their project of ethnic recovery is a political, feminist consciousness, and an insistence on the transformative and redemptive power of creative work. So when writing of her difficult relationship with her mentally ill mother, Louise DeSalvo concludes: "By writing about her, I have begun to know her, and to love her, as I could not when she was alive. What I have learned alters my memories of her, transforms them, transforms her. But it changes my past, and it changes me, as well" (262). DeSalvo here articulates the position of a group of writers who have found in the memoir the means by which to re-read and rewrite not only their lives, but also their cultural history.[8]

In *Vertigo*), DeSalvo views the Italian American literary tradition as worthy and legitimate, and identifies her work, with greater political awareness, as Italian American: a newly acquired sense of ethnic and class identity shapes the narrative of *Vertigo,* as DeSalvo recalls: "In the intervening years [between "The Portrait of the Puttana as a Middle-Aged Woolf Scholar" and *Vertigo*], I read hundreds of works by women, African American, Latina, Native American, etc., who all situated themselves in the context of a particular culture. This alerted me to the fact that there was something I had not dealt with."[9] There was much for DeSalvo to deal with, and she did so in *Vertigo*. In this memoir, she faces issues such as family history, class and ethnic identity, mental illness, physical and sexual abuse, Catholicism, writing, and healing. Her delicate project of excavation, pursued through the use of what she aptly describes as "the scalpel of language" (102), is also a project of recovery and salvation: "My work has changed my life. My work has saved my life. My life has changed my work" (12). *Vertigo* argues for—and provides a powerful example of—the potential for personal and political transformation that memoir affords its writers and readers.

Vertigo delves deep into DeSalvo's working-class origins and the history of the Italian American neighborhood where she grew up in Hoboken, New Jersey. Like *Vertigo, Breathless: An Asthma Journal,* an autobiographical, literary, cultural, and political meditation on asthma, articulates with remarkable clarity DeSalvo's commitment to being an Italian American intellectual. In a polemic fashion, *Breathless* brings to the forefront of literary discussion a burning political issue: the asthma crisis that has struck particularly the inner city, victimizing primarily those who live in conditions of economic deprivation, many of them children. DeSalvo paints a frightening picture of a society that has given up the right to free and clean water and is progressively surrendering the right to free, clean air: "How long will it be," she asks, "until those of us who can afford it will hook ourselves up to portable air purifiers to go outside?" (148–9). This poignant question foregrounds the connection between class privilege and the ability to protect oneself from environmental abuse. It is a power game that the poor are inevitably doomed to lose.[10]

It comes as no surprise that the mainstream press has not given *Vertigo* or *Breathless* their fair share of recognition and that only five years since it was published, *Vertigo* is going out of print. Such neglect, coupled with the current backlash against memoir, a phenomenon that has led some columnists to deride the genre and its practitioners as trendy, illustrates the cooptation of the memoir as a politically radical genre. Such cooptation is illustrated by the popularization of what DeSalvo calls, in *Breathless,* "the recovery narrative":

> I see the perniciousness of the word recovery, for it suggests that the illness or the condition (asthma, whatever) is over, though it isn't. It suggests, too, that people are personally responsible for curing their illnesses. I realize that I am against the neatness and the lie of what I suddenly recognize as the comforting arc of the recovery narrative. The narrative that says, in essence, I was sick, I suffered, I did this and that and the other thing, I figured it out, I made changes, I am now much better, don't worry, there is nothing urgent we really need to do as people to help prevent asthma. (150–51)

Neither *Vertigo* nor *Breathless* subscribes to the recovery narrative; in fact, both texts radically upset the expectations of its "arc." Going against what she calls the "true American tradition of Benjamin Franklin," in *Breathless* DeSalvo proclaims herself "the imperfect asthmatic" who refuses to be blamed for her "imperfection" (151), who indicts rather those who are polluting the air and causing human and environmental trauma at all levels.

The story DeSalvo tells in *Breathless* is one that will not make people feel better; it does not allow us to stay comfortable about the way we have surrendered responsibility for our lives and the lives of others. DeSalvo thus joins authors such as Audre Lorde, Sandra Gilbert, and Nancy Mairs, who have all written eloquently on the politics of illness. Mairs highlights the correlation between popular success and the "feel-good" book—which she does *not* write (and neither, I might add, does DeSalvo). Mairs calls her memoir *Waist-High in the World: A Life Among the Non-Disabled,* "a feel-real book, and reality," she points out, "has never been high on any popular list" (18).

Breathless takes on an almost prophetic tone as DeSalvo comes to view her illness as that which has opened her eyes to the frightful question of environmental abuse:

> I sometimes wonder who is the more highly evolved. The person who responds adversely to chemical fumes, exhaust fumes, cigarette smoke, noxious odors, trauma, or the person who doesn't. Maybe, I tell myself, I'm like the canary [ken-air-ee] in the mine shaft. Maybe my gasping for air is information that other, less sensitive people should heed. Maybe the fate of the planet depends upon people like me whose responsive bodies are telling us all that there is something very wrong around here. (149)

The power of DeSalvo's narrative lies in its insistence that there are people out there who will recognize and respond to the urgency of her words—and of the situation they describe.[11] In this way, literature can serve as a tool for consciousness-raising and community-building.

Louise DeSalvo's most recent book, *Adultery*—in which she combines literary analysis and political commentary, anecdote and history—focuses on an issue that is ancient, cross-cultural (although, DeSalvo points out, not all cultures condemn adultery), and certainly, in the wake of the Clinton-Lewinsky affair—of tremendous relevance to American politics.[12] DeSalvo's work against secrecy leads her to tackle a private issue that is nevertheless bound up with public issues. In her novel *Casting Off,* two married women, instead of two men, engage in adulterous escapades and do not end up dead like Madame Bovary (which might be the very reason why American publishers refused to publish the book in the 1980s—*Casting Off* was published in England). *Adultery* compresses the undertaking of the literary and cultural critic, the biographer, the memoirist. DeSalvo calls herself, ironically but with great seriousness, a "survivor" of adultery, and yet the account of how her husband's affair shaped—and reshaped—her life, her marriage, and, most of all, her literary career and her philosophy of life, provides but one of a multitude of subtexts that, together, comprise a provocative reading of adultery.

Adultery is, in more ways than one, the work of the author of *Vertigo*, the memoir that broke the historical silence that has enveloped the relationship of Italian American women to the family—and to their culture—and transported the primarily private and domestic discourse of Italian American women into a highly politicized realm. Following the publication of *Vertigo*, a number of important memoirs and memoiristic texts that foreground a politicized notion of Italian American identity have been published. Among them, Mary Cappello's *Night Bloom* (1998); *Curaggia: Writing by Women of Italian Descent* (1998), edited by Nzula Angelina Ciatu, Domenica DiLeo, and Gabriella Micallef; Flavia Alaya's *Under the Rose: A Confession* (1999); and Maria Laurino's *Were You Always an Italian? Ancestors and Other Icons of Italian America* (2000) present politically and culturally self-aware voices that put into question the cultural heritage they flaunt.[13] Writing of incest, physical abuse, mental illness, self-hatred, and shame, not only does DeSalvo—as do Cappello, Alaya, Laurino, and the contributors to *Curaggia*—violate the taboos surrounding these subjects, but she also demonstrates the complicated ways in which these forms of violence are interwoven with class and ethnic oppression. *Vertigo*, like Dorothy Allison's *Bastard Out of Carolina* and Michael Ryan's *My Secret Life*, makes it clear that the sexual oppression and exploitation of children is linked to the failure of the family to protect them, even when family members are not directly implicated in the abuse. The family, we are forced to remember, is not an inviolate space, but rather deeply implicated in the politics of gender and sexual oppression.

Mary Cappello's *Night Bloom* unequivocally affirms its radical intent through it continuous concerns with sexual politics and the interconnections with family politics. This familial memoir examines the family as the site of violence and the source of poetry. Cappello finds it necessary to escape the family in more ways than one; she has to reframe her understanding of the category itself: "The family, as most gay people know," she writes in an early version of *Night Bloom*, "can never be confined to the people you shared the house with for twenty years, gay people having always to create community outside the domesticating bloodline in order to survive." Being a reader of the family places one, as Cappello well understands, in a vulnerable, even dangerous position. If one is a reader, she discovers, one also must become a writer.

Cappello's memoir is simultaneously a theoretical reflection that continuously contextualizes the stories the author tells in terms of social history and a poetical meditation that reconsiders personal and cultural past through the imaginative lens of the garden, one of its central images. Indeed, the garden frames and generates the memoir's narrative. Cappello's sources are unconventional and include, in addition to her maternal grandfather's journals, gardening books: The names and lives of flowers and plants overlap with the familial and personal histories she is both uncovering and reinventing. The workings of memory and gardening thus become entwined in poetical images, such as that of the night bloom itself. It is of course relevant that the garden is a classical Italian American trope, and in reelaborating its significance, Cappello rewrites the Italian American narrative.[14] She associates the garden her father cultivates with extraordinary care and devotion with his father's violence, her mother's agoraphobia, her maternal grandfather's poetical and nurturing powers, and her own familial, cultural, and poetical identity.

Night Bloom thus links together individual, family, and community; past and present; class, ethnicity, Catholicism, and sexuality; Sicilian, Neapolitan, Italian, and American; and all of these are woven into a sophisticated and delicately nuanced narrative that reveals a self-conscious understanding of the power of memory: "Maybe none of us has 'our own' memory, but each of us inherits the memories of our ancestors, while what distinguishes us is our interpretation of those pasts" (118). This emphasis on the collective quality of memory characterizes the memoirs of Italian American women writers, even as it seems to link their work to that of African American women and other minority writers. Like DeSalvo, Cappello brings into focus a key function of the memoir: to revisit, to retell, to reframe not *the* true story, but a multifold, provisional account of the truth these particular authors have uncovered, a truth that is both documentary and interpretive, inherited and invented.

Maria Mazziotti Gillan's work is rooted in her Italian American working-class origins and in her understanding of the rightful place of Italian Americans in multiculturalism.[15] The work of this cultural worker is directed at an exploration of ethnic identity that is always biographical and historical, personal and political. Gillan is a poet and editor of *The Paterson Literary Review,* a journal that includes the literary production of multicultural America; she is also the coeditor, with her daughter Jennifer, of *Unsettling America: An Anthology of Contemporary Multicultural Poetry, Identity Lessons,* and *Growing Up Ethnic,* the director of the Poetry Center at Passaic County Community College, and the indefatigable organizer of numerous cultural events. A recognition of

the radical potential of personal power, of the ways in which we can organize ourselves—as students, teachers, parents, writers, and readers—
shapes all aspects of Mazziotti Gillan's work.

In her poem "Coming of Age: Paterson," published in the 1996 anthology *In Defense of Mumia,* Maria Mazziotti Gillan writes:[16]

> In the streets of our cities
> the poor rise again like dough,
> no matter how we push them down. (70)

This poem relies on a familiar Italian American trope—making bread—to
address problems that transcend the Italian American community on
whose behalf Mazziotti Gillan has so eloquently spoken elsewhere. Yet, the
grief expressed in this elegy for the children of Paterson, "beaten to death,"
the children of Micronesia, "born without bones/as the result of nuclear
testing," and "the young men on street corners,/blown like refuse against
Black Bear Liquors" (69), is connected to the grief that pervades her more
overtly Italian American poems, such as "Growing Up Italian," "Public
School No. 18, Paterson, New Jersey," and "Arturo." These poems are
rooted in the search for, and reclaiming of, cultural and ethnic origins.
Each of these poems presents the development of a narrative of shame and
pride: one's self-denial linked to the rejection of working-class and ethnic
origins transforms into powerful self-assertion and reclaiming of one's origins—in terms of family, class, ethnicity, and language. The addressees include the poet's father—invoked in "Arturo" and "Betrayals"—and a
hostile "America," embodied in "Public School No. 18, Paterson, New Jersey," by the "Anglo-Saxon" teachers who silenced the poet's ethnic self. In
Gillan's poems ethnic and class identity are inseparable, so that her exploration of ethnicity is always political: Her understanding of Italian American identity is rooted in the reclaiming of the power of the "broken
tongue" of her immigrant parents (*Where I Come From* 7).

Where I Come From continues the work of recovery and reinvention
that Mazziotti Gillan had initiated with *Taking Back My Name* (1991), a
chapbook that captures the vital place of memory for the poet. It is
through memory that she can trace the painful but important experience
of discrimination suffered by Italian Americans. She describes such an experience in linguistic terms: "English words" fall "thick and sharp as hail"
on the immigrant child. She is silenced as a result:

> I grew silent,
> the Italian word balanced on the edge
> of my tongue and the English word, lost

during the first moment
of every question. (1)

The poet must trace the story of the silencing that occurred in her past in
order to reach a present in which she can proudly claim, as she does at the
end of the poem:

today, I take back my name
and wave it in their faces
like a bright, red flag. (3)

Mazziotti Gillan's well-known activities as a poet and radical cultural worker
thus appear grounded in the intimate connection between her cultural activities and her Italian American working-class roots as well as the early experiences of discrimination she writes about in her poems. In "Growing Up
Italian," the speaker's celebration of her "Italian American" self is inseparable
from her understanding of her place in a country in which

all those black/brown/red/yellow
olive-skinned people
soon will raise their voices (*Where I Come From* 56)

and join in an anthem of cultural reclamation.

Maria Mazziotti Gillan's work foregrounds the importance of origins in
the poet's self-definition, her subject matter, her poetics, and her politics. Recovery and reinvention are instrumental to the formation of Italian American public intellectuals. For such individuals, situating themselves in relation
to ethnic origins represents a radical act, radical in the sense of going back
to the roots: roots of identity, roots of culture, roots of oppression—the roots
where real transformation can and must begin.

The daughter of an African American mother and an Italian American
father, Kym Ragusa is a filmmaker whose work is shaped by a similar understanding of the interconnections between her life and those of her families and communities. Born in New York in 1966, Ragusa was raised by
her grandmothers, although her paternal grandmother did not know of
her existence until she was about two years old. Her father had hidden her
existence from his mother who did not approve of his relationship with
Ragusa's African American mother. Even when she was finally introduced
to her paternal grandmother, she was introduced as the niece of his Puerto
Rican girlfriend. This early "masquerade around [her] . . . origins," as she
describes it in her video *fuori/outside* (1997), informs her work as a filmmaker and a writer. Always keeping a keen eye on issues of class, Ragusa

exposes the interconnections between class and race in U.S. history, especially in *fuori/outside,* as she recalls the exploitation and the lynching of Italian Americans in the early stages of their emigration to the United States. Her racial/cultural allegiance is ambivalent and multiple: Forced to "pass" as "white" in her own Italian American family as a child, Ragusa quickly learned how the dynamics of class and race operate in social as well as familial contexts. Indeed, while all of her work is memoiristic insofar as it focuses on her personal history as well as the history of her communities, it also is historical because it reveals the links between different forms of historical narratives: Tracing her own story makes it possible for her to trace the history of her family, her community, and her country.

The opening question in *fuori/outside* becomes a poignant request: "Do you remember?" That Ragusa's grandmother cannot hear or remember does not diminish the impact of Ragusa's question; indeed, the determination to speak out against secrecy and silence projects that question into a context that is not solely personal. Kym Ragusa's experience of racism and passing transcends the circumstances of her family history and must be understood in the context of the history of race and class in the United States. In addition, Ragusa's grandmother's personal search and questions trigger important revelations of, for example, her father's (Ragusa's great grandfather's) violence. This history of family violence emerges only when Ragusa begins to pose questions to her grandmother; while the old woman seems out of touch with the present, the past powerfully overcomes her and, as she is talking with her granddaughter about her own mother, she lashes out at her father for his violence against her mother. In the background, we hear the voice of Ragusa's father, who remarks that he had never heard this story before. Ragusa's videos demonstrate that it is only when questions are asked that answers can be given and unspoken histories be written. Through provocative questions, Ragusa's work establishes ties between personal story and public history that are crucial to the progressive transformation of the self and the community.

෴   ෴   ෴

Teaching, since 1996, an urban population of primarily working-class and minority students has provided me with useful insights into the radical possibilities offered by memoirs such as the ones I have discussed here. For multiply marginalized students like mine, books like *Vertigo, Breathless, Night Bloom,* and *Where I Come From* trigger a process of understanding their lives and the world in which they live—regardless of whether or not they are Italian American—as intensely political; this is an insight that I take to be fundamental to the possibility of critical social agency and transformation on any level.

My current students may walk into class looking as if they have not slept, but few of them have labored through the artificial trials of fraternity initiation. More often, they come straight from work, since many of them work outside school, often full-time, or juggle two or three part-time jobs; they often have children who keep them up at night and get sick, forcing them to miss school because of the lack of adequate child care; they are frequently single parents; they struggle with financial hardships; they are often abuse survivors; they are characteristically the first in their families to attend college and have come to college in spite of the negative expectations of obtuse high school counselors, and even family members, who outrightly discouraged them from academic pursuits. There also are many so-called nontraditional or returning students, most often women in their forties and older, or foreign nationals, especially from Africa and the developing world. The population is extremely diverse in terms of race/ethnicity, age, nationality, and language. The student population is more homogeneous class-wise, although I want to underscore the diversity even within the class-economic background.

As working-class students, not only are my students not used to writing about themselves, but they also have little experience reading about themselves, or at least reading about their lives in texts that dignify and validate their experiences.[17] It is crucial for me to offer them reading assignments that provide them with frameworks through which they can see their experiences depicted with dignity and authenticity. I am not offering an apology for the ideal students, as teaching these students is not always easy or successful; it can be difficult and frustrating, though it is always, in my mind, worthwhile. The truth is, many of my students, when they first enroll, are not what most teachers would call good writers.

In *Teachers as Intellectuals,* Henry Giroux argues that the transformative intellectual must engage in the task of "making the pedagogical more political"[18]:

> Within this perspective, critical reflection and action become part of a fundamental social project to help students develop a deep and abiding faith in the struggle to overcome economic, political and social injustices, and to further humanize themselves as part of this struggle. (127)

Teaching the memoirs and memoiristic poetry and video I have discussed here has helped make such a political pedagogy possible. Annalisa Ronquillo, a Filipina sophomore, one of my students at New Jersey City University, describes the experience of reading *Vertigo* as profoundly formative: "*Vertigo* has taught me . . . lesson[s] . . . that I will take with me to my dying day. Some of these are: the importance of writing; the control I must gain over my asthma; and the lesson of dealing with the things and people in [my] life." Until she read *Vertigo,* this student did not know, as she puts it in her final exam essay, that she, herself, "had been writing for survival." "Tears formed in my eyes," she continues, "as I began to piece together the meaning of my life. I felt as if [DeSalvo] was speaking for me: for my disturbances, my shame, my failures, my efforts and my will to survive."

In *Writing as a Way of Healing: How Telling Our Stories Transforms Our Lives* (1999), Louise DeSalvo relies on years of experiences as a writer and a teacher of memoir, one who recognizes the power of memory and especially the power that the articulation of memories—personal as well as historical—in writing confers on a writer. "I regularly witness," DeSalvo writes, "The physical and emotional transformation of my students. I see how they change physically and psychically when they work on writing projects—diary, memoir, fiction, poetry, biographical essays—that grow from a deep, authentic place, when they confront their pain in their work" (*Writing* 11). In response to those who dismiss the therapeutic power of writing or the possibility to consider writing as a source of personal and social healing, I want to emphasize how crucial this instrument can be to disenfranchised people, to people who do not have access to other resources.[19] For them, writing can indeed be the means of their survival. As April Sinisi, one of my memoir students, aptly points out in the prologue to her memoir thesis project in which she traces the steps of a writing journey that, she argues, has saved her in more ways than one: ""Do you know how much this has cost me? One 29-cent pen, two 99-cent marble notebooks." Sidonie Smith and Julia Watson argue that "telling the story turn[s] speakers into subjects of narrative who can exercise some control over the meaning of their 'lives'" (14). While I am not arguing that writing memoir represents a panacea for all evils or that it offers a solution to the problems students and educators face, I wish to emphasize the importance of the kind of work that can take place within and beyond the classroom.

Repeatedly, by teaching Italian American women authors—in addition to authors such as Dorothy Allison, Sandra Cisneros, Ana Castillo, Alice Walker, Olga Broumas, Sapphire, Nancy Mairs, and others—I have been able to realize, with my students, the vital political lessons these writers' work can teach. An African American male student was notably moved by "Growing Up Italian": The stark simplicity with which Mazziotti Gillan portrays her experience of cultural marginalization spoke powerfully to him. Another student, Bart Babinski, wrote in response to *Where I Come From:*

> As I write my memoir, and relive as well as re-evaluate my experience, Maria Mazziotti Gillan's work shines like a guiding light. . . . The poems are sweet and short and somewhat quiet. But I can sense the rage and anger and

frustration and mounting explosion boiling just beneath the surface. The fury that she wants to unleash on every person and thing that ever walked all over her, all over her mother and father. All over her heritage. I am touched by each regret and mourning, as I remember my own faults and mistakes. The times I disregarded my mother or father as foreign and dumb. The time I changed my name, and made fun of other odd, exotic, beautiful foreign names. The times I mocked customs of Indians or Chinese, or South Americans, or my fellow Polish companions because they did not find it necessary to hide and become American the way I had.

Reading *Breathless* prompted yet another student to investigate the high incidence of asthma among African American poor. Consistently, my students at New Jersey City University felt that their experiences of marginalization and oppression were validated by these Italian American authors, regardless of the students' ethnic identity or identification.[20] These Italian American women writers thus work to "give students the opportunity to become citizens who have the knowledge and courage to struggle in order to make despair unconvincing and hope practical" (Giroux 128).

After reading the works of writers who truly inspired them, my students come to see the importance of writing memoir. They learn to write about their lives *critically* and, in doing so, come to "own" the very experiences of violence, abuse, and disempowerment that had erased—or partly constituted—their sense of selfhood.[21] I emphasize "critically" because memoir is not simply about writing down the facts of one's life. Memoir requires, as I understand and teach it, the creation of frameworks in which to place one's life, frameworks that enable the writer to shift from the position of object to that of subject, a narrating subject. Here is Laura McKeon, another student, commenting on the course:

> We all suffer from certain degrees of historical, social, and familial amnesia. Through memoir-writing, one can learn to fill in the blanks and, in the process, reclaim his or her past honestly. . . . [T]he greatest gift I received from my course experience was the sense of validation, trust, and community I garnered from my fellow classmates. . . . I came away with the sense that our personal struggles, although different in detail, bound us together as survivors of our own life experiences.

When historically disempowered people write memoirs—in claiming a space for their voices and their memory—they also claim a space for those who are empowered by reading those memoirs. Grace Guandique, a student in the memoir workshop writes:

> The memoir writing workshop let me finally tell the story that I have been carrying around for many years. A story that my family wanted to tell, to

scream, to shout at the top of their lungs, but could not. My family could
not speak English. We did not have a place to be heard because immigration
officials said we did not belong in America. We were not legal residents and
therefore, the United States did not recognize us. To them, we did not exist.

In writing memoir, my students become historians of their families and
communities. This political dimension to writing is one that is, as we have
seen, central to work of the Italian American writers who fulfill, on their
own terms, the function of the public intellectual. It is significant that these
writers are emerging on the literary scene collaterally to the emergence of
the contemporary memoir.

The anger, violence, and sorrow articulated in many Italian American
women's memoirs—combined with a visceral attachment to these authors'
families and cultures—offer different versions of the Italian American immigrant plot. Difficult questions lie at the core of memoir writing: secrecy,
allegiance, betrayal, truth, celebration, and biting attack. This memoir,
which involves both a self-conscious awareness of how one uses memory
and of the radical potential of the uses of memory, necessitates a continuous reimagining and reinventing of the past. For Italian American women,
who are still struggling to come into their own—both inside and outside
their culture—writing memoir is an audacious act. While Italian American
women authors have been producing works of significance and paving the
way for the memoir for decades now, the most recent developments in the
genre suggest that new sites have been uncovered and also that a new kind
of digging needs to be done.[22]

Archival work, for example, might uncover early autobiographical and
memoiristic work produced by Italian American women. This kind of
archeological work would prove vital in sustaining and fostering the development of a tradition that is taking roots. Much like the memoir, poised
between present and past, the Italian American female literary tradition lies
at a crossroads of past and present: The renewed strength of our contemporary production has become a driving force, propelling us toward our
futures. That strength—which derives so much of its power from memory—also serves to awaken in us a greater sense of the need for a vital exploration of our literary and historical pasts.

The work of Italian American women writers opens up important cultural spaces. These authors argue for the necessity of such spaces as the forums in which words can be spoken and change can begin. In doing so,
they politicize their ethnic identity as one of the means that makes it possible to rid communities of the insidious power of silence. Writing, then,
makes it possible to pursue the kind of work that is at the center of the public intellectual's life: To build community even as one seems engaged in dis-

mantling it. *Where I Come From, Night Bloom, Vertigo,* and *fuori/outside* are about family and community, personal and collective: The question of origins, we come to understand through writers such as Mazziotti Gillan, Cappello, DeSalvo, and Ragusa becomes a question of direction. Looking back to the past, then, while "beset with half-involvements and half-detachments, nostalgic and sentimental on one level, an adept mimic or secret outcast on another" (Said 49), paves the way for a future in which the voiceless can learn to transform their own silence into language and action.

Epilogue

Coming Home to Language

*Questi, mi dico, non sono tempi di emigrazione ma di mobilità: la memoria
e il sentimento dell'esilio stanno solo nell'irrequietezza di chi vive altrove.*

*These, I tell myself, are not times of emigration, but of mobility: the memory
and the feeling of exile reside within the restlessness of those who live elsewhere.*

> —Maria Rosa Cutrufelli, Canto al deserto:
> storie di Tina, soldato di mafia—Song to the Desert:
> Story of Tina, Mafia Soldier *(trans. Edvige Giunta)*

*Home for me is in the syntax, in the syllables. In the syncopations and in the
silences. . . .*
*When I write sentences I am at home. When I make shapes. When I do not,
I am damned, doomed, homeless; I know this well—restless, roaming; the actual places I've lived become unrecognizable, and I, too, monstrous, am unrecognizable to myself. In the gloating, enormous strangeness and solitude of the
real world, where I am so often inconsolable, marooned, utterly dizzied—all
I need do is pick up a pen and begin to write—safe in the shelter of the alphabet, and I am taken home.*

La casa per me è nella sintassi, nelle sillabe. Nelle sincopi e nei silenzi. . . .
*Quando scrivo frasi mi sento a casa. Quando creo forme. Se no, sono dannata,
condannata, senza casa; lo so bene—senza riposo, vagabonda; i posti in cui
ho vissuto diventano irriconoscibili, ed anch'io, mostruosa, divengo irriconosci-
bile persino a me stessa. Nella stranezza enorme e arrogante del mondo reale,
in cui così spesso sono inconsolabile, alla deriva, completamente in preda alle
vertigini—devo solo prendere una penna e cominciare a scrivere—sicura, al ri-
paro nell'alfabeto, e sono a casa.*

> —Carole Maso, "The Shelter of the Alphabet"—
> "Al riparo nell'alfabeto" *(trans. Edvige Giunta)*

"To Edvige, another Sicilian in exile": Maria Rosa Cutrufelli inscribes in her book *Canto al deserto,* the novel set in my hometown of Gela. My exile is geographical, like that of Maria Rosa, who left Sicily long ago and lives in Rome: For Sicilians, leaving the island is a form of migration and exile, even if one continues to live in Italy. We leave and take Sicily with us.

But my exile is also linguistic. In language I am perennially homeless. I have managed to remove myself from my language of birth, from the language that I know as intimately as the smell of my baby son's hair, the rhythm of his breath as he falls asleep. I have removed myself so much that I have become a stranger to myself.

⬦⬦⬦   ⬦⬦⬦   ⬦⬦⬦

In May 2000, Maria Rosa Cutrufelli invites me and Caterina Romeo—a young Italian scholar who a few years ago ventured into the field of Italian American women's literature—to put together a special issue of the Italian journal *tutteStorie* on Italian American women writers. I accept enthusiastically: This is the sort of homecoming I have been waiting for. And Maria Rosa and Caterina are the perfect companions for this return; they understand the complications of multiple origins and cultural allegiances.

Caterina does most of the translations. We choose a few other skillful translators for the rest. I will translate Carole Maso, one of the writers I most admire, whose work humbles and inspires me: Carole Maso who performs miracles with language. I dread and look forward to turning into Italian the exquisite prose of "The Shelter of the Alphabet," Maso's meditation on home and language, on language as home.

It has been years since I translated an English text into Italian. Somehow I feel more at ease translating from Italian into English. Paradoxically, I have felt safer, even more competent, navigating the journey from Italian into English, as if venturing among the sounds of my mother tongue might be more dangerous, a journey into a place where familiar signposts suddenly become blank, words that should be easily recognizable disintegrate into shapeless, incomprehensible signs.

How did this happen?

Less than 17 years ago, when I came to the United States as a graduate student, my speech gave out. Whenever I spoke English, for those first long months, I hesitated and stammered. I stood on the edge of each word, then advanced with cautious, circumspect steps. Over the years, through a long and conflicted process, English became mine, like an acquired family member, a partner, a spouse, separate from my origins but nevertheless beloved, at times with even greater passion. Yet, I always felt, and continue to feel, that I can inhabit this other language of mine only as long as I recognize and accept the intricate mix of familiarity and foreignness that is inherent in our relationship.

When I begin to translate Carole Maso, a feeling of comfort and exhilaration takes over as I weigh each word, each phrase, each sentence, and seek the Italian counterpart. I vow to respect the integrity of Carole's writing, to be alert to the temptation to which translators are subject: to become so enamored with the transformative process of language that one forgets the obligation to the original text. Like all translators, I face the challenge of maintaining a delicate balance between remaining within the bounds of the original and transporting that text into another linguistic realm, with all its inevitable semantic and rhythmic variations: be faithful but not pedantic; creative but not disloyal; plunge into each word and turn it inside out before the crossing; turn back and reconsider; be ready to take the leap.

At first, a flood of words, an amorphous mass in which English and Italian fight over who will prevail. Then, I remember Italian words, the right words for this translation, words I have not used in years, words that had become part of my passive vocabulary, much like the English words that sat waiting during my long apprenticeship with the English language.

The contours of language take shape, develop into a fully-formed body. Moving back and forth between English and Italian gives me relief, like stretching a muscle that has been unused for too long: pain turns to discomfort, then to relief, finally to the pleasure of reacquiring that which once was mine. An exhilarating bodily experience. I am surprised by the ease with which Carole Maso's English prose smoothly becomes Carole Maso's prose in Italian.

My apprenticeship with English is not finished yet and here I am, apprenticing in the language that was once my own. But was it? As a toddler, I babbled a few words in Sicilian, but like many children of my generation—especially girls—as my verbal skills developed, I was no longer allowed to speak the dialect, although my parents always spoke Sicilian between themselves. Like other Sicilians, my parents well understood that upward mobility necessitated relinquishing their Sicilian language; it required linguistic assimilation into Italian. I grew up thinking of Sicilian as a lesser language, a language that denoted class distinction, the language of the poor and the uneducated. Traveling to Northern Italy and meeting people from the North who complimented me on the fact that I did not sound Sicilian confirmed my perceptions. These days, I have an unmistakable Sicilian accent in Italian—and even my Sicilian accent is marked by the varieties of the two Sicilian places where I spent most of my life: Gela and Catania.

But if Sicilian was this language to be avoided, an obstacle to being recognized as fully "Italian," it also was the language of my ancestors, the language of intimacy, the language my parents would speak between themselves in soft, musical whispers after a late dinner, while I napped in my mother's lap. *Sciatu miu, sciatuzzu*—my breath, my soul, little breath: a favorite form of address used by Sicilian parents toward their children. Its wide range of phonetic modulations conveys in turn tenderness, passion, compassion, suffering, even a command or rage when abbreviated as "*scià.*" While my parents obeyed the cultural dictates that required the suppression of Sicilian regionalism in favor of the cultural and linguistic homogenization brought about by Italian, they managed to maintain, and instill in their children, a passionate love for all things Sicilian: food, crafts, ritual. Sicilian was offered to me as the language of song, of play, of lullabies, of folk tales and nursery rhymes. Not surprisingly, I have a visceral attachment to Sicilian language.

I cannot help but draw a connection with the ways in which Italian American women writers inhabit the English language, which they own and master—the way I do Italian (or is it "did"?)—while also retaining profound—although often not conscious or even active—ties to the language and culture of their immigrant ancestors. A large number of these ancestors in turn inhabited Italian culture and language as if these were foreign to them. They spoke Italian with an accent: Sicilian, Calabrese, Pugliese, Abruzzese, Sardinian. There are 20 regions in Italy and endless variations of regional dialects.

How long does it take for a literature to take hold, to plant itself firmly in the national cultural terrain? How long does it take for an ethnic group to acquire full cultural and linguistic citizenship?

The body of literature produced by Italian American women has grown by leaps and bounds, as if the writers were determined not to let the century be put to rest without their names clearly imprinted in its history. The process of outgrowing the invisibility, the silence, the lack of recognition, reflects on the literature itself, as the authors feel, whether consciously or not, freer to navigate diverse territories and to explore ethnicity in new and imaginative ways.

A question that women writers have been forever posing—who are our foremothers?—is one that might be relevant for Italian American women writers to address at this point in Italian American cultural history. Yet, one has to ask, is it even important to trace a lineage, to look for literary ancestors, possible models and sources to confront? Who are such foremothers anyway? Chosen foremothers such as Zora Neale Hurston, whose brave embracing of language and culture, of language as culture, makes her a model and source of inspiration not solely for African American women writers; Italian American women whose works may lay buried in dusty libraries and archives of immigrant history; the early-twentieth-century Italian immigrant women whose writings Jennifer Guglielmo has uncovered.

It is significant that the writings of many of these first-generation Italian immigrant women—truly transitional cultural figures—were produced in Italian. But can Italian American women writers also claim a connection with Italian writers in Italy by virtue of distant national origins?

While this subject has not yet been explored in literary criticism, I believe that we must look closely at the possibilities that an encounter between these two groups of writers, past and present, might create. Can Maria Messina's unforgettable narratives of Sicilian life and womanhood resonate for Sicilian American women writers like Sandra M. Gilbert, Rosette Capotorto, and Nancy Caronia? Do these American writers' words in turn resonate for contemporary Italian women writers? If we travel further back, beyond the realm of literature, into that vital part of our cultural heritage represented by storytelling and myth, we encounter Galathea, Arachne, Hecate, Arethusa, Cyane, and, of course, Persephone, Sicilian goddess, ancient traveler, woman-child caught between two worlds, precursor of women immigrants, adept traveler who emerges over and over again in the written words and the cinematic images of so many Italian American women. Perhaps what Italian American women authors must do is not to look for predictable commonalities and conventional literary derivation but instead to explore unexpected, circuitous routes that might lead them to newly fashioned ties with their Italian sisters, writers, filmmakers, and artists from the Italian past, such as Maria Messina, Grazia Deledda, Elvira Notari, or, more recently, Maria Rosa Cutrufelli, Dacia Maraini, Elsa Morante, Silvana La Spina, Annie Messina, Clara Sereni, Lina Wertmuller, and Roberta Torre.

※※※   ※※※   ※※※

In March 2001, I travel back to Italy where I have been invited by Marina Zancan, who oversees the doctoral program in women's writing at the University of Rome. For the first time since I left to come to the United States in 1984, I return as a scholar of Italian American women's literature and art. During this trip, I take part in the presentation of *origini: le scrittrici italo americane,* the special issue of *tutteStorie* I coedited with Maria Rosa Cutrufelli and Caterina Romeo. It is auspicious that we present this volume at the Casa Internazionale della donna in Rome and that our sponsor is the Zora Neale Hurston Multimedia Center. How serendipitous these crossings and re-crossings, these departures and returns. It all comes together as, for the first time, Italian women listen eagerly to the words—on this day spoken in Italian—of their Italian American sisters, and are visibly moved by them: they recognize not sameness, but a connection—creative, fruitful, and complicated.

Accent is a function of two languages in relation; it is a sign of disjunction, but also of connection: It marks being Sicilian and Italian, Italian and

American (or Sicilian, Italian, and American)—and let's not forget that, often, one's ethnic and national mix can be even more varied, inclusive at once of Irish, Jewish, African, Chicana, Argentine, Native American, and many other heritages.

In the late twentieth century, economic and travel conditions have made it possible to witness, in an accelerated manner and within a life, the kind of cultural transformation that has, historically, spanned generations. Recent immigrants—those of the wave of late-twentieth-century intellectual emigration from Italy—maintain geographical, cultural, and linguistic ties both with Italy and the United States. For these immigrants, departure, assimilation, the reclamation of a connection to the ancestral culture, and the struggle to find a voice to tell the story of these experiences, comprise a cycle that can occur within the arc of one or two decades.

Can this particular cultural experience become a bridge of sorts, one across which the cultural disjunction embodied by the accent might help create occasions for dialogue and collaboration? Can it encourage exploratory journeys back and forth, in history and geography, that might in turn lead to the coming together of selves into a new kind of cross-cultural community?

My experience at the Zora Neale Hurston Center in Rome, and on this particular trip to Italy in general, but also my conversations with Italian American women writers on my recent return to the United States, lead me to answer these questions with a resounding yes. And, as I bring this book to a close, it has become quite clear to me that we are, at this particular moment in contemporary cultural history, standing on the brink of just the sort of new creative transformation that such a community of collaboration will indeed make possible.

This is the continuing power of writing with an accent.

Notes

Preface

1. Luisa Pretolani's video, *Things I Take,* which deals with Indian women immigrants, speaks to the experience of emigration in ways that transcend the specific experience of a single ethnic group. The issues the women who appear in this video address relate to the significance of and repercussions on one's sense of self of the separation from one's homeland.

2. See Gilbert and Gubar's feminist classic *The Madwoman in the Attic* (1979), in which they offer a definition of anxiety of authorship, which they juxtapose to the more masculine "anxiety of influence" (50), the title subject of Harold Bloom's study.

3. I began to study Italian American literature and minority literatures not in graduate school, but in the years following my graduation, in the early 1990s.

4. My first actual encounter with Italian American literature actually occurred in 1983, at a conference on Italian American Studies of the AISNA (Italian Association of North American Studies). The conference was organized by my then professor of American Literature at the University of Catania, Maria Vittoria D'Amico. I was one of a handful of undergraduate students involved in the organization of the conference. There, I met several American professors, including John Paul Russo, who would later offer me a teaching assistantship at the University of Miami.

5. Giunta, "The Quest for True Love: Nancy Savoca's Domestic Film Comedy."

6. In 1987, DeSalvo had also published—in England—*Casting Off,* an outrageous novel about Italian American women and adultery.

7. Oddly enough, much like other women and minority writers who, once they started looking, found literary sisters and ancestors, I, too, would later discover two other writers in my family, Giuseppe Minasola and Laura Emanuelita Minasola.

Introduction

1. For a discussion of the problematic status of the term "Italian American," see Fausty and Giunta, "Quentin Tarantino: An Ethnic Enigma" (2001). For historical accounts of and perspectives on the racialization of Southern

Italian immigrants, see Richards (1999), Roediger (1994), and Guglielmo and Salerno.

2. Many Italian American women claim a cultural, if not geographical, connection to Southern Italy and more specifically, Sicily—even if their families are not from the South or Sicily—for example, Roman-born Alessandra Belloni, whose work in music, song, and dance is rooted in the cultural history of the South, or Joanna Clapps Herman, who affirms strong ties to Sicily.

3. For a critical/autobiographical account of the racialization of the Italian South—and especially Sicily—see Giunta, "Figuring Race: Kym Ragusa's *fuori/outside*" (1999). Among Italian American women's texts that explore the issue of race and the identification of Sicilians as people of color, see Nancy Caronia, "Go to Hell" (Ciatu, Micallef and DiLeo 1998, 216–25).

4. Examples would be Filipina writer Jessica Hagedorn and Chicana writer Ana Castillo. For an analysis of American attitudes toward language, see Rosina Lippi-Green's study, *English with an Accent: Language, Ideology, and Discrimination in the United States* (1997). Unfortunately, I did not come across the work of Green-Lippi, a professor of Linguistics, until after this book went to production.

5. Sollors proposes a distinction between "descent"—which he equates with the "hereditary"—and "consent"—which refers to one's choice to establish relationship through law and marriage. Sollors poses the question: "How can consent (and consensus) be achieved in a country whose citizens are of such heterogeneous descent? And how can dissent be articulated without falling back on myths of descent?" (*Beyond Ethnicity* 6).

6. In *Multilingual America* (1998), Werner Sollors laments that "With the exception of some discussion of Spanish, multiculturalism has paid very little attention to linguistic diversity, past or present" (4).

7. This is the translation of the poem by Miuccio and Patricia Donahue as it appears in the bilingual edition: "one time only/mother land/i betrayed you//leaving//each instant/foreign land/i betray you//staying" (Miuccio 7).

8. Giunta, ed., *VIA* Special Issue on Italian American Women (215–8).

9. See Laurino's *Were You Always an Italian?*—especially "Clothes" (54–76) and "Milan, 1997" (94–9).

10. For definitions and discussions of ethnicity in U.S. contexts, see Werner Sollors's *Beyond Ethnicity: Consent and Descent in American Culture* and his edited collections *The Invention of Ethnicity* and *Multilingual America,* and Ishmael Reed, ed., *MultiAmerica.* See also *Varieties of Ethnic Criticism,* two special issues of the journal *MELUS* (1995 and 1998), and Suzanne Oboler, *Ethnic Labels, Latino Lives.*

11. I use the term "minorities" not in its literal significance but in relationship to the political and cultural power held by a specific ethnic group.

12. See Gloria Anzaldúa, ed., *Making Face, Making Soul: Haciendo Caras: Creative and Critical Perspectives by Feminists of Color;* Cherríe Moraga and Gloria Anzaldúa, eds., *This Bridge Called My Back: Writings by Radical Women of*

Color; and Lisa Albrecht and Rose M. Brewer, eds., *Bridges of Power: Women's Multicultural Alliances.* Davida J. Alperin, arguing in favor of "the interactive model and alliances based upon it," as opposed to the pluralist or separatist models, suggests that "oppressed groups need to have separate spaces in which to gain their self-respect, name themselves, and discover their own history. These same groups need to form alliances with other groups in order to compare, contrast, and identify the connections among different types of oppression" in order to develop possibilities for social change (Albrecht and Brewer 31).

13. Telephone conversation with Louise DeSalvo, 2 April 1996.
14. Edvige Giunta, e-mail correspondence with Caronia and Cappello, June 2000.
15. Conversation with Jennifer Guglielmo, December 2000.
16. Telephone conversation with Kym Ragusa, 27 April 2001.
17. E-mail correspondence from Saracino to Giunta, 5 July 2000.
18. Blurb on the back cover of *The Dream Book.*
19. On regional provenance, see Micaela di Leonardo, *The Varieties of Ethnic Experience: Kinship, Class, and Gender among California Italian-Americans.* On the North–South dichotomy, see Antonio Gramsci's *The Southern Question.*
20. See my essays "Figuring Race" and "Dialects, Accents, and Other Aberrations."
21. Another important book that deals with environmental politics and public health is Susanne Antonetta's *Body Toxic: An Environmental Memoir,* published after this book had gone to production.
22. The contribution of the following scholars should be highlighted: Fred Gardaphé, Anthony Tamburri, Mary Jo Bona, Robert Viscusi, Mary Frances Pipino, Caterina Romeo, Annette Wheeler Cafarelli, Peter Carravetta, Mary Ann Mannino, Carol Bonomo Albright, John Paul Russo, Julia Lisella, Martino Marazzi, Blossom Kirschenbaum, and Franco Mulas.
23. The phrase "spazio/space" is the title of Giuliana Miuccio's book of poems.

Chapter 1

1. Mary Ann Fusco, "Telling Her Story in Italian American."
2. In the "Clothes" chapter of her memoir *Were You Always an Italian?* (54–76), Maria Laurino offers a compelling analysis of Versace's career and self-fashioning, foregrounding issues of class and regional origins (Versace was, notably, from Calabria). Laurino intertwines this analysis with a memoiristic narrative on the impact of clothes on her own upbringing in suburban New Jersey.
3. It is rare that women writers and filmmakers show an interest in the subject, although when they do, they demonstrate the subversive ways in which the subject can be approached, as Sandra Mortola Gilbert does in her poem "Mafioso" (*The Dream Book* 348–9) or Louise DeSalvo in a passing reference in *Vertigo.* In "Mafioso," the haunting question addressed by

the speaker to presumed Mafiosi uncles obliquely exposes the fictitious connections between all Italian Americans and the mafia forced on this ethnic group by American culture. DeSalvo matter-of-factly and shrewdly implies that *some* Italian Americans she knew growing up might have been involved with the mafia: yet this simple fact does not drag all Italian Americans into organized crime, a fantasy carefully cultivated by Hollywood and American media. But DeSalvo has no need to dwell on this, as her life narrative in *Vertigo* illustrates that while she had to deal with many troubling issues in her life, the mafia was not one of them. Self-conscious and self-parodic representations also can help to change the aesthetics of stereotyping because they call attention to their culturally and historically determined existence.

In the Preface to *Benedetta in Guysterland,* Fred Gardaphé notes that "What Mario Puzo romanticized in *The Godfather* (1969), what Gay Talese historicized in *Honor Thy Father* (1971), Giose Rimanelli has parodied in *Benedetta*" (16–7). Gardaphé rightly notes that this novel enables Rimanelli to transcend "the Italian/American subject" (17). At the same time, through its parodic focus on mafia, it also "tells the story of America's relationship with Italy and debunks the traditional stereotype of the Italian/American gangster" (Rimanelli 19).

4. Texts such as Leonardo Sciascia's *La Sicilia come metafora* and Giovanni Falcone's *Cose di cosa nostra* should be necessary homework for anyone wanting to understand the history of the mafia phenomenon, including its most recent developments.

5. Ed Guerrero argues that, rather than challenging Hollywood conventions concerning race, in *Jungle Fever* Lee perpetuates them in the most conservative manner. For a discussion of representation of Italian Americans in Spike Lee's movies, see articles by Aste, Bensoussan, and Pierson in *Shades of Black and White,* eds. Ashyk, Gardaphé, and Tamburri. See also Verdicchio, "Spike Lee's Guineas."

6. Nancy Savoca's film *True Love* offers an imaginative alternative to the stereotypes of the Italian American family presented by *Moonstruck.* The same can be said of Cara DeVito's *Ama l'uomo tuo,* Christine Noschese's *Mary Therese,* Susan Caperna Lloyd's *The Baggage.* Innovative works by Italian American women filmmakers were presented at *Malafemmina: A Celebration of the Cinema of Italian American Women,* curated by Kym Ragusa. For a videography, see the festival's program.

7. On Italian American cinema see Anna Camaiti Hostert and Anthony J. Tamburri, eds., *Screening Ethnicity: Cinematographic Representations of Italian Americans in the United States.* On representations of ethnicity in cinema, see Lester D. Friedman, *Unspeakable Images.*

8. See Fredric Jameson, *The Political Unconscious.*

9. If the silencing of ethnic voices transcends gender, and even class boundaries, it also works most powerfully when gender, class, sexuality, and ethnicity intersect. This does not mean that all Italian American women who

do not write explicitly about their ethnicity suffer from the effects of cultural silencing. Italian American literature exceeds the bounds of the immigrant narrative and includes a wide spectrum of experiences and narratives.

10. See my essay on *Dogfight*, "Narratives of Loss: Voices of Ethnicity in Agnes Rossi and Nancy Savoca."

11. In *Household Saints*, Savoca draws on her dual—Sicilian and Argentinean—cultural heritage. A magical realism characteristic of Latin American literature pervades this film. On Savoca, see Baker and Vitullo, Giunta ("The Quest for True Love), Fausty and Giunta ("An Interview with Nancy Savoca"), Messina, Nardini, and Reich.

12. See Fawzia Afzal-Khan's study of the Indo-English novel.

13. While strongly anchored to the contemporary U.S. memoir of the late twentieth century, *Adultery* develops some of its premises even further, by establishing multiple narrative levels and voices. On the contemporary memoir, described by some as a new kind of autobiography, see Barrington, DeSalvo (*Writing as a Way of Healing*), Giunta ("Teaching Memoir at New Jersey City University" and "Honor Thy Students"), McDonnell, and Rainer. On Italian American women's memoirs, see Romeo and the last chapter of this book.

14. See Mary Cappello, Wallace Sillanpoa, and Jean Walton's interview with Roberta Torre.

15. Victims of the harshest forms of prejudice and persecution in the early stages of their immigration, like other southern and eastern European groups that experienced similar forms of discrimination, Italian Americans quickly learned that "whiteness" was the key to assimilation in Anglo-America. The trial of the Italian anarchists Nicola Sacco and Bartolomeo Vanzetti, and the lynching of Italian Americans in New Orleans in 1891, represent two chapters in the history of Italian Americans in the United States. In "Dago Street" (a poem in *The Wop Factor*), Rose Romano remembers, as if she had witnessed it, the 1891 lynching. Bona points out that the interweaving of past and present "allows Romano to reinforce the insidious persistence of ethnic prejudice in America" ("Learning to Speak Doubly" 165). See Nazzaro's article, "*L'Immigration Quota Act del* 1921, *la crisi del sistema liberale e l'avvento del fascismo in Italia.*"

16. See Rose Romano's controversial essay on her relationship to the lesbian community, "Where is Nella Sorellanza?" and her poem "This is Real" (*The Wop Factor* 12–3).

17. See Scelsa and Milione.

18. Candeloro notes that the Italian Americans in Chicago, for example, have achieved better economic status, but they have not yet reached a much sought after "respect" (Holli 247–8).

19. For a discussion of race and the changing significance of whiteness, particularly in connection to political, cultural, and legal definitions of citizenship, see Roediger, *Towards the Abolition of Whiteness*. On Italian Americans and

the question of race, see Richards, *Italian American: The Racializing of an Ethnic Identity,* and Guglielmo and Salerno, eds., *Italians and the Politics of Race-Making in the United States.* On the dichotomy between European and non-European in the United States and a myopic reading of European identity, see Danuta Zadworna Fjellestad's approach to the literature produced by Central European immigrants in the United States in "'The insertion of the self into the space of borderless possibilities: Eva Hoffman's Exiled Body." Fjellestad argues that "the first assumption encouraging a homogenizing view on European American literature seems to be the persistent myth of the so-called 'European model' of voluntary immigration, acculturation and assimilation that leads directly to a seamless if not quite painless absorption. . . . The second . . . is the naïve yet stubborn belief that Europe is a cultural—if not political—unity" (134).

20. For an account of Italian American working-class history see Cohen, Gabaccia's *From Sicily to Elizabeth Street,* Guglielmo, and Vecoli.

21. Guglielmo notes how such stereotypes persist even in the literature on "Italian American working class activism, which privileges the voices and actions of men" ("Lavoratrici coscienti").

22. The poet Vittoria repetto explores the issue of racism in Italian American communities in "a line of 7 olive and black stories," in which she writes about hearing of the assault on Abner Louima: "I hold my breath/hoping/there will be no Italian names/but there he is/he says/he's not a racist/he has a black fiancée/he just/had to break a man/he's paisan/a countryman/I'd rather not have."

23. See Vittoria repetto's chapbook, *Heading for the Van Wyck.*

24. See Lucia Chiavola Birnbaum, in Tamburri, Giordano, and Gardaphé, eds., *From the Margin* 282–93.

25. See Viscusi, "Narrative and Nothing: The Enterprise of Italian American Writing" and "A Literature Considering Itself: The Allegory of Italian America" (Giordano, Tamburri, and Gardaphé, eds., *From the Margin* 265–81). In 1994, the *New York Times Book Review* published an article by Gay Talese entitled, "Where Are the Italian American Novelists?" Talese's article has been criticized by a number of Italian American writers. See the responses of some Italian American scholars and writers to Talese's article in *Italian Americana,* "Where Are the Italian American Novelists?" by Dana Gioia and others.

26. For an overview of Italian American literature, see Fred Gardaphé, *Italian Signs, American Streets.* Anthony J. Tamburri's *A Semiotic of Ethnicity* examines the work of Italian American male authors such as Tony Ardizzone, Luigi Fontanella, and Giose Rimanelli, in addition to women authors such as Helen Barolini and Gianna Patriarca. On Italian American literature, see also *Beyond the Margin: Readings in Italian Americana,* edited by Giordano and Tamburri.

27. Ciresi's *Blue Italian* and *Pink Slip* are considerably less layered in their exploration of ethnic identity than her first book, *Mother Rocket,* and her lat-

est book, *Sometimes I Dream in Italian.* See also Louise DeSalvo's essay, "A Portrait of the Puttana as a Middle-Aged Woolf Scholar" (Barolini, *The Dream Book* 93–9; a revised and expanded version can be found in *Vertigo*). On Frances Winwar, see Barolini's Introduction to *The Dream Book,* 6.

28. See my essay, "Persephone's Daughters."

29. Gioia Timpanelli talked about her grandparents during the 2000 Symposium on Italian and Italian American women organized by the Collective of Italian American Women with the cosponsorship of Casa Italiana Zerilli Marimò and the Department of Italian at New York University.

30. After the reprint of *Paper Fish,* De Rosa would repudiate Italian American identity (see Chapter 3 of this book). The contradictions inherent to working-class origins do not, obviously, pertain only to Italian Americans. In an essay on "Reclaiming Our Working-Class Identities: Teaching Working-Class Studies in a Blue-Collar Community," Linda Strom writes of the painful gap that her "education" created between her and her family, although her family had encouraged her in her pursuits (131–2).

31. Referring to her response to reading Carole Maso's *Ghost Dance* (1986), De Rosa commented that after searching for a long time, reading Maso she heard an echo, a voice that resonated for her (Fausty and Giunta, "Interview with Tina De Rosa"). DeSalvo, "An Appreciation of *Paper Fish.*"

32. Apart from *The Dream Book,* the following anthologies include Italian American women authors: *la bella figura: a choice* (1993), a selection of poetry and prose from a now-defunct journal devoted to Italian American women edited by Rose Romano; *From the Margin* (1991), edited by Tamburri, Giordano, and Gardaphé; Mary Jo Bona's *The Voices We Carry: Recent Italian American Women's Fiction* (1994); and the Fall 1996 issue of *VIA,* which I guest-edited, devoted to Italian American women authors. *Curaggia,* an anthology of women of Italian descent published by the Canadian Women's Press gathers together many new voices and foregrounds lesbian identity as an urgent issue for women authors of Italian descent to address. The same can be said of *FUORI* and *Hey Paesan,* two anthologies of writings by gays and lesbians of Italian descent. The latest collection is a special issue of *tutteStorie,* an Italian literary journal on women authors, devoted to Italian American women writers, which I coedited with Maria Rosa Cutrufelli and Caterina Romeo. See also the forthcoming anthology of Italian American women writing about food, edited by DeSalvo and Giunta.

33. See Barbara Grizzuti Harrison's review of Alaya and Ferriss's review of Rossi. See also Harrison's review of the just-published *Recollections of My Life as a Woman* by Diane di Prima.

34. While most nineteenth- and early-twentieth-century Italian women immigrants, being illiterate and non-English-speaking, could not write, many did write in Italian. Sustained archival research needs to be undertaken on Italian women who wrote prior to and contemporaneously to Sister Blandina Segale, Frances Winwar, Rosa Marinoni, Mari Tomasi, and a

handful of others. These are the reasons why contemporary Italian American women have written in virtual isolation, feeling they have neither a tradition nor a community with which to connect. *The Dream Book,* crucial as it was to the development of an Italian American female literary tradition, did not foster the literary explosion and critical recognition that the recovery of Zora Neale Hurston's *Their Eyes Were Watching God* by Alice Walker did. Only several years after the publication of Barolini's anthology, a greater public awareness of the existence of a community of writers and artists has begun to develop.

35. See Gioseffi, "Breaking the Silence for Italian-American Women." From the introduction to *The Dream Book* to "*Umbertina* and the Universe" and "Becoming a Literary Person Out of Context," Barolini has resorted to a blending of autobiographical essay and literary reading to legitimize her work.

36. This quotation is taken from a longer, unpublished version of Lisella's essay on Marinoni.

37. See Walker, *In Search of Our Mothers' Gardens.*

38. On Pola, see Barolini's comments in *The Dream Book* (161–2).

39. On Rosa Marinoni, see Julia Lisella's article in *A Tavola,* eds. Giunta and Patti. On Segale, see Romeo, "Sister Blandina alla conquista del West."

40. Mary Jo Bona, Mary Ann Mannino, and Mary Frances Pipino have recently published studies of Italian American women writers. Caterina Romeo's study of Italian American women's memoirs demonstrates also the emerging interest, on the part of young Italian scholars, in Italian American women's literature. These texts were all released as I was approaching the completion or after the completion of this study.

41. See Cafarelli, "No Butter on Our Bread: Anti-Intellectual Stereotyping of Italian Americans."

42. See Gardaphé, "The Evolution of Italian American Literary Studies."

Chapter 2

1. For a discussion of the historical exclusion of Italian American authors from the canon, see Chiavola Birnbaum, "red, a little white, a lot of green, on a field of pink: a controversial design for an Italian component of a multicultural canon for the United States," in Tamburri et al., eds., *From the Margin* 282–93. For a broader critique of the canon, see Robinson and Lauter. Many feminist critics have rewritten literary history, embracing wider criteria that validate the specificity of female literary experience. In *Women of the Left Bank,* for example, Shari Benstock recovers the work of the women who participated in the creation of Modernism in ways that are not recognized as legitimately literary.

2. Diana Di Sorella, the protagonist of Helen DeMichiel's film *Tarantella,* inherits a dream book from her mother, and that book serves as the means of recovery of familial and cultural memory.

3. In *In Search of Our Mothers' Gardens,* Walker writes of her fortuitous encounter with Hurston's work, which in turn led to her pilgrimage to Hurston's unmarked grave in a Florida cemetery, to the reprint of *Their Eyes Were Watching God,* and to its enormous impact on African American literature as well as, more broadly, on American literature. See especially "Saving the Life That Is Your Own. The Importance of Models in the Artist's Life" (3–14), "Zora Neale Hurston: A Cautionary Tale and a Partisan Review" (83–92), and "Looking for Zora" (93–116). See also Mary Helen Washington's Foreword and Henry Louis Gates Jr.'s Afterword to *Their Eyes Were Watching God* (vii–xiv and 185–95). Barolini's own journey in search of Italian American women literary predecessors, described in her essay "Looking for Mari Tomasi" (*Chiaroscuro* 73–82), parallels, in some ways, Walker's journey in search of Hurston.
4. A hardcover edition of *Umbertina* was published by Seaview in 1979. Promoted as a family saga, it achieved modestly respectable sales, but went out of print after three years. Two more editions were subsequently published. The first, a mass-market paperback by Bantam issued in March 1982, depicted on the cover, in the author's words, "three women, blouses undone, hair streaming romantically . . . [the cover] spoke of a world the book did not represent." In the fall of 1982, Bantam informed Barolini that the book would be shredded. The American Italian Historical Association bought several hundred copies, which allowed for some distribution of the book among its members, but, as the author recounts, over 100,000 copies were destroyed. Another paperback edition was published by Ayer in 1988, but its type was reduced to an almost illegible size.
5. While *Umbertina* was reviewed by numerous newspapers in smaller cities with large ethnic populations, it was virtually ignored by the kind of prestigious publications capable of setting a novel on the path toward contemporary canonization.
6. In *The Cheese and the Worms,* Carlo Ginsburg describes such histories as "microhistories." Catherine L. Albanese uses Ginsburg's theory in her work of recovery of immigrant history, *A Cobbler's Universe.*
7. See Tamburri's essays on *Umbertina* and the two chapters on Barolini in *A Semiotic of Ethnicity* (17–64 and 81–93), which incorporate and expand on the earlier essays. See also Beranger, and Gardaphè, "Autobiography as Piecework" as well as the section on *Umbertina* in "The Later Mythic Mode: Reinventing Ethnicity Through the Grandmother Figure" in *Italian Signs, American Streets,* 123–31. See also Bona, *Claiming a Tradition,* 126–45.
8. Marguerite's class transition is complicated by her geographical move to Italy. See Tamburri, "Helen Barolini's 'Comparative' Woman: The Italian American Woman" and "Looking Back: The Image of Italy in *Umbertina*" in *A Semiotic of Ethnicity.*
9. The protagonist of Antonia Pola's *Who Can Buy the Stars?* (an excerpt is included in *The Dream Book*), Marietta, is also an immigrant entrepreneur

whose story challenges the expectation of economic passivity and dependence, much like the story of Umbertina. On the issue of work in *Umbertina,* see Carol Bonomo Albright, "From Sacred to Secular in *Umbertina* and *A Piece of Earth.*"

10. These hardships were the direct result of brutal exploitation by feudal landlords and the Italian government. In fact, Umbertina's story of inherited poverty is the story of Calabrian peasants and shepherds abused by absentee landlords of the Calabrian *latifondi* (latifundia). In the nineteenth century, "partnerships" between landlords and peasants and shepherds, always mediated by *fattori* (land agents) and *caporali* (estate guards), were an integral part of the feudal economy of the Italian South. Such "partnerships"—in which the baron provided grazing land and flocks to shepherds (like Umbertina and Serafino), and the shepherds provided labor—proved "immensely profitable for the baron." "The baron's income was assured even in bad years when the 'gain' in 'fruits of the flock' was meager and corresponded to starvation wages for the shepherds" (Petrusewicz 118–19).

11. Anna Giordani's family leaves Italy for political reasons. In the introduction to his translation of Gramsci's *The Southern Question,* Pasquale Verdicchio writes: "Gramsci's analysis of North/South implicates the history of Italian unification, the first phase of which took place in 1860 with Garibaldi's 'liberation' of Sicily and the South from Bourbon rule. It soon became obvious to the Southern masses that the effort was to benefit them much less than they had been led to believe. The collaboration of Northern 'liberators' with Southern landowners further rooted the imbalances that had been established by the Bourbons" (4).

12. On the myth of Persephone, see Carl Kerényi, *Eleusis: Archetypal Image of Mother and Daughter;* Christine Downing, *The Long Journey Home: Re-visioning the Myth of Demeter and Persephone for Our Time;* and Kathie Carlson, *Life's Daughter/Death's Bride: Inner Transformation Through the Goddess Demeter/Persephone.*

13. For a discussion of the myth of Persephone in the works of Italian American women authors, see my essay "Persephone's Daughters." See also Mariarosy Calleri's video *Hidden Island/L'isola sommersa.*

14. On the idea of place and displacement see, in addition to Bartkowski, *Travellers' Tales: Narratives of Home and Displacement,* edited by George Robertson and others. See also Angelika Bammer, *Displacements,* and Iain Chambers, *Migrancy, Culture, Identity.*

15. See Gilbert and Gubar, *The Madwoman in the Attic.*

16. On Lily Bart's role as an artist, see Dittmar.

17. See Bartkowski.

18. See Anthony Tamburri, "Looking Back: The Image of Italy in *Umbertina*" in *A Semiotic of Ethnicity,* 81–93.

19. Yet, Weezy's political commitment seems articulated in the novel without much complexity or depth, reflecting more a trend of the times than any

kind of serious elaboration of feminist thinking or politics. On Italian feminism, see Giovanna Miceli Jeffries, *Feminine Feminists: Cultural Practices in Italy,* and Carol Lazzaro-Weis, *From Margins to Mainstreams: Feminism and Fictional Mode in Italian Women's Writing 1968–1990.* Among texts by Italian feminists published in the 1970s, see Maria Rosa Cutrufelli, *L'invenzione della donna* and *Disoccupata con onore.* See also *Donna, cultura e tradizione,* edited by Pia Bruzzichelli and Maria Luisa Algini.

20. "If the legal and social history of Jim Crow often turned on the question 'Who Was Black?,'" writes David Roediger, "the legal and social history of immigration often turned on the question 'Who Was White?'" (182).

21. "In asserting that race and racial difference are socially constructed, I do not minimize their social and political reality, but rather insist that their reality is, precisely, social and political rather than inherent or static. . . . Jewish Americans, Italian Americans, and Latinos have, at different times and from varying political standpoints, been viewed as both 'white' and 'nonwhite.' And as the history of 'interracial marriage and sexual relationships also demonstrates, 'white' is as much as anything else an economic and political category maintained over time by a changing set of exclusionary practices, both legislative and customary" (Frankenberg 13–14). On the social constructions of whiteness, in addition to Roediger and Frankenberg, see Dye and Richards.

22. Most critics who have written about *Umbertina* have discussed Barolini's use of autobiographical material. See, for example, Gardaphé's essay, "Autobiography as Piecework."

23. On the female *kunstlerroman,* see Jones.

24. Class transition is less an issue for Tina, who is born into the material comfort of bourgeois life as well as the social legitimacy of her father's Venetian family.

25. Barolini traces the genesis of the book to a trip to Calabria in 1969 during which she came across a traditional Calabrian bedspread, much like the one described in *Umbertina,* which in turn triggered a childhood memory of her grandmother: The bedspread she found in Calabria, woven by women from the mountain villages on huge handlooms, was for Barolini "the most authentic" link to the times in which her grandmother had left Calabria. Indeed, the seeds of the story Barolini tells in the "Umbertina" section are to be found in an autobiographical essay, "A Circular Journey," published in 1978, in which the author writes of her search for the story of her own grandmother Nicoletta (Greenberg 100).

26. See Barolini, "Becoming a Literary Person Out of Context."

27. *Umbertina* has, over the years, been taught in several colleges and universities and been written about extensively by Italian American scholars such as Anthony Tamburri, Mary Jo Bona, Fred Gardaphé, Mary Ann Mannino, Mary Frances Pipino, Carol Bonomo Albright, Caterina Romeo, Rose De Angelis, and Robert Viscusi, among others. These critics have focused on such issues as the negotiation between Italian and American cultures and

the figure of the grandmother as a recurring device that Italian American writers employ to mediate their relationship to ethnicity, as well as the quest for female selfhood that places *Umbertina* within the tradition of the feminist *bildungsroman*.

Chapter 3

1. A prepublished portion of the manuscript received the Illinois Arts Council Literary Award, and it was nominated for the Carl Sandburg Award.
2. This comment appears on the back cover of the first edition of *Paper Fish*.
3. A roman a clef, *HERmione* was written in 1927, but was published posthumously, not only because of its overt autobiographical elements but also for the centrality of lesbian love in the novel. See Friedman and Du Plessis. The late recognition of *Their Eyes Were Watching God* has received much critical attention. See Washington's Foreword (vii–xiv), Gates's Afterword to the book (185–95), and Walker's "Zora Neale Hurston: A Cautionary Tale and a Partisan View" and "Looking for Zora" (83–116).
4. In 1995, I included Tina De Rosa's *Paper Fish* in the syllabus for my undergraduate course on Italian American culture and literature. I turned to my colleague Fred Gardaphé, who had long known De Rosa, to help me get in touch with her to make sure that she would receive a monetary compensation for the sale of photocopies of her novel. In the months to come, during long telephone conversations, I learned from De Rosa more about the story of *Paper Fish*. I became determined to find a publisher willing to reprint it, although I knew that Gardaphé, a long-time supporter of this novel—and of Italian American literature—had in the past tried to find a publisher himself, to no avail. One publisher, he told me, found *Paper Fish* too "literary" and esoteric to warrant a successful reprint. In May 1995, in the aftermath of a conference on "The Lost Radicalism of Italian Americans," organized by the historian Phil Cannistraro in New York, while sipping cappuccino in Brooklyn with Fred and my then-partner, now husband, Josh Fausty, I shared with them my idea that The Feminist Press could provide an ideal home for De Rosa's orphaned book. This was a press that had made it its mission to reprint forgotten, particularly working-class, literature by women: *Paper Fish* was an ideal fit. Gardaphé had his doubts. He also seemed certain that the De Rosa would not be willing to reprint her work with a press that had "feminism" not only on its agenda but also in its name. (In light of later comments made by De Rosa, who has rejected both feminism and Italian American identity, I can understand Gardaphé's concern.) Perhaps I could persuade her. And I did. A few weeks later, as I was drafting a letter for Florence Howe, Director of The Feminist Press, Gardaphé called me from Ohio to tell me that, while attending the Working Class Studies conference in Youngstown, he had found himself sitting next to Howe herself. He had told her about *Paper Fish* and my idea to send it to the Press. I mailed a photocopy of *Paper Fish* to Florence Howe. Kim

Mallett, then editorial assistant at the Feminist Press, called me to inform me that The Feminist Press wanted to publish *Paper Fish*. A year later, De Rosa's novel was back in print with a blurb on the front cover by Louise DeSalvo: "The best novel by an Italian American woman in this century."

5. Ramholz received a grant from the National Endowment for the Arts to publish *Paper Fish*.

6. A Mexican family lives on the floor below the BellaCasa family (*Paper Fish* 16).

7. The biographical information is based on Gardaphé's interview with the author as well as my conversations with her.

8. On di Donato, see Gardaphé's introduction to the reprint and, also by Gardaphé, "Pietro di Donato's Revolutionary Revision of Christ" (*Italian Signs, American Streets* 66–75).

9. The struggle between the family and the individual in Italian American culture has been examined in various disciplines. See Caroli et al., eds., *The Italian Immigrant Woman in North America*.

10. See Werner Sollors's classic distinction in *Beyond Ethnicity*. Although that distinction has undergone much criticism (see Brenkman 98–9), it nevertheless maintains a broad epistemological validity.

11. Grandmother Doria's storytelling enables Carmolina to "make her inevitable journey away from the family and into her self . . . To help her reach this goal," Gardaphé argues, "Grandma Doria teaches Carmolina to turn memory into strength" (*Italian Signs* 133). In "Feminism, Family, and Community," Jeanne Bethke Elshtain sheds light on the creative and radical potential within the family, which, she contends, stands in opposition to "the 'needs' of capitalism" and the "market images of human beings" created by capitalism (260). *Feminism and Community*, the collection of essays edited by Penny A. Weiss and Marilyn Friedman in which Elshtain's essay appears, provides a multiplicity of perspectives on the function of various kinds of communities in shaping women's self-definition. The question of whether or not ethnicity, race, and nation define one's identity is one De Rosa indirectly takes up in *Paper Fish*, a book that emphasizes the instrumental role of ethnic heritage in forging the author's artistic talent.

12. On working-class literature, see the special issue of *Women's Studies Quarterly* devoted to working-class studies edited by Janet Zandy, and *Calling Home: Working-Class Women's Writings* and *Liberating Memory: Our Work and Our Working-Class Consciousness*, also edited by Zandy.

13. On the subject of homelessness, see Rachel Amodeo's film *What About Me?*

14. In 1996 a selection of De Rosa's poems appeared in a special issue of *Voices in Italian Americana*, which was devoted to women authors (Giunta, *VIA* 233–9).

15. The information on the composition of *Paper Fish* was given to me by De Rosa during telephone conversations that took place in 1995.

16. Of course, as in the connection that Barolini draws between herself and Gertrude Stein in the acknowledgments in the 1999 reprint of *Umbertina*,

one should not neglect to emphasize the centrality of class issue when discussing expatriation and emigration. See Bartkowski, *Travelers, Immigrants, Inmates: Essays in Estrangement.*

17. Interestingly enough, H.D.'s experimental fiction is represented primarily by a number of romans à clef, a category that can be used to describe *Paper Fish.* *HERmione*, written in 1927, was published in 1981, a year after the publication of *Paper Fish*, while other novels by H.D were published later: *Bid Me to Live* in 1983, *The Gift* in 1984, and *Asphodel* in 1992. *The Gift* is especially akin to the child's perspective of *Paper Fish*, with its focus on the memories of Hilda Doolittle's childhood in her hometown of Bethlehem, Pennsylvania.

18. On the structure of *Paper Fish*, see Bona, "Broken Images," and Gardaphé, "The Later Mythic Mode" in *Italian Signs, American Streets* (131–41).

19. According to Henry Louis Gates Jr.'s definition, the "speakerly text" is "a text whose rhetorical strategy is designed to represent an oral literary tradition. . . . the narrative strategy signals attention to its own importance, an importance which would seem to be the privileging of oral speech and its inherent linguistic features" (181). See also Gardaphé, "From Oral Tradition to Written Word: Toward an Ethnographically Based Criticism" in Tamburri, Giordano, and Gardaphé, eds., 294–315.

20. See *Grandmothers, Mothers, and Daughters: Oral Histories of Three Generations of Ethnic American Women*, ed. Corinne Azen Krause.

21. On the relationships between sisters, see *Sister to Sister: Women Write About the Unbreakable Bond*, ed. Patricia Foster. The stream of consciousness of De Rosa's prose and the crucial function of topography in the novel recalls the experiments and the representation of urban setting by modernist authors such as James Joyce, Virginia Woolf, and Jean Rhys. Sandra Cisneros's *The House on Mango Street* (1984) places Esperanza Cordero, a girl growing up in the Latino section of Chicago, at the center of the narrative. A comparative study of *Paper Fish* and *The House on Mango Street*, including a reception study, might shed light both on ethnic self-representation and on the cultural construction of ethnicities in American culture.

22. *Alice's Adventures in Wonderland* and *The Wizard of Oz* come to mind as possible—although distant—literary antecedents, especially because of their combination of enchantment and darkness.

23. "It is truly no secret that life for ethnic groups in America has been equated to a Dantean hell; that alongside the usual hardships of poverty and hunger come serious and debilitating mental illnesses that arise in America and cannot be cured there; that the family, however much loved and passionately honored by men, is often unrelentingly painful for women" (Bona, *Voices* 13).

24. See Bartkowski, *Travelers, Immigrants, Inmates* and Angelika Bammer, *Displacements.*

25. Other Italian American writers, such as Julia Savarese in *The Weak and the Strong* and Pietro di Donato in *Christ in Concrete*, and other writers of other ethnic backgrounds, have explored the intersection of class and ethnicity and

delved into the devastating consequences of city living. Sandra Cisneros, for example, foregrounds the juxtaposition between a landscape in which nature prevails and a desolate urban landscape in *The House on Mango Street*.

26. For a discussion of *Paper Fish* as a *bildungsroman* see Bona, "Broken Images, Broken Lives: Carmolina's Journey in Tina De Rosa's *Paper Fish*," and Gardaphé, "The Later Mythic Mode" in *Italian Signs, American Streets* (131–41).

27. See Candeloro in Holli 244. Ironically, the neighborhood was destroyed to make room for the University of Illinois, where De Rosa would receive her M.A. in English and where she would begin to outline *Paper Fish*. To this day, the few surviving residents blame the university for the destruction of the community and the uprooting of its members.

28. "Turning to crime," argues Humbert Nelli, "was not a denial of the American way of life, but rather comprised an effort by common laborers who lacked skills to find 'success'" (quoted in Holli and Jones 241).

29. Telephone conversation with the author, 26 September 1995. Referring to Humbert Nelli's research, Candeloro points out that during the Capone era, "the members of the corrupt syndicates were *American*-born practitioners of the *American*-ethic of success" (Holli and Jones 241).

30. *Paper Fish* is the first novel about Italians in Chicago, although several sociological studies about Italians in Chicago exist. See Nelli, *Italians in Chicago* and *Role of the Colonial Press in the Italian-American Community in Chicago*. Candeloro's essay, "Chicago Italians: A Survey of the Ethnic Factor, 1850–1990," provides much information about the history and changing status of the Italians in Chicago (Holli and Jones 229–59).

31. During a telephone conversation I had with the author in August 1995, she described *Paper Fish* as a "song from the ghetto," akin to Anne Frank's *Diary*, and enthusiastically agreed with my idea that I use it as a title for my afterword to the reprint of the book.

32. Telephone conversation with the author, August 1995.

33. See interview with De Rosa by Lisa Meyer.

Chapter 4

1. "The difference is between a malintegration one has learned to cope with or whose hopelessness is fully understood and a more radical malintegration exacerbated by the greenhorn status" (Ostendorf 577).

2. Micaela DiLeonardo points out that "critics and advocates alike implicitly or explicitly assume that contemporary identity politics categories—gender, race or ethnicity, nationality, sexual orientation—are *ur*-identities, the most fundamental divisions in human experience, but depending on which era in American history we consider, we would want to later alter or expand this list" (109).

3. On the relationship between geographical and cultural displacement and cultural identity, see *Displacements: Cultural Identities in Question,* edited by Angelika Bammer.

4. See Gardaphé, "What's Italian About Italian/American Literature."

5. Anthony Tamburri has argued that the experience of hyphenation is literally reproduced in the signs used to refer to Americans of Italian descent. See *To Hyphenate or Not To Hyphenate*.

6. Gardaphé argues that authors such as Don DeLillo and Frank Lentricchia either suppress ethnic clues or portray ethnicity obliquely through other ethnicities in their work. See his article "(In)visibility."

7. "The evocation of the trip foregrounds the ambiguity of racial identity—and identification: the uncertainty of the customers in the diner about the woman's racial identity is articulated through their relentless question: 'What side of the tracks are you from?' At first, she does not understand what they mean; then, the repetition of the words, spoken again and again, begins to unveil their significance. Repeatedly, she avoids the question, having become aware of the possibility and imminence of danger. But before leaving, she turns defiantly towards her questioners and tells them: 'Well, you just served a nigger!'" (Giunta, "Figuring Race," in Guglielmo and Salerno).

8. On names and naming in an Italian American context, see Rose De Angelis, "'What's in a Name?' Conflicted Identities in Black and White," in Ashyk, Gardaphé, and Tamburri, *Shades of Black and White* (78–86).

9. *Primitive Obsessions: Men, Women, and the Quest for Ecstasy* (1997) was published under the name Marianna Torgovnick.

10. For a discussion of the political implications of naming—and name-calling—see Elaine K. Chang, "A Not-So-New Spelling of My Name: Notes Towards (and Against) a Politics of Equivocation" in Bammer 251–66.

11. See the review of *The American Woman in the Chinese Hat* by Fausty.

12. On Carole Maso, see John O' Brien, ed., *The Review of Contemporary Fiction*. Special Issue on Raymond Queneau and Carole Maso.

13. Denise Giardina's novel *Storming Heaven* (1987) contains a memorable account of the life of coal miners, many of Italian origins (Rosa Angelelli, a Sicilian immigrant, is one of the book's four narrators), in West Virginia at the beginning of the twentieth century. Giardina is one of the authors who has presented a different picture of Italian American settlements. In her novella "Drowning" (1995), Mary Bucci Bush depicts the life of Italian immigrants in the plantations of the South at the beginning of the century.

14. "My father and his sister made a quick leap into the middle class and were the success story in their working-class family. But they maintained close ties with their working-class cousins." Telephone conversation with Agnes Rossi, 22 April 2001.

15. Letter from Agnes Rossi to the author, 5 January 1994. Early drafts of *The Houseguest* also contained Italian American references. In 1995, Rossi claimed that she had only in the recent past developed a self-awareness of her ethnicity ("On Being Italian American," unpublished notes, 2). Her characters thus actualize their author's relationship to Italian ethnicity.

16. Rossi claims that the omission of the Italian American reference had to do exclusively with the direction the narrative had taken. Telephone conversation, 28 February 1994.

17. For a discussion of white ethnicity, see Micaela di Leonardo. See also Noel Ignatiev's study of the racialization of Irish immigrants.

18. See my essay "Persephone's Daughters."

19. "Perhaps the most revealing cultural difference between southern Italy and America, especially relating to literary representations of selfhood, is the Southern Italian's distrust of words itself. A firm belief in the value of deeds over words was held sacrosanct by the peasant stock in southern Italy. . . . the southern Italians' traditional distrust of words perpetuated a heritage of silence for both genders" (Bona, "Broken Images" 89).

20. For a discussion of identity politics and white ethnicity, see di Leonardo.

21. Noting that what she has in common with Gilbert, Torgovnick, and Davidson—besides Italian origins—is the fact the four of them are "*cryptoethnic professors of English,*" Hutcheon poses the following question: "But what does it mean to become an *English* professor when you grow up in an Italian household where 'the English' were seen to possess a distinct and different ethnic identity, where roast beef and Yorkshire pudding were considered foreign but ossobuco and polenta were the norm. 'The English' were as different, as strange to us as no doubt we were to them; they were too 'ethnic,' other, alien—at least from our point of view. This is ethnicity as positionality" (Ciongoli and Parini 248).

22. Yet Davidson's memoir significantly focuses on the experience of living outside one's culture—Japan—and language. "As the Americanized child and grandchild of immigrants from various countries who had married, intermarried, and remarried but who never liked one another very much (Italian and Poles, Catholics and Jews), I had learned over the years to get by on inklings of cultural differences, scraps of words, the interstices between America and some other culture—some history—far away but never forgotten" (Davidson 195). Recollecting an incident relating to her Italian grandmother, Davidson poignantly writes: "Translation was something like love" (196).

23. Rita Ciresi, author of three novels of Italian American subject, *Blue Italian, Pink Slip,* and *Sometimes I Dream in Italian,* made her literary debut with a collection of short stories, *Mother Rocket* (1993), winner of the Flannery O'Connor Award for Short Story.

24. Interestingly enough, the recent publication of ethnic memoirs by second- and third-generation Italian American critics such as Frank Lentricchia, Louise DeSalvo, Marianna De Marco Torgovnick, Cathy N. Davidson, and Sandra M. Gilbert, suggests that the cycle has come full circle, recreating the early literary forms of the immigrant experience.

25. Tusmith's common though somewhat facile distinction neglects to take into account ethnic intersections. Her juxtaposition of two large, broadly defined groups, European American and non-European American, oversimplifies

differences among various European American groups and subgroups, such as the Northern Italians and Southern Italians. In addition, her juxtaposition ignores the way in which immigration policies have shaped the idea of "Americanness" developed by certain ethnic groups, including Italian Americans. To overlook the history of discrimination suffered by certain European American groups, especially Eastern and Southern European, would mean to ignore the history of citizenship in the United States. In the early twentieth century, "preparedness" experts argued that "military service was the only way to 'yank the hyphen out of the Italian Americans' and other 'imperfectly assimilated immigrants'" (Vaughan 450). "The history of citizenship," Brenkman argues, "is also the history of the denial of citizenship" (89). See Brenkman's critique of Sollors's classic distinction between descent and consent (98–9).

26. See Judith Roof and Robyn Wiegman, *Who Can Speak? Authority and Critical Identity.*

27. In the Note to the Reader in *The Houseguest,* Rossi writes: "These facts [of my mother's family] shaped my mother's life and so my own. I grew up hearing stories. This story, however, is invented. The characters herein, *all* of them, are figments of my imagination, though some of them are named for and share certain other biographical markers with my relations."

28. Gardaphé argues that when writers are free from "the chain of the immigrant's memory and reality, and have . . . to rely on imagination . . . their writing reaches into the more mythic quality of the Italian-American experience, thus creating literature that transcends a single ethnic experience" ("Italian American Fiction" 83).

Chapter 5

1. In addition to Lucia Chiavola Birnbaum's study of the Black Madonna, two recent texts by Italian American women that deal with Madonna worship are Louisa Ermelino's *Black Madonna* and Beverly D'Onofrio's *Looking for Mary.*

2. Saint Agatha is also celebrated in Palermo, the two cities competing over which one was her birthplace.

3. Because of obvious cultural connections, they also appear in Latin American culture. An interesting analogy can be drawn between the blending of Catholic and indigenous spiritual elements in Latin American Catholicism—a classic example would be the Virgin of Guadalupe—and the blending of pre-Christian and Christian elements in Southern Italian Catholicism. See Ana Castillo, ed., *Goddess of the Americas.*

4. In his essay "Debate in the Dark: Love in Italian-American Fiction," Robert Viscusi writes: "When parents and children do not speak the same language, they learn to communicate through bedposts and quilts, houses and trees, deeds and dollars" (170). This is true of Italian American immigrants and their descendants, as the literary works testify.

5. In a provocative study of embroidery from the Middle Ages to today, entitled *The Subversive Stitch,* Roszika Parker delves into the complex relation between domestic work, women's oppression, and women's creativity. For a discussion of women's art, especially sewing and quilting, see Hedges and Wendt, "Everyday Use" (1–73), and Alice Walker, *In Search of Our Mothers' Gardens.*

6. In *Disoccupata con onore: lavoro e condizione della donna* (1975), a groundbreaking study of women's work in Sicily, Maria Rosa Cutrufelli offered invaluable insights into the exploitation of women in the workplace, paying particular attention to women hired to work at home: *ricamatrici*—embroiderers—figured prominently in this group. The tragically notorious Triangle Shirtwaist Factory Fire of March 1911 in New York resonates powerfully in contemporary contexts in which the sweatshop is alive and well. Maria Terrone is one of a handful of poets who has captured the contradictions of this form of female work in a poem on the Triangle Fire, entitled "Unmentionable." On the Triangle Fire see Leon Stein, *The Triangle Fire;* Janet Zandy, "Fire Poetry on the Triangle Shirtwaist Factory Fire of March 25, 1911" and "Sisters of the Fire," that gathers a number of poems written on the Fire (Special Issue of *Women's Studies Quarterly* on working-class studies); Annelise Orleck, *Common Sense and a Little Fire;* and Jennifer Guglielmo, "Learning from Seamstresses: Past and Present."

7. On Italian American material culture, see Robert Anthony Orsi, *The Madonna of 115th Street.*

8. Joseph Sciorra, "Imagined Places, Fragile Landscapes: Italian American Presepi in New York City."

9. See Gloria Feman Orenstein, "An Ecofeminist Perspective on the Demeter-Persephone Myth," in *The Long Journey Home: Re-visioning the Myth of Demeter and Persephone for Our Time,* edited by Christine Downing (262–70).

10. See my essay "Persephone's Daughters."

11. Mysticism is what De Rosa is concerned with and what provides a key to understanding the world of her novel. Both Carmolina and Doriana are portrayed as Christ-like figures, sacrificial victims, although Doriana is the one for whom there is no redemption or rescue.

12. Other authors, besides De Rosa, endow the quotidian and monotonous domestic activities with a creative function, for example, in the poetry of Anne Marie Macari, which is pervaded by a deep vein of mysticism, as in the prose poem "Clare and Francis": "God in your icy fingertips, God in the bird droppings, in the fog walking the hills, the pebbles under your feet" (55). In the poetry of Sandra M. Gilbert, domestic chores become poetical subject matter, as in "Doing Laundry," where the tediousness of the chore is ritualized and infused with mystical quality (Barolini, *The Dream Book* 349). The peculiar brand of mysticism of De Rosa's work lacks the irony underscoring the works of authors such as Gilbert. De Rosa's quotidian world is mystical in a "serious" way.

13. "In Italian tradition, the daughter (and quite often the son) does not leave home until she is married. Marriage is the ritual through which a young woman establishes her independence from her family. However, it also means shifting from an identification with family to an identification with a male who then becomes her new patriarch. De Rosa's presentation of this scene signifies a defiance of the Italian tradition" (Gardaphé, *Italian Signs* 137).

14. For a feminist analysis of Catholicism, and specifically the Marian cult, see Maurice Hamington, *Hail Mary? The Struggle for Ultimate Womanhood in Catholicism.* See also Karen Jo Torjesen, *When Women Were Priests.* Scorsese's *The Last Temptation of Christ* (based on the novel by Kazantzakis), a film that attempted to capture the paradox of the divine in the human (or vice versa), caused one of the most explosive controversies in film history because of the virulent responses of many Christian groups.

15. De Rosa's poem indicts male violence and the patriarchal laws of the Old Testament, according to which adulterous women were stoned to death, through the words of Mary. The presence of Jesus is evoked in the concluding line when Mary, now on the ground, hears "someone ask a question" (Giunta, *VIA* 237). In speaking to the violent crowd on Mary's behalf, Jesus is contrasted with, and separated from, the realm of male violence.

16. See Aaron Baker and Juliann Vitullo, "Mysticism and the Household Saints of Everyday Life." Food occupies an important place in Savoca's *Household Saints,* as in *True Love,* another film of Italian American subject.

17. Carole Maso's forthcoming book focuses on Frida Kahlo.

18. Catholicism makes its way in more irreverent ways in the pages of Rosette Capotorto's *Bronx Italian,* especially in "Mother of a Priest," "Confession," and "Heathen," all pervaded by a profane Catholicism, which is not uncommon in Italian literature—a literature that boasts a number of distinguished anti-clerical writers—and in folk culture, especially Southern Italian, in which devotion and irreverence go hand in hand.

19. Rosa Angelelli, one of the protagonists/narrators of Denise Giardina's *Storming Heaven,* remarks, as one of the significant facts of her life in America: "The priest comes to our house because there is not yet a church. We cannot talk to him because he is the Irish" (50).

20. Perrotta's story unfolds in desolate places such as Stop and Shop and the Wiener Man's Frankmobile with its anonymous trailer kitchen: Food has lost all of its ritualistic power for Perrotta's Italian American characters.

21. The speaker of "Box of Broken Things" addresses his father relentlessly: "Place yourself at the dinner table/like a place setting you tinkle/against your teeth; I'm the fork,/I'm the fork, my sister's a spoon.// . . . . Quarter yourself and feed/yourself to yourself on those nights/you are hungry, feed yourself,/feed yourself. Feed yourself/to the generations of yourself,/the generations of *us,* in this box with you." Covino's rendition of the Italian American table offers an important, if terrifying, alternative to the celebrated narrative of conviviality.

22. Contemporary Italian American women authors' emphasis on food also must be understood within the context of the ethnic revival of the 1960s, which put ethnics in the position to have "to undo the cultural effects of three generations of cultural assimilation. Not surprisingly, food became an integral part of that effort" (Gabaccia, *We Are What We Eat* 176). See also Camille Cauti, "'Pass the Identity, Please': Culinary Passing in America" in Giunta and Patti, *A Tavola: Food, Tradition and Community Among Italian Americans* (10–19).

23. For a discussion of recipes as cultural and literary narratives, see Goldmann and Leonardi.

24. On the Italian American cookbook, see Annette Wheeler Cafarelli, "Cena Trimalchionis: Identity in the Publishing Industry" in Giunta and Patti: 33–48.

25. Barolini writes of the response of the students at Sarah Lawrence College, where the screening took place: "Being liberated from imposed roles, they could romanticize the heart-warming Italian Americans who were represented as living confining roles" ("Becoming a Literary Person" 272).

26. Through *Festa,* Barolini negotiates her position between American and Italian culture, but this cookbook also furthers her authorial assertion as a woman who cooks *and* writes. See my article, "Blending 'Literary' Discourses: Helen Barolini's Italian/American Narratives."

27. Cookbooks have always been an accessible genre to women, even Italian American women: Marcella Hazan, Cathy Luchetti, Anna Del Conte, Biba Caggiano, Anne Casale, Viana La Place—women with Italian names make it in this specialized section of the publishing market. "Write an Italian cookbook, author Nives Cappelli was told when she tried to market an ethnic novel, but don't write about Italian Americans because they don't read" (*The Dream Book* 44–5). For an analysis of the cookbook as a cultural and literary text, see Leonardi and Goldman. By asserting the author's "cultural specificity" and "ethnic difference," a cookbook "provides the self with authority to speak" (Goldman 179).

28. Romano's poems cited here appear in her two volumes of poetry, *Vendetta* and *The Wop Factor.*

29. On the interconnections between food and violence in *The Godfather,* see John Paul Russo, "The Hidden Godfather."

30. Michele Linfante's play *Pizza* similarly defies expectations of conviviality linked to this dish.

Chapter 6

1. Remarks given by Jennifer Guglielmo at "Speaking of Jersey: Italian American Women on the Garden state," Poetry Center, Paterson, New Jersey, March 2001.

2. That contemporary American culture seems fascinated by all sorts of life narratives is evident from the controversial popularity of the memoir.

Sidonie Smith and Julia Watson, the editors of *Getting a Life: Everyday Uses of Autobiography,* see "autobiographical discourse" as that which, in the past as in the present, functions as "a palpable means through which Americans know themselves to be American and not-American in all the complexities and contradictions of that identity" (5–6).

3. On issues of public health, in addition to DeSalvo's *Breathless,* see Sandra M. Gilbert's memoir, *Wrongful Death* and Audre Lorde's *The Cancer Journals.*

4. Filmmakers such as Nancy Savoca, Susan Caperna Lloyd, and Kym Ragusa also have tackled the conflicted nature of women's relationships to community, in films such as Savoca's *True Love* and *Household Saints,* Ragusa's *fuori/outside* and *Passing,* and Lloyd's *The Baggage.* On Savoca's *True Love,* see my essay "The Quest for True Love: Nancy Savoca's Domestic Film Comedy"; on *Household Saints,* see Baker and Vitullo. On Ragusa, see my essay "Figuring Race: Kym Ragusa's *fuori/outside.*"

5. On the politics of recognition, see Taylor.

6. For a theoretical discussion of various notions of community, see Weiss.

7. See the other essays in *FUORI,* the first collection of writings by Italian American gays and lesbians, edited by Anthony Tamburri. See also Mary Cappello's exploration of lesbian identity in *Night Bloom.*

8. From Sister Blandina Segale's *At the End of the Santa Fe Trail,* first published in 1932 and currently out of print, to *Rosa,* a transcription of the life of the first-generation illiterate immigrant Rosa Cavalleri narrated to Marie Hall Ets, published in 1970, the autobiographies of early Italian American women writers have offered an important record of immigrant life from a female perspective and demonstrated an understanding of the function of personal and cultural memory. *Rosa,* in particular, raises issues of authorial mediation, oral narrative, translation, and compels the reader to reflect on how such issues relate to class identity and to the formation of an autochthonous Italian American literature. On Segale, see Caterina Romeo, "Sister Blandina all conquista del west."

9. Telephone conversation with Louise DeSalvo, 10 February 1997.

10. Susanne Antonetta's memoir *Body Toxic: An Environmental Memoir* (2001) explores the devastating consequences of environmental disasters on the life of the author and the New Jersey communities in which she grew up.

11. See DeSalvo's *Writing as a Way of Healing.*

12. In 1981, the Italian legislators put an end to a shameful chapter in Italian legislative history. Article 587 of the penal code, "Omicidio e lesione personale a causa di onore" (Homicide and personal injury on grounds of honor), commonly referred to as "delitto d'onore"—honor killing—was repealed as a result of the controversial three-year sentence given to a Mr. Furnari for the murder of a Professor Speranza, a well-known university professor, who was having an affair with a student of his, Furnari's daughter. My mother, who herself was a student of Speranza, recalls that public opinion was divided around this sentence, the minimum punishment given under the notorious article 587—the maximum was seven years, although

in the case of a physical confrontation between the relative who had dis-covered an illicit affair of his spouse, sister, or daughter, the sentence could be even milder than the three years given to Furnari. The *Delitto d'onore* enlarged the concept of sexual property and betrayal to a sphere that went beyond the marital bed, and gave spouses, parents, and brothers the right to embrace the emotional responses, and the legal rights, of the betrayed husband. Article 587 was established in its latest form in the Codice Rocco in 1930, and survived fascism, the postwar period, and even the feminist movement of the 1970s.

13. "Curaggia" is the feminization of the word "curaggiu," which in Southern Italian dialect means "courage." Another important memoir is Diane di Prima's *Recollections of My Life as a Woman,* which was published after this book had gone to production.

14. See Helen DeMichiel's film *Tarantella* and Jeanette Vuocolo's video *Three Graces.*

15. On this issue, see Vecoli.

16. This multicultural anthology, edited by S. E. Anderson and Tony Medina, includes the artwork and writings of 140 international activists who came together in support of the journalist Mumia Abu-Jamal, who is widely rec-ognized as a political prisoner allegedly accused of murder and currently sitting on death row in Eastern Pennsylvania.

17. On representations of the working class, see Zandy's introductions to her two anthologies and the special issue of *Women's Studies Quarterly* devoted to working-class studies that she edited.

18. By the same token, the political must be made more pedagogical. See Giroux, "Teachers as Tranformative Intellectuals" in *Teachers as Intellectuals* (125–8).

19. I do not confuse the function of the therapist and that of the writing teacher. A ground rule in my memoir workshop concerns the fact that no-body is allowed to *talk* about one's life or make comments about other stu-dents' lives. We can only discuss lives within the context of the writing in which they are framed. This distinction is, for me, fundamental and tremendously useful.

20. Annie Lanzillotto, a performance poet whose work centers on the recov-ery and transformation of public spaces for the purpose of progressive community building, also envisions "autobiography as resistance" in her writing workshops, conducted in settings that range from college class-rooms to prisons.

21. An excellent text on writing and trauma is Brenda Daly, *Authoring a Life: A Woman's Survival in and through Literary Studies.* For a theoretical perspective on trauma and memory, see Judith Lewis Herman, *Trauma and Recovery.*

22. A number of Italian American women have engaged the genre of the memoir in other ways, by writing autobiographical essays, fiction, and po-etry, and by producing videos, in which they rely on the act of remem-bering, of evoking past experiences through the creative workings of

memory: Tina De Rosa's autobiographical novel, *Paper Fish,* as well as her essays published in the 1980s, Rose Spinelli's *Baking Bread,* Renata Gangemi's *The Journey Back,* and Gia Amella's *La mia isola sacra,* exemplify the kind of work Italian American women do when they tackle the territory of memory: It is a work of meticulous piecing together of the cultural pasts of working-class people.

Bibliography

Addonizio, Kim. *Tell Me.* Rochester, NY: BOA, 2000.

———. *In the Box Called Pleasure.* Normal, IL and Tallahassee, FL: FC 2, 1999.

———. *Jimmy and Rita.* Rochester, NY: BOA, 1997.

Afzal-Khan, Fawzia. *Cultural Imperialism and the Indo-English Novel: Genre and Ideology in R. K. Narayan, Anita Desai, Kamaya Markandaya, and Salman Rushdie.* University Park: The Pennsylvania State University Press, 1993.

Ahearn, Carol Bonomo. "Interview: Helen Barolini." In *Fra Noi* (September 1986): 47.

Alaya, Flavia. *Under the Rose: A Confession.* New York: The Feminist Press, 1999.

Albanese, Catherine L., ed. *A Cobbler's Universe: Religion, Poetry and Performance in the Life of a South-Italian Immigrant: Frank S. Spiziri.* New York: Continuum, 1997.

Albrecht, Lisa, and Rose M. Brewer, eds. *Bridges of Power: Women's Multicultural Alliances.* Philadelphia: New Society, 1990.

Albright, Carol Bonomo. "From Sacred to Secular: *Umbertina* and *A Piece of Earth.*" In *MELUS* 20.2 (Summer 1995): 93–103.

Allison, Dorothy. *Two or Three Things I Know for Sure.* New York: Dutton, 1995.

———. *Bastard Out of Carolina.* New York: Dutton, 1992.

Alvarez, Julia. *How the García Girls Lost Their Accent.* New York: Penguin, 1992.

Ama l'uomo tuo. Cara DeVito, 22 min., 1975, videocassette.

Amore, B. *Lifeline, "filo della vita": An Italian American Odyssey 1901–2001.* Exhibit. Museum of Immigration at Ellis Island. October–March 2001.

Anderson, S. E., and Tony Medina, eds. *In Defense of Mumia.* New York: Writers and Readers: 1996.

Antonetta, Susanne. *Body Toxic: An Environmental Memoir.* Washington, D.C.: Counterpoint, 2001.

Anzaldúa, Gloria. *Borderlands. La Frontera: The New Mestiza.* San Francisco: Aunt Lute, 1987.

Anzaldúa Gloria, ed. *Making Face, Making Soul: Haciendo Caras: Creative and Critical Perspectives by Feminists of Color.* San Francisco: Aunt Lute, 1990.

Angelou, Maya. *I Know Why the Caged Bird Sings.* New York: Bantam, 1971.

Arcade, Penny. "La miseria." Theater performance (videotaped, 113 min), Performance Space 122, New York, 1991. (Performed for the first time at Franklin Furnace, New York, 1989)

Ardizzone, Toni. *Taking It Home: Stories from the Neighborhood.* Urbana and Chicago: University of Illinois Press, 1996.

Ashyk, Dan, Fred L. Gardaphé, and Anthony J. Tamburri, eds. *Shades of Black and White: Conflict and Collaboration Between Two Communities.* Staten Island, NY: American Italian Historical Association, 1999.

Azara, Nancy. "Fire." Collage: 18" x 24"; paint, wood, and pencil fragment wih gold leaf on paper. 2000.

———. *Catalogue of Exhibition* curated by Ronald Sosinki. Essay by Flavia Rando. Prose poem by Arlene Raven. 1994–95.

The Baggage, Susan Caperna Lloyd, 32 min., Susan Caperna Lloyd, 2001, videocassette.

Baker, Aaron, and Juliann Vitullo. "Mysticism and the *Household Saints* of Everyday Life." In *VIA: Voices in Italian Americana.* Special Issue on Women Authors 7.2 (Fall 1996): 55–68.

Baking Bread, Rose Spinelli, 30 min., Rose Spinelli, 2001, videocassette (in progress).

Bammer, Angelika, ed. *Displacements: Cultural Identities in Question.* Bloomington and Indianapolis: Indiana University Press, 1994.

Barolini, Helen. *Chiaroscuro: Essays of Identity.* 1997. Madison: University of Wisconsin Press, 1999.

———. *Aldus and His Dream Book.* New York: Italica Press, 1992.

———. *Festa: Recipes and Recollections of Italian Holidays.* New York: Harcourt Brace Jovanovich, 1988.

———. "Becoming a Literary Person Out of Context." In the *Massachusetts Review* 27.2 (1986): 262–74.

———. *Love in the Middle Ages.* New York: William Morrow, 1986.

———. "A Circular Journey." In the *Texas Quarterly* 21.2 (1979): 109–26.

———. *Umbertina.* 1979. New York: The Feminist Press at CUNY, 1999. Afterword by Edvige Giunta.

———. "Margaret Fuller, an American Heroine of the Italian Risorgimento." Radiodrama broadcast by RAI. Rome. 1971.

———, ed. *The Dream Book: An Anthology of Writings by Italian American Women.* 1985. New York: Shocken, 1987. Reprinted: Syracuse: Syracuse University Press, 2000.

———, and Antonio Barolini. *Duet.* Poems in English and Italian. Venice: Neri Pozza Editore, 1966.

Barreca, Regina. *They Used to Call Me Snow White . . . But I Drifted: Women's Strategic Uses of Humor.* New York: Penguin, 1991.

Barresi, Dorothy. *The Post-Rapture Diner.* Pittsburgh, PA: University of Pittsburgh Press, 1996.

———. *All of the Above.* Introduction by Olga Broumas. Boston: Beacon, 1991.

Barrington, Judith. *Writing the Memoir: From Truth to Art.* Portland, OR: The Eighth Mountain Press, 1997.

Bartkowski, Frances. *Travelers, Immigrants, Inmates: Essays in Estrangement.* Minneapolis: University of Minnesota Press, 1995.

Belloni, Alessandra. *Tarantata: Dance of the Ancient Spider.* CD. Sounds True. 2000.

Benasutti, Marion. *No Steady Job for Papa.* New York: Vanguard, 1966.

Benstock, Shari. *Women of the Left Bank: Paris 1900–1940.* Austin: University of Texas Press, 1986.

Beranger, Jean. "*Umbertina* d'Helen Barolini: une odyssee italienne de Castagna a Cape Cod." In *Annales du Centre de Recherches sur l'Amerique Anglophone* 15 (1990): 153–67.

Bernardi, Adria. *The Day Laid on the Altar.* Hanover, NH, and London: University Press of New England, 2000.

Between Black and White, Giannella Garrett, 26 min., GG Productions, 1994, videocassette.

Big Night, Stanley Tucci and Campbell Scott, 107 min., Rysher Entertainment, 1996, videocassette.

Birnbaum, Lucia Chiavola. *Black Madonna.* Boston: Northeastern University Press, 1993.

Bona, Mary Jo. *Claiming a Tradition: Italian American Women Writers.* Carbondale: Southern Illinois University Press, 1999.

———. "Learning To Speak Doubly: New Poems by Gianna Patriarca and Rose Romano." In *VIA: Voices in Italian Americana* 6.1 (Spring 1995): 161–8.

———, ed. *The Voices We Carry: Recent Italian/American Women's Fiction.* Montreal and New York: Guernica, 1994.

———. "Broken Images, Broken Lives: Carmolina's Journey in Tina De Rosa's *Paper Fish.*" In *MELUS* 14.3–4 (Fall/Winter 1987): 87–106.

Bonetti, Kay. "Interview with Helen Barolini." American Audio Prose Library. 1982.

Brenkman, John. *Multiculturalism and Criticism: Inside and Out: The Places of Literary Criticism.* Eds. Susan Gubar and Jonathan Kamboltz. New York and London: Routledge, 1993. 87–101.

Broumas, Olga. *Rave: Poems 1975–1999.* Port Townsend, WA: Copper Canyon Press, 1999.

Brugo, Isabella, Guido Ferraro, Caterina Schiavon and Manuela Tartari. *Al sangue o ben cotto: Miti e riti intorno al cibo.* Roma: Meletemi, 1998.

Bruno, Giuliana. *Streetwalking on a Ruined Map: Cultural Theory and the City Films of Elvira Notari.* Princeton, NJ: Princeton University Press, 1993.

Bruzzichelli, Pia, and Maria Luisa Algini. *Donna, cultura e tradizione.* Milano: Gabrielle Mazzotta, 1976.

Bryant, Dorothy. *Confessions of Madame Psyche.* 1986. New York: The Feminist Press at CUNY, 1998. Afterword by J. J. Wilson.

———. *Miss Giardino.* 1978. New York: The Feminist Press at CUNY, 1997. Afterword by Janet Zandy.

———. *Ella Price's Journal.* 1972. New York: The Feminist Press, 1997. Afterword by Barbara Horn.

Bush, Mary Bucci. *Drowning.* Berkeley: Parentheses Writing Series, 1995.

———. *A Place of Light.* New York: William Morrow, 1990.

Cafarelli, Annette Wheeler. "No Butter on Our Bread: Anti-Intellectual Stereotyping of Italian Americans." In *VIA: Voices in Italian Americana* 7.1 (Spring 1996): 39–47.

Calcagno, Anne. *Pray for Yourself and Other Stories.* Evanston, Il: Triquarterly Books, 1993.

Camaiti Hostert, Anna, and Anthony J. Tamburri, eds. *Screening Ethnicity: Cinematographic Representations of Italian Americans in the United States.* Boca Raton, FL: Bordighera, 2001.

Capone, Giovanna (Janet), Denise Nico Leto, and Tommi Avicolli Mecca, eds. *Hey Paesan! Writing by Lesbians & Gay Men of Italian Descent.* Oakland, CA: Three Guineas Press, 1999.

Caponegro, Mary. *Five Doubts.* New York: Marsilio, 1998.

Capotorto, Rosette. "Broke." In *The Milk of Almonds.* Eds. Louise DeSalvo and Edvige Giunta. New York: The Feminist Press at CUNY. Forthcoming.

———. *Bronx Italian.* Unpublished manuscript.

Cappello, Mary. *Night Bloom.* Boston: Beacon, 1998.

———. "Nothing to Confess: A Lesbian in Italian America." In *FUORI: Essays by Italian/American Lesbians and Gays.* Ed. Anthony J. Tamburri. West Lafayette, IN: Bordighera, 1996. 89–108.

Cappello, Mary, Wallace Sillanpoa, and Jean Walton. "Roberta Torre: Filmmaker of the Incoscienza." In *The Quarterly Review of Film and Video* 17.4 (November 2000): 317–331.

Carlson, Kathie. *Life's Daughter/Death's Bride: Inner Transformation through the Goddess Demeter/Persephone.* Boston: Shambhala, 1997.

Caroli, Betty Boyd, Robert F. Harney, and Lydio F. Tomasi, eds. *The Italian Immigrant Woman in North America.* Toronto: The Multicultural History Society of Ontario, 1978.

Caronia, Nancy. "Go to Hell." In *Curaggia: Writing by Women of Italian Descent.* Eds. Nzula Angelina Ciatu, Domenica DiLeo, and Gabriella Micallef. Toronto: Women's Press, 1998. 216–25.

———, ed. *the girlSpeak journals.* New York: Women's Words Press, 1997.

Carravetta, Peter. "Naming Identity in the Poetry of Maria Mazziotti Gillan." In *Estudios de la mujer* 3 (1998): 1–23.

Castillo, Ana, ed. *Goddess of the Americas: Writings on the Virgin of Guadalupe.* New York: Riverhead, 1996.

———. *Massacre of the Dreamers: Essays on Xicanisma.* New York: Penguin, 1995.

Cavallo, Diana. *A Bridge of Leaves.* New York: Atheneum, 1961. Reprint: Toronto and Buffalo: Guernica, 1997. Afterword by Mary Jo Bona.

Chambers, Iain. *Migrancy, Culture, Identity.* London and New York: Routledge, 1994.

Chernin, Kim. *In My Mother's House.* New York: Harper, 1983.

Chin, Frank, Jeffrey Paul Chan, Lawson Fusao Inada, and Shawn Hsu Wong, eds. *Aiiieeeee! An Anthology of Asian American Writers.* New York: Penguin, 1991.

Chopin, Kate. *The Awakening.* 1899. Ed. Nancy A. Walker. New York: St. Martin's Press, 1993.

Ciatu, Nzula Angelina, Domenica DiLeo, and Gabriella Micallef, eds. *Curaggia: Writing by Women of Italian Descent.* Toronto: Women's Press, 1998.

Ciongoli, Kenneth A., and Jay Parini, eds. *Beyond The Godfather: Italian American Writers on the Real Italian American Experience.* Hanover, NH: University Press of New England, 1997.

Ciresi, Rita. *Sometimes I Dream in Italian.* New York: Delacorte, 2000.

———. *Pink Slip.* New York: Delacorte, 1999.

———. *Blue Italian.* Hopewell, NJ: Ecco, 1996.

———. *Mother Rocket.* Athens: The University of Georgia Press, 1993.

———. "Paradise Below the Stairs." *Italian Americana* 12.1 (Fall/Winter 1993): 17–22.

Cisneros, Sandra. *The House on Mango Street.* New York: Random House, 1984.

Cohen, Miriam. *Workshop to Office: Two Generations of Italian Women in New York City, 1900–1950.* Ithaca, NY: Cornell University Press, 1992.

Continents Apart, Franca Barchiese. Black and white: 16 mm, 20 min. Franca Barchiesi, 1993.

Conwill Majozo, Estella. *Come Out the Wilderness: Memoir of a Black Woman Artist.* New York: The Feminist Press at CUNY, 1999.

Covino, Peter. *Cut Off the Ears of Winter.* Unpublished manuscript.

Cusumano, Camille. *The Last Cannoli: A Sicilian-American Family Comes of Age through the Ancient Power of Storytelling.* New York: Legas, 2000.

Cutrufelli, Maria Rosa. *Canto al deserto: Storia di Tina. soldato di mafia.* Milano: Longanesi, 1994.

———. *Disoccupata con onore: Lavoro e condizione della donna.* Milano: Gabriele Mazzotta, 1975.

———. *L'invenzione della donna: Miti e tecniche di uno sfruttamento.* Milano: Gabriele Mazzotta, 1974.

———, Edvige Giunta, and Caterina Romeo, eds. *TutteStorie Origini: le scrittrici italoa americana* 8 (March–May 2001).

Daly, Brenda. *Authoring a Life: A Woman's Survival in and through Literary Studies.* Albany: SUNY Press, 1998.

Danticat, Edwidge. *Krik? Krak!* New York: Random House, 1996.

Davidson, Cathy N. *36 Views of Mount Fuji: On Finding Myself in Japan.* New York: Penguin, 1994.

De Ferrari, Gabriella. *Gringa Latina.* Boston: Houghton Mifflin, 1995.

Demetrick, Mary Russo. *First Pressing: Poems.* Syracuse, NY: Hale Mary Press, 1994.

———, and Maria Famà. *Italian Notebook: Poems.* Syracuse, NY: Hale Mary Press, 1995.

De Rosa, Tina. *Bishop John Baptist Scalabrini, Father to the Migrants.* Darien, CT: Insider Publications, 1987.

———. "My Father's Lesson." In *Fra Noi* (September 1986): 15.

———. "Silent Night, Homeless Night." In *Fra Noi* (January 1986): 1, 8. A revised version in *Volunteer News: A Publication of the Chicago Emergency Volunteer Organization* 2.2 (Fall 1987): 3–8.

———. "Career Choices Come From Listening to the Heart." In *Fra Noi* (October 1985): 9.

———. "An Italian American Woman Speaks Out." In *Attenzione* (May 1980): 38–9.

———. *Paper Fish.* 1980. New York: The Feminist Press at CUNY, 1996. Afterword by Edvige Giunta.

DeSalvo, Louise. *Adultery.* Boston: Beacon, 1999.

———. *Writing as a Way of Healing: How Telling Our Stories Transforms Our Lives.* New York: Harper San Francisco, 1999.

————. "Digging Deep." In *Coming to Class: Pedagogy and the Social Class of Teachers.* Eds. Alan Shepard, John Macmillan, and Gary Tate. New York: Boynton/Cook, 1998. 13–22.

————. *Breathless: An Asthma Journal.* Boston: Beacon, 1997.

————. *Vertigo.* New York: Dutton, 1997.

————. "*Paper Fish:* An Appreciation." In *VIA: Voices in Italian Americana.* Special Issue on Women Authors. 7.2 (Fall 1996).

————. *Virginia Woolf: The Impact of Childhood Sexual Abuse on Her Life and Work.* New York: Random House, 1989.

————. *Casting Off.* Brighton, UK: Harvester, 1987.

————. "A Portrait of the Puttana as a Middle-Aged Woolf Scholar." In *Between Women: Biographers, Novelists, Critics, Teachers and Artists Write About Their Work on Women.* Eds. Carol Ascher, Louise DeSalvo, and Sara Ruddick. Boston: Beacon, 1984. 35–53.

DeSalvo, Louise and Edvige Giunta, eds. *The Milk of Almonds: Italian American Women Writers on Food and Culture.* New York: The Feminist Press at CUNY, 2002. Forthcoming.

de Vries, Rachel Guido. *How To Sing to a Dago and Other Canzonetti.* Toronto and New York: Guernica, 1996.

————. *Tender Warriors.* Ithaca, NY: Firebrand, 1986.

di Donato. *Christ in Concrete.* 1937. Preface by Studs Terkel. Introduction by Fred L. Gardaphé. New York: Penguin, 1993.

di Leonardo, Micaela. *The Varieties of Ethnic Experience: Kinship, Class, and Gender among California Italian-Americans.* Ithaca: Cornell University Press, 1984.

di Prima, Diane. *Recollections of My Life as a Woman.* New York: Viking, 2001.

————. *Dinners and Nightmares.* San Francisco: The Last Gasp, 1998.

————. *Memoirs of a Beatnik.* San Francisco: The Last Gasp, 1969.

Dittmar, Linda. "When Privilege is No Protection: The Woman Artist in Quicksand and *The House of Mirth.*" In *Writing the Woman Artist: Essays on Poetics, Politics, and Portraiture.* Ed. Suzanne W. Jones. Philadelphia: University of Pennsylvania Press, 1991. 133–54.

D'Onofrio, Beverly. *Looking for Mary (or the Blessed Mother and Me).* New York: Viking, 2000.

————. *Riding in Cars with the Boys: Confessions of a Bad Girl Who Makes Good.* New York: Penguin, 1990.

Downing, Christine, ed. *The Long Journey Home: Re-visioning the Myth of Demeter and Persephone for Our Time.* Boston: Shambhala, 1994.

Dyer, Richard. *White.* London and New York: Routledge, 1997.

Elshtain, Jean Bethke. "Feminism, Family, and Community." In *Feminism and Community.* Eds. Penny A. Weiss and Marilyn Friedman. Philadelphia: Temple University Press, 1995. 259–272.

Ermelino, Louisa. *The Black Madonna.* New York: Simon and Schuster, 2001.

————. *Joey Dee Gets Wise: A Novel of Little Italy.* New York: St. Martin's Press, 1991.

Esquivel, Laura. *Like Water for Chocolate.* Trans. Carol Christensen and Thomas Christensen. New York: Doubleday, 1992.

Ets, Marie Hall. *Rosa: The Life of an Italian Immigrant.* Minnesota: University of Minneapolis Press, 1970. Foreword by Rudolph J. Vecoli. Reprinted in 1999 with an introductory note by Helen Barolini.

Falcone, Giovanni. In collaboration with Marcelle Padovani. *Cose di cosa nostra.* Milano: Rizzoli, 1991.

Fante, John. *The Brotherhood of the Grape.* Santa Rosa: Black Sparrow, 1993.

Fausty, Joshua. Review of Carole Maso's *The American Woman in the Chinese Hat.* In *VIA: Voices in Italian Americana.* Special Issue on Women Authors 7.2 (Fall 1996). 283–85.

———. Review of Rita Ciresi's *Mother Rocket.* In *VIA: Voices in Italian* Americana 6.2 (Fall 1995): 204–207.

———, and Edvige Giunta. "An Interview with Nancy Savoca." In *VIA: Voices in Italian Americana* 12.2 (2001). Forthcoming.

———, and Edvige Giunta. "Quentin Tarantino: An Ethnic Enigma." In *Screening Ethnicity: Cinematographic Representations of Italian Americans in the United States.* Boca Raton, Fl: Bordighera, 2001. 210–221.

———, and Edvige Giunta. "An Interview with Tina De Rosa." Unpublished.

Felman, Shoshana and Doris Laub. *Testimony: Crises of Witnessing in Literature, Psychoanalysis, and History.* New York: Routledge, 1992.

Ferriss, Lucy. "The Bad Father." Review of Agnes Rossi's *The Houseguest.* In the *New York Times* (6 February 2000).

Fjellstad, Danuta Zadworna. "'The insertion of the self into the space of borderless possibilities': Eva Hoffman's Exiled Body." In *MELUS* 20.2 (Summer 1995): 93–103.

Foster, Patricia ed. *Sister to Sister: Women Write About the Unbreakable Bond.* New York: Doubleday, 1995.

Frankenberg, Ruth. *White Women, Race Matters: The Social Construction of Whiteness.* Minneapolis: University of Minnesota Press, 1993.

Friedman, Lester D., ed. *Unspeakable Images: Ethnicity and the American Cinema.* Urbana and Chicago: University of Illinois Press, 1991.

Friedmann, Susan, and Rachel Blau Du Plessis. "'I Had Two Loves Separate': The Sexualities of H.D.'s "Her.'" In *Montemora* 8 (1981): 7–30.

fuori/outside, Kym Ragusa, 15 min., Ibla Productions, 1997, videocassette.

Furst, Lilian R., and Peter W. Graham, eds. *Disorderly Eaters: Texts in Self-Empowerment.* University Park: The Pennsylvania State University Press, 1992.

Fusco, Mary Ann. "Telling Her Story in Italian American." In the *New York Times.* New Jersey Section. June 4 2000: 4.

Gabaccia, Donna R. *We Are What We Eat: Ethnic Food and the Making of Americans.* Cambridge: Harvard University Press, 1998

———. *From the Other Side. Women, Gender, and Immigrant Life in the U.S., 1820–1990.* Bloomington: Indiana University Press, 1994.

———. "Italian American Women: A Review Essay." In *Italian Americana* 12.1 (Fall/Winter 1993): 38–61.

———. *From Sicily to Elizabeth Street: Housing and Social Change Among Italian Immigrants, 1880–1930.* Albany: SUNY Press, 1984.

García, Cristina. *Dreaming in Cuban.* New York: Ballantine, 1993.

Gardaphé, Fred L. "Continuity in Concrete: (Re)Constructing Italian American Writers." In *Industry, Technology, Labor and the Italian American Communities.* Eds. Mario Aste, Jerome Krase, Louise Napolitano-Carman, and Janet E. Worrall. Staten Island, NY: American Italian Historical Association, 1997. 245–54.

————. "The Evolution of Italian/American Literary Studies." In *The Italian American Review. Italian-American Studies: The State of the Field and New Directions for Development.* Part I. 5.1 (Spring 1996): 23–35.

————. *Italian Signs, American Streets: The Evolution of Italian American Narrative.* Durham, NC: Duke University Press, 1996.

————. "Breaking and Entering: An Italian American's Literary Odyssey." In *Forkroads* 1.1 (Fall 1995): 5–14.

————. *The Italian-American Writer: An Essay and an Annotated Checklist.* Spencertown, NY: Forkroads, 1995.

————. "(In)visibility: Cultural Representation in the Criticism of Frank Lentricchia." In *Differentia.* Special Issue on Italian American Culture 6–7 (Spring-Autumn 1994): 201–18.

————. "What's Italian About Italian/American Literature." Paper presented at the Purdue University Conference on Romance Languages, Literatures and Film. Purdue University. West Lafayette, IN. 13–15 October 1994.

————. "Autobiography as Piecework: The Writings of Helen Barolini." In *Italian Americans Celebrate Life, the Arts and Popular Culture.* Eds. Paola A. Sensi Isolani and Anthony Julian Tamburri. American Italian Historical Association, 1990. 19–27.

————. "Italian American Fiction: A Third Generation Renaissance." In *MELUS* 4.3–4 (Fall/Winter 1987): 69–85.

————. "An interview with Tina De Rosa." In *Fra Noi* (May 1985): 23.

Gates, Henry Louis Jr. *The Signifying Monkey: A Theory of African American Literary Criticism.* New York: Oxford University Press, 1988.

Giardina, Denise. *Storming Heaven.* New York: Ivy, 1987.

Gilbert, Sandra M. *Kissing the Bread: New and Selected Poems 1969–1999.* New York: W.W. Norton, 2000.

————. *Ghost Volcano.* New York: W.W. Norton, 1995.

————. *Wrongful Death: A Memoir.* New York: Norton, 1994.

————. "Piacere Conoscerla: On Being an Italian-American." In *From the Margin: Writings in Italian Americana.* Eds. Anthony Julian Tamburri, Paolo A. Giordano, and Fred L. Gardaphé. West Lafayette, IN: Purdue University Press, 1991. 116–20.

————. *Emily's Bread.* New York: W.W. Norton, 1984.

————. *The Madwoman in the Attic: The Woman Writer and the Nineteenth-Century Literary Imagination.* New Haven, CT, and London: Yale University Press, 1979.

———— and Susan Guber. *No Man's Land: The Place of the Woman Writer in the Twentieth Century.* Volume 3. *Letters from the Front.* New Haven, CT, and London: Yale University Press, 1996.

————— and Susan Guber. *No Man's Land: The Place of the Woman Writer in the Twentieth Century.* Volume 2. *Sexchanges.* New Haven, CT, and London: Yale University Press, 1989.

————— and Susan Guber. *No Man's Land: The Place of the Woman Writer in the Twentieth Century.* Volume 1. *The War of the Words.* New Haven, CT, and London: Yale University Press, 1989.

Gillan, Maria Mazziotti. *Things My Mother Told Me.* Toronto: Guernica, 1999.

—————. "Why I Took Back My Name." In *VIA: Voices in Italian Americana* 9.1 (Spring 1998): 31–4.

—————. *Where I Come From: Selected and New Poems.* Toronto: Guernica, 1995.

—————. *Taking Back My Name.* Franklin Lakes, NJ: Lincoln Springs, 1991.

—————and Jennifer Gillan, eds. *Growing Up Ethnic in America: Contemporary Fiction About Learning to Be American.* New York: Penguin, 1999.

—————and Jennifer Gillan, eds. *Identity Lessons: Contemporary Writing About Learning to Be American.* New York: Penguin, 1999.

—————and Jennifer Gillan, eds. *Unsettling America: An Anthology of Contemporary Multicultural Poetry.* New York: Penguin, 1994.

Gilman, Charlotte Perkins. *The Yellow Wallpaper.* 1899. New York: The Feminist Press at CUNY, 1973. Afterword by Elaine R. Hedges.

Ginsburg, Carlo. *Il formaggio e i vermi: Il cosmo di un mugnaio del '500.* Torino: Einaudi, 1976.

Gioia, Dana et al. "Where Are the Italian American Novelists?" In *Italian Americana* 12.1 (Fall–Winter 1993): 7–37.

Giordano, Paolo A., and Anthony Julian Tamburri, eds. *Beyond the Margin: Readings in Italian Americana.* Madison, NJ: Fairleigh Dickinson University Press, 1998.

Gioseffi, Daniela. "Breaking the Silence for Italian-American Women: Maligned and Stereotyped." In *VIA: Voices in Italian Americana* 4.1 (Spring 1993): 1–14.

—————. *The Great American Belly Dance.* New York: Doubleday, 1977.

—————, ed. *On Prejudice: A Global Perspective.* New York: Doubleday, 1993.

Girls Like Us, Tina Di Feliciantonio and Jane C. Wagner, 58 min., Naked Eye Productions, 1997, videocassette.

Giroux, Henry A. *Teachers as Intellectuals.* Westport, CT: Bergin and Garvey, 1988.

Giunta, Edvige. "Honor Thy Students: The Power of Writing." In *What We Hold in Common: Working-Class Studies.* Ed. Janet Zandy. New York: The Feminist Press at CUNY, 2001. 265–68.

—————. "Teaching Memoir at New Jersey City University." In *Transformations* 11.1 (Spring 2000): 80–89.

—————. "Figuring Race: Kym Ragusa's *fuori/outside.*" In *Shades of Black and White: Conflict and Collaboration Between Two Communities.* Eds. Dan Ashyk, Fred L. Gardaphé, and Anthony J. Tamburri. Staten Island, NY: American Italian Historical Association, 1999. 262–71

—————. "Blending 'Literary' Discourses: Helen Barolini's Italian/American Narratives." In *Beyond the Margin: Readings in Italian Americana.* Eds. Paolo A. Giordano and Anthony Julian Tamburri. Madison, NJ: Fairleigh Dickinson University Press, 1998. 114–30.

————. "Dialects, Accents, and Other Aberrations." In *New Jersey Mosaic* (Spring 1997): 4, 7.

————. "The Quest for True Love: Nancy Savoca's Domestic Film Comedy." In *MELUS* (Summer 1997): 75–89.

————. "Crossing Critical Borders in Italian/American Women's Studies." In *The Italian American Review. Italian-American Studies: The State of the Field and New Directions for Development Part II* 5.2 (Autumn–Winter 1996–97). 79–94.

————. "Narratives of Loss: Voices of Ethnicity in Agnes Rossi and Nancy Savoca." In the *Canadian Journal of Italian Studies*. Special Issue on Italian American Culture 19 (1996): 164–83.

————. "Persephone's Daughters." Unpublished essay.

————, ed. "Writing Memoir." In Special Issue of *Women on Campus*. New Jersey City University. Spring 2000.

————, ed. In *VIA: Voices in Italian Americana*. Special Issue on Women Authors 7.2 (Fall 1996).

————, and Samuel J. Patti, eds. *A Tavola: Food, Tradition, and Community Among Italian Americans. Selected Essays from the 29th Annual Conference of the American Italian Historical Association Conference*. Staten Island, NY: American Italian Historical Association, 1998.

Goldman, Anne. "'I Yam What I Yam': Cooking, Culture, and Colonialism." In *De-Colonizing the Subject: The Politics of Gender in Women's Autobiography*. Minneapolis: University of Minnesota Press, 1992. 169–95.

Gramsci, Antonio. *The Southern Question*. Translation. and introduction. by Pasquale Verdicchio. West Lafayette, IN: Bordighera, 1995.

————. *Selections from the Prison Notebooks*. Ed. and trans. Quintin Hoare and Geoffrey Nowell Smith. New York: International Publishers, 1971.

Greenberg, Dorothée von Heune. "A *MELUS* Interview: Helen Barolini." In *MELUS* 18.2 (Summer 1992): 91–108.

Guerrero, Ed. "Spike Lee and the Fever in the Racial Jungle." In *Film Theory Goes to the Movies: Cultural Analyses of Contemporary Film*. Eds. Ava Collins, Jim Collins, and Hilary Radner. London: Routledge, 1992. 170–81.

Guglielmo, Jennifer. "Donne Ribelli: Recovering the History of Italian Women's Radicalism in the United States." In *The Lost World of Italian American Radicalism: Culture, Politics, History*. Eds. Philip V. Cannistraro and Gerald Meyer. Westport, CT: Praeger Forthcoming.

————. "Lavoratrici Coscienti: Italian Women Garment Workers and the Politics of Labor Organizing in New York City, 1890s–1940s." In *Foreign, Female, Fighting Back: Women in the Italian Diaspora*. Eds. Donna Gabaccia and Franca Iacovetta. Toronto: University of Toronto. Forthcoming.

————. In progress. Negotiating Gender, Race, and Coalition: Italian Women and Working-Class Politics in New York City, 1880–1945. Ph.D. diss., University of Minnesota.

————. "Pietre, Parole e Circoli Politici." In *TutteStorie* 8 (March–May 2001): 21–24.

————. "Italian American Women's Political Activism in New York City, 1900–1950." In *The Italians of New York, Five Centuries of Struggle and Achieve-*

ment. Ed. Philip V. Cannistraro. New York: New York Historical Society, 1999. 103–113.

———. "Donne Sovversive: The History of Italian American Women's Radicalism." In *Italian America. The Official Publication of the Order of the Sons of Italy in America* (September 1997): 8–11.

———, and Sal Salerno, eds. *Italians and the Politics of Race-Making in the United States.* In progress.

H.D. *The Gift.* New York: New Directions, 1982.

———. *HERmione.* New York: New Directions, 1981.

Hagedorn, Jessica. *Dogeaters.* 1990. New York: Penguin, 1991.

Hamington, Maurice. *Hail Mary? The Struggle for Ultimate Womanhood in Catholicism.* New York and London: Routledge, 1995.

Hammad, Suheir. *Drops of This Story.* New York and London: Harlem River Press, 1996.

Harrison, Barbara Grizzuti. Review of Diane di Prima's *Recollections of My Life as a Woman.* In *The New York Times Book Review* (6 May 2001): 25.

———. Review of Flavia Alaya's *Under the Rose: A Confession.* In *The New York Times Book Review* (23 January 2000).

———. *An Accidental Autobiography.* Boston: Houghton Mifflin, 1996.

Hedges, Elaine, and Ingrid Wendt. *In Her Own Image: Women Working in the Arts.* New York: The Feminist Press at CUNY, 1980.

Hendin, Josephine Gattuso. *The Right Thing To Do.* 1988. New York: The Feminist Press at CUNY, 1999. Afterword by Mary Jo Bona.

Herman, Joanna Clapps. "The Discourse of un' Propria Paparone." In *Curaggia: Writing by Women of Italian Descent.* Eds. Nzula Angelina Ciatu, Domenica DiLeo and Gabriella Micallef. Toronto: Women's Press, 1998. 176–79.

Herman, Judith Lewis. *Trauma and Recovery.* New York: Basic Books, 1992.

Hidden Island/L'isola sommersa, Calleri, Mariarosy, 48 min., Kore Productions, 1998, videocassette.

Hoffman, Eva. *Lost in Translation.* New York: Penguin, 1989.

Holli, Melvin G., and Peter d'A. Jones, eds. *Ethnic Chicago: A Multicultural Portrait.* 1977. Grand Rapids, MI: William B. Eerdmans, 1995.

Hongo, Garrett, and Catherine Parke. "A Conversation with Sandra M. Gilbert." In *The Missouri Review* 9.1 (1985–86): 89–109.

Household Saints, Nancy Savoca, 124 min., Columbia TriStar, 1993, videocassette.

Hurston, Zora Neale. *I Love Myself When I am Laughing . . . And Then Again When I Am Looking Mean and Impressive.* Ed. Alice Walker. Introduction by Mary Helen Washington. New York: The Feminist Press at CUNY, 1989.

———. *Their Eyes Were Watching God.* 1937. Foreword by Mary Helen Washington. Afterword by Henry Louis Gates, Jr. New York: Harper and Row, 1990.

Hutcheon, Linda. *The Politics of Postmodernism.* London and New York: Routledge, 1989.

The Incredibly True Adventure of Two Girls in Love, Maria Maggenti, 91 min., Fine Line Features, 1995, videocassette.

Ignatiev, Noel. *How the Irish Became White.* New York: Routledge, 1995.

Italian American Presence(s), Luisa Pretolani, 10 min., PHANI Productions, 1996, videocassette.

Jameson, Fredric. *The Political Unconscious: Narrative as a Socially Symbolic Act.* Ithaca, NY: Cornell University Press, 1981.

Jeffries, Giovanna Miceli, ed. *Feminine Feminists: Cultural Practices in Italy.* Minneapolis: University of Minnesota Press, 1992.

Jones, Suzanne W., ed. *Writing the Woman Artist: Essays on Poetics, Politics, and Portraiture.* Philadelphia: University of Pennsylvania Press, 1991.

The Journey Back, Renata Gangemi, Renata Gangemi and Ruben Gonzales, videocassette (in progress).

Kadi, Joanna. *Thinking Class: Sketches from a Cultural Worker.* Boston: South End Press, 1996.

————, ed. *Food for Our Grandmothers: Writings by Arab-American and Arab-Canadian Feminists.* Boston: South End Press, 1994.

Kerényi, Carl. *Eleusis: Archetypal Image of Mother and Daughter.* 1960. Trans. Ralph Manheim. Princeton, NJ: Princeton University Press, 1967.

Kingston, Maxine Hong. *The Woman Warrior.* New York: Random House, 1995.

Kirschenbaum, Blossom. "Mary Caponegro: Prize-Winning American Writer in Rome." In *Italian Americana* 13.1 (Winter 1995): 24–31.

————. "Diane di Prima: Extending *La Famiglia.*" In *MELUS* 14.3–4 (Fall–Winter 1987): 53–67.

Krause, Corinne Azen, ed. *Grandmothers, Mothers, and Daughters: Oral Histories of Three Generations of Ethnic American Women.* Boston: Twayne, 1991.

La Barre, Adele Regina. "Biencherie." Presentation given at 28th American Italian Historical Association Conference. "Industry, Technology, Labor and the Italian American Communities." Lowell, Ma. 11–13 November 1995.

La mia isola sacra, Gia Amella, film (in progress).

Labozzetta, Marisa. *Stay with Me, Lella.* Toronto: Guernica, 1999.

Lanzillotto, Annie. "Confessions of a Bronx Tomboy." Performance. *Italian American and Italian Women on Cultural Politics.* Casa Italiana Zerilli Marimò at New York University. New York. 20 May 2000.

La Spina, Silvana. *Penelope.* Milano: La Tartaruga, 1998.

————. *L'amante del paradiso.* Milano: Mondadori, 1997.

Lauerman, Connie. "Lady in Waiting." In the *Chicago Tribune* (2 September 1996); 1,3.

Laurino, Maria. *Were You Always an Italian? Ancestors and Other Icons of Italian America.* New York: Norton, 2000.

Lazzaro-Weis Carol. *From Margins to Mainstream: Feminism and Fictional Modes in Italian Women's Writing 1968–1990.* Philadelphia: University of Pennsylvania Press, 1993.

Lentricchia, Frank. *The Edge of Night: A Confession.* New York: Random House, 1984.

Leonardi, Susan J. "Recipes for Reading: Summer Pasta, Lobster à la Riseholme, and Key Lime Pie." In *PMLA* 104.3 (May 1989): 340–47.

Leshko, Lisa. "Interview with *Two Girls in Love* Writer/Director Maria Maggenti." In *Sojourner: The Women's Forum* 20.10 (June 1995).

Linfante, Michele. "Pizza." In *The Dream Book: An Anthology of Writings by Italian American Women*. Ed. Helen Barolini. 1985. New York: Shocken, 1987. 270–96.

Ling, Amy. "I'm Here: An Asian American Woman's Response." In *Feminisms: An Anthology of Literary Theory and Criticism*. Eds. Robyn R. Warhol and Diane Price Herndl. New Brunswick: Rutgers University Press, 1991. 738–45.

Lipari, Loryn. "Cracked." In *The Milk of Almonds: Italian American Women Writers on Food and Culture*. Eds. Louise DeSalvo and Edvige Giunta. New York: The Feminist Press at CUNY. Forthcoming.

Lippi-Green, Rosina. *English with an Accent: Language, Ideology, and Discrimination in the United States*. London and New York: Routledge, 1997.

Lisella, Julia. "Radicalizing an Uncertain Past: The Poetry of Rosa Zagnoni Marinoni." In *A Tavola: Food, Tradition and Community Among Italian Americans. Selected Essays from the 29th Annual Conference of the American Italian Historical Association Conference*. Eds. Edvige Giunta and Samuel J. Patti. Staten Island, NY: American Italian Historical Association, 1998. 114–25.

Lloyd, Susan Caperna. *No Pictures in My Grave: A Spiritual Journey in Sicily*. San Francisco: Mercury, 1992.

Lorde, Audre. *Sister Outsider: Essays and Speeches*. Freedom, CA: The Crossing Press, 1984.

———. *Zami: A New Spelling of My Name*. 1982. Freedom, CA: The Crossing Press, 1994.

———. *The Cancer Journals*. San Francisco: Aunt Lute, 1980.

Macari, Anne Marie. *Ivory Cradle: Poems*. Philadelphia: The American Poetry Review, 2000.

Maggio, Theresa. *Mattanza: Love and Death in the Sea of Sicily*. Cambridge, MA: Perseus, 2000.

Mairs, Nancy. *Waist-High in the World: A Life Among the Non-Disabled*. Boston: Beacon, 1996.

Manfredi, Renée. *Where Love Leaves Us*. Iowa City: University of Iowa Press, 1994.

Mangione, Jerre. *Mount Allegro: A Memoir of Italian American Life*. 1942. New York: Harper and Row, 1989.

———, and Ben Morreale. *La Storia: Five Centuries of the Italian American Experience*. New York: HarperCollins, 1992.

Mannino, Mary Ann Vigilante. *Revisionary Identities: Strategies of Empowerment in the Writing of Italian/American Women*. New York: Peter Lang, 2000.

———. "Blurred Racial Borders in the Poetry of Maria Mazziotti Gillan and Rose Romano." In *Shades of Black and White: Conflict and Collaboration Between Two Communities*. Ed. Dan Ashyk, Fred L. Gardaphé, and Anthony J. Tamburri. Staten Island, NY: American Italian Historical Association, 1999. 331–39.

———. "The Empowered and Empowering Grandmother in the Poetry of Italian-American Women." In *VIA: Voices in Italian Americana* 8.2 (Fall 1997): 29–36.

Maraini, Dacia. *La lunga vita di Marianna Ucrìa*. Milano, Rizzoli, 1990.

Maraini, Dacia. *The Silent Duchess*. 1990. Trans. Dick Kitto and Elspeth Spottiswood. New York: The Feminist Press at CUNY, 1990. Afterword by Anna Camaiti Hostert.

Marazzi, Martino. "Le fondamenta sommerse della narrativa italoamericana." In *Belfagor* 3.327 (31 May 2000): 277–96.

———. "Pietro di Donato e John Fante: un racconto dimenticato e una lettura inedita." In *Acoma: Rivista Internazionale di studi nordamericani.* 19 (Spring–Summer 2000): 55–59.

Marcus, Jane. "Still Practice: A/Wrested Alphabet." In *Feminist Issues in Literary Scholarship.* Ed. Shari Benstock. Bloomington: Indiana University Press, 1997. 79–97.

———. *Virginia Woolf and the Languages of Patriarchy.* Bloomington: Indiana University Press, 1987.

Marinoni, Rosa Zagnoni. *Side Show.* Philadelphia: McKay, 1938.

———. *Behind the Mask.* New York: Harrison, 1927.

Mary Therese, Christine Noschese, black and white,7 min., Women Interart Center, 1977, 16 mm., videocassette.

Maso, Carole. *Beauty is Convulsive: The Passion of Frida Kahlo.* Washington, DC: Counterpoint. Forthcoming.

———. *Break Every Rule: Essays on Language, Longing & Moments of Desire.* Washington, DC: Counterpoint, 2000.

———. *The Room Lit by Roses: A Journal of Pregnancy and Birth.* Washington DC: Counterpoint, 2000.

———. *Defiance.* New York: Dutton, 1998.

———. *The American Woman in the Chinese Hat.* Normal, IL: Dalkey Archive Press, 1994.

———. *Ghost Dance.* San Francisco: North Point Press, 1986.

Mazza, Cris. *Your Name Here _____.* Minneapolis, MN: Coffee House Press, 1995.

———. *Exposed.* Minneapolis, MN: Coffee House Press, 1994.

———. *How To Leave a Country.* Minneapolis, MN: Coffee House Press, 1992.

MELUS: Varieties of Ethnic Criticism 23.2 (Summer 1998).

MELUS: Varieties of Ethnic Criticism 20.2 (Summer 1995).

Messina, Annie. *Il mirto e la rosa.* Palermo: Sellerio, 1982.

Messina, Elizabeth. "Soul-Food and Psychologically Transcendent Ways of Knowing." In *A Tavola: Food, Tradition, and Community Among Italian Americans. Selected Essays from the 29th Annual Conference of the American Italian Historical Association Conference* Eds. Edvige Giunta and Samuel J. Patti. Staten Island, NY: American Italian Historical Association, 1998. 68–82.

Messina, Maria. *Piccoli gorghi.* Palermo: Sellerio, 1997.

———. *Ragazze siciliane.* Palermo: Sellerio, 1997.

Meyer, Lisa A. "Breaking the Silence: Interview with Tina De Rosa." In *Italian Americana* 17.1 (Winter 1999): 58–83.

Minasola, Giuseppe. *Cantici e canti.* Roma: Edizioni Passaporto, 2000.

Minasola, Laura Emanuelita. *Il mio mondo in rime.* Capo d'Orlando, 1993.

Minh-ha, Trinh T. *Woman, Native, Other: Writing Postcoloniality and Feminism.* Bloomington: Indiana University Press, 1989.

Miuccio, Giuliana. *Spazio Space.* With bilingual Italian and English text. Trans. by Giuliana Miuccio and Patricia Donahue. Roma: Nuova Impronta edizioni, 1992.

Monardo, Anna. *The Courtyard of Dreams.* New York: Doubleday, 1993.

Moraga, Cherríe. *Loving in the War Years: Lo que nunca pasó por sus labios.* Boston: South End Press, 1983.

Moraga, Cherríe, and Gloria Anzaldúa, eds. *This Bridge Called My Back: Writings by Radical Women of Color.* Foreword by Toni Cade Bambara. New York: Kitchen Table—Women of Color Press, 1981.

Morrison, Toni. *Beloved.* New York: Knopf, 1987.

Mulas, Francesco. *Studies on Italian-American Literature.* Staten Island, NY: Center for Migration Studies, 1995.

Nazzaro, Pellegrino. "L'Immigration Quota Act del 1922, la crisi del sistema liberale e l'avvento del fascismo in Italia." In *Gli italiani negli Stati Uniti: l'emigrazione e l'opera degli italiani negli Stati Uniti d'America. Atti del III Symposium di Studi Americani.* New York: Arno, 1975. 323–64.

Nardini, Gloria. "Is It *True Love?* or Not? Patterns of Ethnicity and Gender in Nancy Savoca." In *VIA: Voices in Italian Americana* 2.1 (Spring 1991): 9–17.

Nelli, Humbert Steven *Italians in Chicago, 1880–1930: A Study in Ethnic Mobility.* New York: Oxford University Press, 1970.

———. 1965. The Role of the "Colonial" Press in the Italian-American Community of Chicago, 1886–1921. Ph.D. diss., University of Chicago.

Nerenberg, Ellen. "Overlooking and Looking Over Ida Lupino." In *VIA: Voices in Italian Americana.* Special Issue on Women Authors 7.2 (Fall 1996): 69–81.

Oboler, Suzanne. *Ethnic Labels, Latino Lives: Identity and the Politics of (Re)Presentation in the United States.* Minneapolis: University of Minnesota Press, 1995.

O'Brien, John, ed. *The Review of Contemporary Fiction.* Special Issue on Raymond Queneau and Carole Maso. Guest editors Mary Campbell-Sposito and Victoria Frenkel Harris. 17.3 (Fall 1997).

Orleck, Annelise. *Common Sense and a Little Fire: Women and Working-Class Politics in the United States, 1900–1965.* Chapel Hill: University of North Carolina Press, 1995.

Orsi, Robert Anthony. *The Madonna of 115th Street: Faith and Community in Italian Harlem, 1880–1950.* New Haven, CT: Yale University Press, 1985.

Ostendorf, Berndt. "Literary Acculturation: What Makes Ethnic Literature 'Ethnic.'" In *Callaloo* 8.3 (Fall 1985): 577–86.

Pagani, Daria. *Mercy Road.* New York: Delacorte, 1998.

Pallotta, Lina. *Piedras Negras* (Catalogue of photographic exhibit). New York: New York Foundation for the Arts, 1999.

Paola, Suzanne. *Bardo.* Madison: The University of Wisconsin Press, 1998.

Parenti, Michael. *Dirty Truths: Reflections on Politics, Media, Ideology, Conspiracy, Ethnic Life and Class Power.* San Francisco: City Lights, 1996.

Parini, Jay. *Some Necessary Angels: Essays on Writing and Politics.* New York: Columbia University Press, 1997.

Parker, Roszika. *The Subversive Stitch: Embroidery and the Making of the Feminine.* 1984. New York: Routledge, 1989.

Passing, Kym Ragusa, 9 min., Kym Ragusa, 1996, (16 mm and 8mm film edited on video) videocassette.

Patriarca, Gianna. *Italian Women and Other Tragedies*. Toronto and New York: Guernica, 1994.

Pearlman, Mickey ed. *A Place Called Home: Twenty Writing Women Remember.* New York: St. Martin's Press, 1996.

Penzato, Sadie. *Growing Up Sicilian and Female: In America, in a Small Town, in the Thirties.* New York: Bedford Graphics, 1991.

Perillo, Lucia. *The Oldest Map with the Name America: New and Selected Poems.* New York: Random House, 1999.

Perrotta, Tom. *Bad Haircut: Stories of the Seventies.* 1994. New York: Berkeley, 1995.

Petrusewicz, Marta. *Latifundium: Moral Economy and Material Life in a European Periphery.* 1989. Trans. Judith C. Green. Ann Arbor: The University of Michigan Press, 1996.

Pipino, Mary Frances. "Creating a Context: The Fiction and Criticism of Helen Barolini." In *I Have Found My Voice: The Italian American Woman Writer.* Currents in Comparative Romance Languages and Literatures. Vol. 71. Peter Lang, 1998.

———. "*Ella Price's Journal:* The Subv/mersion of Ethnic and Sexual Identity." In *VIA: Voices in Italian Americana.* Special Issue on Italian American Women 7.2 (Fall 1996): 35–54.

Pola, Antonia. *Who Can Buy the Stars?* New York: Vantage, 1957.

Processione, Susan Caperna Lloyd, 28 min., Susan Caperna Lloyd, 1989, videocassette.

Ragusa, Kym. "Ritorni." In *Tuttestorie. Origini: le scrittrici italo Americana* 8 (March–May 2001): 70–72.

Rainer, Tristine. *Your Life as a Story: Writing the New* Autobiography. New York: G.P. Putnam's Sons, 1997.

Rando, Flavia. "'My Mother Was a Strong Woman': Respect, Shame, and the Feminine Body in the Sculpture of Nancy Azara and Antonette Rosato." In *VIA: Voices in Italian Americana.* Special Issue on Italian American Women. 7.2 (1996): 225–9.

———. "Sacred Dwellings: The Work of Nancy Azara." In *Nancy Azara.* Catalogue. 1994–1995.

Raptosh, Diane. *West of Now.* Montreal: Guernica, 1992.

Redmond, Layne. *When the Drummers Were Women: A Spiritual History of Rhythm.* New York: Three Rivers Press, 1997.

Reed, Ishmael, ed. *MultiAmerica: Essays on Cultural Wars and Cultural Peace.* New York: Viking, 1997.

Reich, Jacqueline. "Nancy Savoca: An Appreciation." In *Italian Americana* 13.1 (Winter 1995): 11–15

repetto, Vittoria. *Heading for the Van Wyck.* New York: Monkey Cat Press, 1994.

Richards, David A. J. *Italian American: The Racializing of an Ethnic Identity.* New York: New York University Press, 1999.

Rimanelli, Giose. *Benedetta in Guysterland: A Liquid Novel.* Montreal and New York: Guernica, 1993.

Robertson, George, Melinda Mash, Lisa Tickner, Jon Bird, Barry Curtis and Tim Putnam. *Travellers' Tales: Narratives of Home and Displacement.* London and New York: Routledge, 1994.

Roediger, David. *Towards the Abolition of Whiteness: Essays on Race, Politics, and Work-ing-Class History.* London:Verso, 1994.

Romano, Rose. "Where Is Nella Sorellanza When You Really Need Her?" In *New Explorations in Italian American Studies: Proceedings of the 25th Annual Conference of the American Italian Historical Association. Washington, DC, November 12–14 1992.* Eds. Richard N. Juliani and Sandra P. Juliani. Staten Island, NY: American Ital-ian Historical Association, 1994. 147–54.

———. *The Wop Factor.* Brooklyn/Palermo: malafemmina press, 1994.

———. *Vendetta.* San Francisco: malafemmina press, 1990.

Romeo, Caterina. "Sister Blandina alla conquista del West." In *TutteStorie* 6 (Sep-tember–November 2000): 85–86.

———. "*Vertigo* di Louise DeSalvo: vertigine della memoria." In *Acoma* 19 (Spring–Summer 2000): 33–39.

———. 1999–2000. Esplorare il passato, riscrivere il presente: tradizione e inno-vazione nel memoir delle scrittrici italo americane. Ph.D. diss in Storia delle scritture femminili, University of Rome, la Sapienza.

Roof, Judith, and Robyn Wiegman, eds. *Who Can Speak? Authority and Critical Identity.* Urbana and Chicago: University of Illinois Press, 1995.

Rossi, Agnes. *The Houseguest.* New York: Dutton, 2000.

———. *Split Skirt.* New York: Random House, 1994.

———. *The Quick: A Novella and Stories.* New York: W.W. Norton, 1992.

———. *Athletes and Artists.* New York: Persea, 1987.

———. "On Being Italian American." Unpublished notes.

Rushdie, Salman. *Imaginary Homelands: Essays and Criticism 1981–1991.* New York: Penguin, 1991.

Russo, John Paul. "Italian American Filmmakers: No Deal on Madonna Street." In *Italian Americana* (Winter 1995): 5–9.

———. "From Italophilia to Italophobia: Representations of Italian Americans in the Early Gilded Age." In *Differentia* 6.7 (Spring/Autumn 1994): 45–76.

———. "The Hidden Godfather: Plenitude and Absence in Francis Ford Coppola's *Godfather I* and *II.*" In *Support and Struggle: Italians and Italian Americans in a Com-parative Perspective.* Eds. Joseph L. Tropea, James E. Miller, and Cheryl Beattie-Repetti. Staten Island, NY: The American Italian Historical Association, 1986.

Ryan, Michael. *Secret Life.* New York: Random House, 1995.

Said, Edward. *Representations of the Intellectual.* New York: Random House, 1994.

Santiago, Esmeralda. *When I Was Puerto Rican.* New York: Vintage, 1994.

Sapphire. *Push.* New York: Alfred A. Knopf, 1996.

Saracino, Mary. "Sunday Rounds." In *Hey Paesan! Writing by Lesbians and Gay Men of Italian Descent.* Eds. Giovanna (Janet) Capone, Denise Nico Leto, Tommi Avi-colli Mecca. Oakland, CA: Three Guineas Press, 1999. 43–53

———. *No Matter What.* Minneapolis, MN: Spinsters Ink, 1993.

———. *Talk it with the Moon.* Unpublished manuscript.

Savarese, Julia. *The Weak and the Strong.* New York: G. P. Putnam's Sons, 1952.

Scelsa, Joseph V., and Vincenzo Milione. "High School Dropout Rate Indicators for Italian American and Other Race/Ethnic Population." In *To See the Past More*

Clearly: The Enrichment of the Italian Heritage 1890–1990. Ed. Harral E. Landry. Austin, TX: Nortex Press, 1994. 1–18.

Sciascia, Leonardo. *La Sicilia come metafora: Intervista di Marcelle Padovani.* Milano: Mondadori, 1979.

Sciorra, Joseph. "Imagined Places, Fragile Landscapes: Italian American Presepi in New York City." Unpublished paper.

Segale, Blandina. *At the End of the Santa Fe Trail.* 1912. Milwaukee, WI: Bruce Publishers, 1948.

Sereni, Clara. *Casalinghitudine.* Torino: Einaudi, 1987.

Silko, Leslie Marmon. *Ceremony.* New York: Penguin, 1977.

Smith, Barbara, ed. *Home Girls: A Black Feminist Anthology.* New Brunswick, NJ: Rutgers University Press, 2000.

Smith, Sidonie, and Julia Watson, eds. *Getting a Life: Everyday Uses of Autobiography.* Minneapolis: University of Minnesota Press, 1996.

Sollors, Werner. *Beyond Ethnicity: Consent and Descent in American Culture.* New York: Oxford University Press, 1986.

———, ed. *The Invention of Ethnicity.* New York and Oxford: Oxford University Press, 1989.

———, ed. *Multilingual America: Transnationalism, Ethnicity and the Languages of American Literature.* New York: New York University Press, 1998.

Squier, D. Ann, and Jill S. Quadagno. "The Italian American Family." In *Ethnic Families in America: Patterns and Variations.* Eds. Charles H. Mindel, Robert W. Habenstein, and Roosevelt Wright, Jr. New York: Elsevier. 109–37.

Stay of Execution, Lilith Dorsey, 10 min., 1991, videocassette.

Stefanelli, Filomena LoCurcio. *The Stromboli Legacy.* Nutley, NJ: Stromboli American Heritage Society, 1998.

Stein, Leon. *The Triangle Fire.* 1962. Ithaca, NY: Cornell University Press, 2001. Introduction by William Greider.

Strom, Linda. "Reclaiming Our Working-Class Identity: Teaching Working-Class Studies in a Blue-Collar Community." In *Women's Studies Quarterly: Working-Class Studies* 23.1–2 (Spring–Summer 1995): 131–41.

Talese, Gay. Where Are the Italian American Novelists? In the *New York Times Book Review* (14 March 1993): 1, 23, 25, 29.

Talking Back, Renata Gangemi, 17 min., Third World Newsreel, 1992, videocassette.

Tamburri, Anthony J. *A Semiotic of Ethnicity: In (Re)Cognition of the Italian/American Writer.* Albany: SUNY Press, 1998.

———. *To Hyphenate or Not to Hyphenate. The Italian/American Writer: An "Other" American.* Montreal: Guernica, 1991.

———. "Helen Barolini's Umbertina: The Gender/Ethnic Dilemma." In *Italian Americans Celebrate Life, the Arts and Popular Culture.* Eds. Paola A. Sensi Isolani and Anthony Julian Tamburri. American Italian Historical Association, 1990. 29–44.

———, ed. *FUORI: Essays by Italian/American Lesbians and Gays.* Introduction by Mary Jo Bona. West Lafayette, IN: Bordighera, 1996.

———, Paolo A. Giordano, and Fred L. Gardaphé, eds. *From the Margin: Writings in Italian Americana.* West Lafayette, IN: Purdue University Press, 1991.

Tan, Amy. *The Kitchen God's Wife.* New York: Ivy, 1991.

——. *The Joy Luck Club.* New York: Ivy, 1989.

Tarantella. Helen DeMichiel, color: 88 min., Tarantella Productions, 16 mm., 1996.

Taylor, Charles. *Multiculturalism: Examining the Politics of Recognition.* Ed. Amy Gutman. Princeton, NJ: Princeton University Press, 1994.

Terrone, Maria. "Unmentionable." Unpublished poem.

Things I Take, Luisa Pretolani, 9 min., PAHNI Productions, 1997, videocassette.

Three Graces, Jeanette Vuocolo, 22 min., Jeanette Vuocolo, 1996, videocassette.

Timpanelli, Gioia. *Sometimes the Soul: Two Novellas of Sicily.* New York: W.W. Norton, 1998.

——. *Stories.* Audiotape. Yellow Moon Press, 1990.

Tomasi, Mari. *Like Lesser Gods.* 1949. Shelburne, VT: The New England Press, 1988.

——. *Deep Grow the Roots.* Philadelphia: J.B. Lippincott, 1940.

Torgovnick, Marianna. *Primitive Obsessions: Men, Women, and the Quest for Ecstasy.* Chicago: University of Chicago Press, 1997.

——. *Crossing Ocean Parkway.* Chicago: University of Chicago Press, 1994.

Torjesen, Karen Jo. *When Women Were Priests: Women's Leadership in the Early Church and the Scandal of Their Subordination in the Rise of Christianity.* San Francisco: Harper, 1995.

True Love, Nancy Savoca, 100 min., MGM/USA, 1990, videocassette.

Turner, Kay. *Beautiful Necessity: The Art and Meaning of Women's Altars.* New York: Thames and Hudson, 1999.

Tusmith, Bonnie. *All My Relatives: Community in Contemporary Ethnic American Literatures.* Ann Arbor: The University of Michigan Press, 1994.

The Twenty-Four Hour Woman, Nancy Savoca, 92 mins. Redeemable Features/Exile Films, 1999, videocassette.

Valerio, Anthony. *Anita Garibaldi: A Biography.* Westport, CT: Praeger, 2000.

——. *Valentino and the Great Italians.* Toronto: Guernica, 1996.

——. *The Mediterranean Runs Through Brooklyn.* New York: H.B. Davis, 1982.

Vaughan, Leslie J. "Cosmopolitanism, Ethnicity and American Identity: Randoplh Bourne's 'Trans-National' America." In the *Journal of American Studies* 25 (1991): 433–59.

Vecoli, Rudolph J. "Italian Immigrants and Working Class Movements in the United States: A Personal Reflection on Class and Ethnicity." In the *Journal of the Canadian Historical Association* (1993): 293–305.

Verdicchio, Pasquale. "Spike Lee's Guineas." In *Differentia.* Special Issue on Italian American Culture 6.7 (Spring–Autumn 1994): 177–91.

Viscusi, Robert. *Astoria.* Toronto and New York: Guernica, 1996.

——. "Debate in the Dark: Love in Italian-American Fiction." In *American Declarations of Love.* Ed. Ann Massa. New York: St. Martin's Press, 1990. 155–73.

——. "Narrative and Nothing: The Enterprise of Italian American Writing." In *Differentia: Review of Italian Thought,* Special Double Issue on Italian American Culture 6–7 (Spring–Fall, 1994): 77–99.

——. "Il Caso della Casa: Stories of Houses in Italian America." In *The Family and Community Life of Italian Americans.* Ed. Richard N. Juliani. Staten Island, NY: The Italian American Historical Association, 1983. 1–9.

Waldo, Octavia Capuzzi. *A Cup of the Sun.* New York: Harcourt, 1961.

388

Walker, Alice. *The Color Purple.* New York: Harcourt Brace, 1992.

———. *In Search of Our Mothers' Gardens: Womanist Prose.* San Diego, New York, and London: Harcourt Brace Jovanovich, 1983.

Weiss, Penny A., and Marilyn Friedman, eds. *Feminism and Community.* Philadelphia: Temple University Press, 1995.

Wharton, Edith. *The House of Mirth.* 1905. New York: Charles Scribner's Sons, 1969.

What About Me?, Rachel Amodeo. Black and white: Amodeo Productions, 87 min., 16mm., 1993.

Williams, Patricia J. *Seeing a Color-Blind Future: The Paradox of Race.* New York: Farrar, Strauss, and Giroux, 1997.

Wing, Diane Yen-Mei, and Emilya Cachapero, eds. *Making Waves: An Anthology of Writings by and about Asian American Women.* Boston: Beacon, 1989.

Winwar, Frances. *Wings of Fire: A Biography of Gabriele D'Annunzio and Eleonora Duse.* London: Alvin Redman, 1957.

———. *The Last Love of Camille.* New York: Harper and Brothers, 1954.

———. *The Eagle and the Rock.* New York: Harper and Brothers, 1953.

Women Forward / Mujeres Adelante, Liliana Fasanella, 30 min., Liliana Fasonella, 1998, (shot on digital video), videocassette.

Zandy, Janet. "My Children's Names." In *The Milk of Almonds: Italian American Women Writers on Food and Culture.* Eds. Louise DeSalvo and Edvige Giunta. New York: The Feminist Press at CUNY. Forthcoming.

———. "Fire Poetry on the Triangle Shirtwaist Company Fire of March 25, 1911." In *College Literature* 24.3 (October 1997).

———, ed. *What We Hold in Common: An Introduction to Working-Class Studies.* New York: The Feminist Press at CUNY, 2001.

———, ed. *Liberating Memory: Our Work and Our Working-Class Consciousness.* New Brunswick, NJ: Rutgers University Press, 1995.

———, ed. *Women's Studies Quarterly.* Issue on Working-Class Studies 23.1–2 (Spring–Summer 1995).

———, ed. *Calling Home: Working Class Women's Writings.* New Brunswick, NJ: Rutgers University Press, 1990.

Index

absence, 35–6
Abu-Jamal, Mumia, 167 n16
abuse, 106
    environmental, 120, 126, 127
    sexual, 103
academics, working-class, 96
accent, 2–3 29, 78, 79, 143–4
    "writing with an," 3
acculturation, 72
activism, 119, 120
    cultural, 29
    radical, 22
    social, 118
addiction, drug, 106
Addonizio, Kim, 10, 18, 20, 24, 33, 35, 105;
    The Box Called Pleasure, 20;
    "Generations," 35
African American
    grandmother, 19
    identity, 74
    maternal grandmother, 74
    mother, 131
    origins, 88
    poor, 135
    women, 51, 95, 125, 129, 142
    women writers, 29–30
    writers, 24
African Americans, 69
African, heritage, 144
Afzal-Khan, Fawzia, 149 n12
agrarian culture, 58
Ahearn, Rosemary, 33
Alaya, Flavia, 15, 28, 123, 128; Under the
    Rose: A Confession, 15, 28, 128
Albanese, Catherine L., 153 n4; A Cobbler's
    Universe, 153 n4
Albright, Carol Bonomo, 147 n22, 155 n27
allegiances, cultural, 140

Allison, Dorothy, 48, 128, 134; Bastard Out
    of Carolina, 48, 128
Alvarez, Julia, 3, 5; How the García Girls Lost
    Their Accents, 3
Amella, Gia, 5, 167–8 n21; La mia isola
    sacra, 167–8 n21
The American Italian Historical
    Association, xxii, 153 n4;
    conference, xix
American Italian Historical Association
    Newsletter, 54
Amodeo, Rachel, 19; What About Me?, 19
Amore, B., 93, 96, 117; Lifeline—filo della
    vita: An Italian American Odyssey, 93,
    117
Anania, Michael, 55
ancestry, Southern Italian, 104
Anderson, S. E., 167 n16
Angelou, Maya, 6, 120
Anglo-American
    expatriates, 37
    tradition, 107
anorexic, 110
Antonetta, Susanne, 33, 88, 121, 123, 147
    n21, 166 n10; Body Toxic: An
    Environmental Memoir, 147 n21, 166
    n10
Anzaldúa, Gloria, 2, 5, 6, 27; Borderlands La
    Frontera: The New Mestiza, 2; Making
    Face, Making Soul: Haciendo Caras:
    Creative and Critical Perspectives by
    Feminists of Color, 27; This Bridge
    Called My Back: Writings by Radical
    Women of Color, 27
Arab-American feminists, 95
Arab-Canadian feminists, 95
Arcade, Penny, 8, 20, 96, 121; La Miseria,
    20, 121

archival work, 136
Ardizzone, Toni, 104
Argentine heritage, 144
art, 96
    women's, 163 n5
artist, culinary, 110
artistic movement, 98
artistry, female, 95
artists, working-class, 96
Asian American writers, 24
Asian Americans, 69
assimilation, 21, 72, 149 n15
    linguistic, 141
Ata Press, 28
Attenzione, 26, 73–4
audience, implied, 84
authorial legitimization, 27
authorial self-creation, 115
authorial voice, 39
authors, working-class, 57
autobiographical documentary, 105
autobiographical text, 109
autobiographical video, 76
Avella, Caterina Maria, 31
Azara, Nancy, xxii, 11, 19, 96, 97, 117;
    "Dwelling," 97; "Fire," 117;
    "Goddess Wall," 97; "Spirit House
    of the Mother," 97; "Tree Altar," 97

background, ethnic, 31
Bantam, 153 n4
Barchiesi, Franca, 76, 105; *Continents Apart,*
    76
Barolini, Antonio, 36, 46; *Duet,* 36
Barolini, Helen, 4, 7, 8, 9, 10, 12, 23, 24–5,
    27, 28, 30, 31–2, 32, 33, 35–51, 54,
    56, 69, 75, 80, 83, 95–6, 105, 106,
    122, 125, 152 n35, 153 n3, 153 n4,
    155 n22, 155 n25, 157–8 n16, 163
    n12, 165 n25, 165 n26; *Aldus and His
    Dream Book,* 36; "Becoming a
    Literary Person Out of Context,"
    24–5, 36, 47, 105; *Chiaroscuro: Essays
    of Identity,* 30, 32, 35, 36, 46, 122, 153
    n3; "A Circular Journey," 155 n25;
    *The Dream Book: An Anthology of
    Writings by Italian American Women,* 7,
    8, 10, 27–8, 30, 31, 32, 35, 36, 43, 54,
    125, 151 n32, 151–2 n34, 153–4 n9,
    163 n12; *Duet,* 36; *Festa: Recipes and*

Recollections of Italian Holidays, 36,
    105, 106, 165 n26; "The Finer Things
    in Life," 4; "How I Learned to Speak
    Italian," 4, 46; *The Last Abstraction,* 38;
    Love in the Middle Ages, 36; "Looking
    for Mari Tomasi," 153 n3;
    "Reintroducing *The Dream Book,*"
    12; "Turtle Out of Calabria," 4;
    Umbertina, 4, 8, 9–10, 27, 30, 35–6,
    38, 39–51, 54, 56–7, 65, 80, 95–6, 153
    n4, 155 n22, 155 n25, 155 n27,
    157–8 n16; "*Umbertina* and the
    Universe," 36; "Writing to a Brick
    Wall," 122
Barreca, Regina, 18, 19–20; *They Used to
    Call Me Snow White . . . But I
    Drifted,* 18–9, 19–20
Barresi, Dorothy, 33
Bartkowski, Frances, 45, 46, 47, 68; *Travelers,
    Immigrants, Inmates: Essays in
    Estrangement,* 45
Beacon, 33
Belloni, Alessandra, xvi, 146 n2
Benasutti, Marion, 30; *No Steady Job for
    Papa,* 30
Bensonhurst, 18, 22–3, 74
Bernardi, Adria, 4, 5, 33; *The Day Laid on
    the Altar,* 5
betrayal, 4
bias, ethnic, 18
bicultural experience, 36
bildungsroman, 39, 66, 80, 155–6 n27, 159 n26
Birnbaum, Lucia Chiavola, 23, 162 n1
Black Madonna, 162 n1
Boelhower, William, 85
Bona, Mary Jo, 31, 74, 147 n22, 151 n32, 152
    n40, 155 n27; *The Voices We Carry:
    Recent Italian American Women's Fiction,*
    151 n32
breads, 108
    cultural, 107–8
breadmakers, 107
Brenkman, John, 88
Brontë, Emily, 107
Brontë sisters, 28
Broumas, Olga, 134
Bryant, Dorothy Calvetti, 26, 27, 28, 30, 33,
    53; *Confessions of Madame Psyche,* 30;
    Ella Price's Journal, 30; *Miss Giardino,*
    26, 30, 53

Bush, Mary Bucci, 23, 160 n13; "Drowning," 160 n13

Cachapero, Emilya, 27; *Making Waves: An Anthology of Writings by and about Asian American Women*, 27
Cafarelli, Annette Wheeler, 147 n22
Calcagno, Anne, 33, 105
Calleri, Mariarosy, 96, 105, 106; *Hidden Island/l'isola sommersa*, 106
Candeloro, Dominic, 149 n18, 159 n29
Cannistraro, Phil, 119, 156 n4; "The Lost Radicalism of Italian Americans," 156 n4
Capello, Phyllis, xxii, 27, 81, 117
Capone, Al, 67
Capone, Giovanna (Janet), 27, 29, 80, 104, 106; "A Divided Life: Being a Lesbian in an Italian American Family," 106; *Hey Paesan: Writing by Lesbians and Gay Men of Italian Descent*, 27, 151 n32
Caponegro, Mary, 4, 5, 33; *Five Doubts*, 5
Capotorto, Rosette, xxii, 6, 8, 11, 23, 96, 105, 106, 112–3, 121, 123, 124, 143, 164 n18; "Broke," 113; "Bronx Italian," 121, 164 n185; "Confession," 164 n18; "Dealing with Broccoli Rabe," 113; "Heathen," 164 n18; "Mother of a Priest," 164 n18; "The Oven," 106, 112–3; "Red Wagon," 124
Cappello, Mary, xvi, 6, 8, 10, 11, 23, 26, 32, 33, 80, 88, 96, 105, 106, 121, 122, 123, 124, 128–9, 137; *Night Bloom*, 26, 32, 96, 121, 122, 128–9, 132, 137; "Nothing to Confess: A Lesbian in Italian America," 106
Caronia, Nancy, 6, 23, 29, 105, 106, 121, 122, 123, 143; "Go to Hell," 122; *the girlSpeak journals*, 29; "Setting the Table," 29, 106
Carravetta, Peter, 147 n22
Carroll, Lewis, xvii; *Alice's Adventures in Wonderland*, 158 n22
Casa Italiana Zerilli Marimò at New York University, xxii, 118, 151 n29
Casale, Anne, 165 n27
Casella, Jean, xxii, 33
Cassettari, Rosa, 103–4

Castillo, Ana, xix, 5, 134, 145 n4
Catholic
  icons, 114
  rituals, 99
Catholicism, 164 n14, 164 n18
  Latin American, 102
  Southern Italian, 97, 104
Cauti, Camille, 74
Cavalieri, Grace, 32
Cavallo, Diana, 30, 63; *A Bridge of Leaves*, 30, 63
Chan, Jeffrey Paul, 27; *Aiiieeeee! An Anthology of Asian American Writers*, 27
characters
  Irish American, 89
  Latina, 89
Chassman, Deborah, 33
Chicana
  heritage, 144
  women, 51
Chicano culture, 75
Chin, Frank, 27; *Aiiieeeee! An Anthology of Asian American Writers*, 27
Chopin, Kate, 49; *The Awakening*, 49
Ciatu, Nzula Angelina, 27, 128; *Curaggia: Writing by Women of Italian Descent*, 27, 29, 128, 151 n32
Ciresi, Rita, 20, 24, 25, 33, 86, 150–1 n27, 161 n23; *Blue Italian*, 20, 150–1 n27, 161 n23; *Mother Rocket*, 20, 86, 150–1 n27, 161 n23; "Paradise Below the Stairs," 25; *Pink Slip*, 150–1 n27, 161 n23; *Sometimes I Dream in Italian*, 20, 150–1 n27, 161 n23
Cisneros, Sandra, xix, 3, 5, 6, 48, 51, 53, 64, 75, 134, 158 n21, 158–9 n25; *The House on Mango Street*, 3, 10, 48, 53, 64, 158 n21, 158–9 n25
class, 39, 48
  and ethnicity, 75–6
  identity, 106, 125
  migration, 49
  oppression, 128
il Collettivo la Maddalena, xix
Collective of Italian American Women, xxii, 118, 151 n29
Colonna, Dora, 31
comedy, 102

Conference on Italian Americans and
African Americans, xxii
Conference on Italian Americans and
Publishing, xxii
Conference on the Lost Radicalism of
Italian Americans, xxii
consciousness
feminist, 48
working-class, 7
contemporary memoir, 119–37
context, middle-class, 49
cookbooks, 105, 106, 165 n27
Italian American, 165 n24
Coppola, Francis Ford, xix, 67, 107, 122;
The Godfather, xix
Covino, Peter, 104, 123, 164 n21; "Box of
Broken Things," 104, 164 n21; "The
Poverty of Language," 123; "Rice,"
104
cross-cultural identity, 55
culinary artist, 110
cult, matriarchal, 98
cultural
allegiances, 4, 140
breads, 107–8
constructs, 22
dislocation, 47, 56
disorientation, 26
displacement, 78, 79, 80, 82, 90, 159 n3
experience, 39
heritage, 149 n11
history, 125
icon, 105
identities, xv, 5
initiatives, 31
invisibility, 24, 67
isolation, 125
legitimation, 83
marginalization, 134
material, 95–6
memory, 44, 95
minority writers, 27
movement, 98
reclamation, 24, 95, 131
recovery, 103
role, 82
silencing, 86, 149 n9
spaces, 136
transformation, 144
workers, xxi, xxii, 119–37

cultural/familial definition, 80–1
culture
agrarian, 58
Chicano, 75
ghost, 82
homophobic American, 106
Italophobic American, 106
material, 100, 109, 114
misogynist American, 106
Southern Italian, 71
Cuomo, Mario, 73
custom, Sicilian, 108
Cusumano, Camille, 29
Cutrufelli, Maria Rosa, 17, 139, 140, 143,
151 n32, 163 n6; *Canto al deserto:
storia di Tina, soldato di mafia/Song to
the Desert: Story of Tina, Mafia
Soldier,* 139, 140; *Disoccupata con
onore: lavoro e condizione della donna,*
163 n6

D'Amico, Maria Vittoria, 145 n4
D'Onofrio, Beverly, 32, 33, 121, 162 n1;
Looking for Mary, 32, 162 n1; *Riding
in Cars with Boys,* 121
Daly, Brenda, 167 n21; *Authoring a Life: A
Woman's Survival in and through
Literary Studies,* 167 n21
Dante, 50–1; *Commedia,* 50–1
Danticat, Edwidge, 5
Dash, Julie, 6
Davidson, Cathy (Notari), 85, 161 n21, 161
n22, 161 n24; *36 Views of Mount
Fuji,* 85
De Angelis, Rose, 155 n27
DeLillo, Don, 160 n6
DeMichiel, Helen, 96, 167 n14; *Tarantella,*
152 n2, 167 n14
definition, cultural/familial, 80–1
Del Conte, Anna, 165 n27
Deledda, Grazia, 143
Delitto d'onore, 166–7 n12
Demeter, 44, 98, 99
Demetrick, Mary Russo, 4, 29; *Italian
Notebook,* 4
depression, 110–1
De Rosa, Tina, xx, 8, 9, 23, 26, 27, 29, 30,
33, 39, 48, 51, 53–69, 73–4, 80,
99–101, 102, 105, 111–2, 112, 151
n30, 151 n31, 156 n3, 156 n4, 157

n11, 158 n21, 159 n27, 163 n11,
163 n12, 164 n15, 167–8 n21;
"Career Choices Come from
Listening to the Heart," 61; "An
Italian American Woman Speaks
Out," 26, 55, 57–8, 69, 74, 112;
"Mary of Magdala," 101–2; "My
Father's Lesson," 57–8; *Paper Fish,*
xx, 8, 9–10, 27, 29, 30, 39, 53–7, 80,
99–101, 111–2, 151 n30, 156 n2,
156 n3, 157 n11, 157 n5, 157 n15,
158 n17, 158 n18, 158 n21, 159
n26, 159 n27, 159 n30, 159 n31,
167–8 n21; "Silent Night, Homeless
Night," 58; "Therese," 101–2
DeSalvo, Louise, xx, 6, 8, 10, 11, 18, 19,
20–1, 23, 25, 26, 27, 29, 31, 32, 33,
48, 74, 84, 88, 94–5, 96, 102–3, 105,
106, 109–10, 111, 114, 121, 122,
123, 124, 125, 127–8, 134, 137, 145
n6, 147–8 n3, 156–7 n4, 161 n24,
166 n3; *Adultery,* 19, 20, 127–8, 149
n13; "Anorexia," 106, 109–11, 113;
*Between Women: Biographers, Novelists,
Critics, Teachers and Artists Write About
Their Work on Women,* 125; *Breathless:
An Asthma Journal,* 8, 18, 19, 20, 122,
124, 126–7, 132, 135, 166 n3;
Casting Off, 19, 31, 84, 94–5, 109,
114, 127–8, 145 n6; "Digging
Deep," 26; "A Portrait of the *Puttana*
as a Middle-Aged Woolf Scholar,"
74, 124–5; *Vertigo,* xi, xx, 6, 9, 19, 29,
31, 32, 48, 74, 102–3, 109–10, 111,
121, 122, 125–7, 128, 132, 133–4,
137, 147–8 n3; *Writing as a Way of
Healing: How Telling Our Stories
Transforms Our Lives,* 134
descent, Southern Italian, 94
De Sica (Vittorio), xix; *La ciociara,* xix
development, female, 48
DeVito, Cara, 8, 105, 148 n6; *Ama l'uomo
tuo,* 8, 148 n6
DeVries, Rachel Guido, 32
di Donato, Pietro, 57, 104, 157 n8, 158 n25;
Christ in Concrete, 57, 158 n25
di Leonardo, Micaela, 159 n2
di Prima, Diane, 27, 32, 33, 81, 167 n13;
Recollections of My Life as a Woman,
167 n13

Dickinson, Emily, 107
DiLeo, Domenica, 27, 128; *Curaggia: Writing
by Women of Italian Descent,* 27, 29,
128, 151 n32
discrimination, 23
ethnic, 68
dislocation, 4, 45
cultural, 47, 56
dual, 4
disorientation, cultural, 26
displacement, 4, 26, 37, 45, 46, 64–5, 76, 77,
cultural, 78, 79, 80, 82, 90, 159 n3
geographical, 159 n3
documentary, autobiographical, 105
domestic
activities, 163 n12
chores, 163 n12
life, 102, 109
space, 46, 97, 105, 109
work, 95
domesticity, 102
Donahue, Patricia, 146 n7
Dorsey, Lilith, 10
drug addiction, 106
dual heritage, 46, 77, 149 n11
Dunye, Cheryl, 6
dynamics, familial power, 106

Easter Procession in Trapani, 98, 99
eating disorders, 110
ecofeminism, 98
Elshtain, Jeanne Bethke, 157 n11;
"Feminism, Family, and
Community," 157 n11
embroidery, 163 n5
environmental abuse, 120, 126, 127
environmental racism, 120
erasure, 124
Ermelino, Louisa, 21, 33, 162 n1; *Black
Madonna,* 162 n1; *Joey Dee Gets
Wise,* 21
Esquivel, Laura, 93; *Like Water for Chocolate,*
93
ethnic, 5
background, 31–2
bias, 18
discrimination, 68
experience, 87
identity, 10, 77, 109, 115, 125
intersections, 161 n25

invisibility, 86
memory, 89
oppression, 128
recovery, 125
revival, 39
self-silencing, 21
space, 89
voice, 85
writers, 87
ethnicity, 66, 82
white, 161 n17, 161 n20
Ets, Marie Hall, 30, 166 n8; *Rosa,* 30, 166 n8
exile, 37
expatriates, Anglo-American, 37
expatriation, 37
experience
bicultural, 36
cultural, 39
ethnic, 87
immigrant, 35
working class, 19
exploitation of children, 128

Falcone, Giovanni, 17, 148 n4; *Cose di cosa nostra,* 148 n4
Famà, Maria, 4, 29, 32; *Italian Notebook,* 4
familial memoir, 128
familial power dynamics, 106
Fante, John, 104
Fasanella, Liliana, 10, 19, 105; *Women Forward, Mujeres Adelante,* 19
father-daughter relationship, 57, 81
Fausty, Joshua, 86, 156 n4
Felman, Shoshana, 120
female
artistry, 95
development, 48
oppression, 80
perspective, 35
feminine/feminist spirituality, 102
The Feminist Press, xx, 33, 67, 156–7 n4
feminists, 113
Arab-American, 95
Arab-Canadian, 95
awakening, 39
consciousness, 48
movement, xix–xx
practices, 124
scholars, 38
scholarship, 95

Ferlinghetti, Lawrence, 32
fiction
memoiristic, 80
maternal, 81
filmmakers, 19, 98, 105, 107, 131, 148 n6, 166 n4
Argentinean American, 10
Italian American, 10
working-class, 96
films, 96, 102, 106, 148 n6
folk tales, 31
food, 95, 96, 103, 104–3, 114, 164 n16, 164 n20, 165 n22
and violence interconnections, 165 n29
recipes, 102
rituals, 104
Sicilian family's, 105
food-writing, 105
foreign nationals, 133
foremothers, 142
fragmented identity, 78
Franciscan mysticism, 100
Frank, Anne, 68, 159 n31; *The Diary of a Young Girl,* 68, 159 n31
Freeperson, Kathy, 105
Friedman, Marilyn, 157 n11; *Feminism and Community,* 157 n11
Fuller, Margaret, 36
Furst, Lilian R., 110; *Disorderly Eaters: Texts in Self-Empowerment,* 110

Gabaccia, Donna, 43, 87–8, 110, 119; *We Are What We Eat: Ethnic Food and the Making of Americans,* 110
Gangemi, Renata, 5, 8, 10, 121, 123, 167–8 n21; *The Journey Back,* 167–8 n21; *Talking Back,* 8, 121
Garcia, Cristina, 5, 38, 84, 89; *Dreaming in Cuban,* 84, 89
Gardaphé, Fred, xx, 54, 63, 73, 89, 101, 106, 147 n22, 148 n3, 151 n32, 155 n27, 156 n4, 157 n11, 160 n6, 162 n28; *From the Margin,* 43, 151 n32; *Italian Signs,* 63, 157 n11
gardening, 129
Garrett, Giannella, 10
Gates, Jr., Henry Louis, 158 n19
gays
Italian American, 106, 166 n7
writers, 96, 123, 151 n32

geographical displacement, 159 n3
ghost culture, 82
Giardina, Denise, 76–7, 160 n13, 164 n19;
    Storming Heaven, 160 n13, 164 n19
Gilbert, Sandra Mortola, 8, 18, 23, 27, 28,
    32, 33, 74–5, 85, 96, 105, 107–9,
    111, 115, 121, 124, 127, 143, 147–8
    n3, 161 n21, 161 n24, 163 n12;
    "Doing Laundry," 163 n12; *Emily's
    Bread,* 107, 108; "The
    Grandmother's Dream," 109;
    Kissing the Bread, 108; "The
    Kitchen Dream," 108; *The
    Madwoman in the Attic,* 107–8;
    "Mafioso," 107, 147–8 n;3;
    "Mysteries of the Hyphen: Poetry,
    Pasta, and Identity Politics," 108;
    No Man's Land, 107; "Still Life:
    Woman Cooking," 108–9; *Wrongful
    Death: A Memoir,* 8, 18, 124
Gillan, Jennifer, 32, 129; *Growing Up Ethnic
    in America,* 32, 129; *Identity Lessons,*
    32, 129; *Unsettling America: An
    Anthology of Contemporary
    Multicultural Poetry,* 32, 129
Gillan, Maria Mazziotti, xxii, 10, 11, 23, 27,
    32, 33, 63, 73, 85–6, 86, 96, 121,
    122, 123, 124, 129–32, 134–5, 137;
    "Arturo," 130; "Betrayals," 130;
    "Coming of Age: Paterson," 129;
    Growing Up Ethnic in America, 32,
    129; "Growing Up Italian," 86, 130,
    134; *Identity Lessons,* 32, 129; *The
    Paterson Literary Review,* 129; "Public
    School No. 18/Paterson, New
    Jersey," 63, 85–6, 130; *Taking Back
    My Name,* 86, 130–1; *Unsettling
    America: An Anthology of
    Contemporary Multicultural Poetry,* 32,
    129; *Where I Come From,* 86, 122,
    130, 132, 134–5, 137
Gillman, Charlotte Perkins, 49; *The Yellow
    Wallpaper,* 49
Ginsburg, Carlo, 153 n4; *The Cheese and the
    Worms,* 153 n4
Giordano, Paolo, xx, 151 n32; *From the
    Margin,* 43, 151 n32
Gioseffi, Daniela, 19, 23, 27, 28, 31, 33, 88,
    121; *The Great American Belly Dance,*
    19, 31

Giroux, Henry, 133; *Teachers as Intellectuals,*
    133
goddess, 99
Gomez, Jewelle, 6
Gordon, Mary, 27
Gotti, John, 17
Gramsci, Antonio, 122, 154 n11; *The Prison
    Notebooks,* 122; *The Southern
    Question,* 154 n11
grandmother
    African American, 19
    African American maternal, 74
Great Depression, 39
Great Migration, 39
Guandique, Grace, 135–6
Gubar, Susan, 107–8; *The Madwoman in the
    Attic,* 107–8; *No Man's Land,* 107
Guerrero, Ed, 148 n5
Guglielmo, Jennifer, xxii, 6, 22, 31, 118,
    119, 120, 142–3, 150 n21, 165 n1

H. D., xvii, 54, 60, 158 n17; *Asphodel,* 158
    n17; *Bid Me to Live,* 158 n17; *The
    Gift,* 158 n17; *HERmione,* 54, 156
    n3, 158 n17
Hagedorn, Jessica, 6, 146 n4
Hak-Kyung-Cha, Theresa, 6
Hale Mary Press, 29
Hammad, Suheir, 120
Harjo, Joy, 6
Harrison, Barbara Grizzuti, 28
Hawkins, Yusef, 74
Hendin, Josephine Gattuso, 30, 81; *The
    Right Thing to Do,* 30, 81
heritage
    African, 144
    Argentine, 144
    Chicana, 144
    cultural, 149 n11
    dual, 46, 77, 149 n11
    Irish, 144
    Jewish, 144
    Native American, 144
Herman, Joanna Clapps, xxii, 123, 146 n2
Herman, Judith, 120
hierarchy, patriarchal, 99
historical recovery, 118–9
historical silence, 128
histories
    unspoken, 132

working-class, 120
history
    cultural, 125
    immigrant, 90
    social, 129
Hoffmann, Eva, xiv, 2; *Lost in Translation,*
    xiv, 2
home, 57, 59, 76, 77, 80, 82, 123–4, 140
homeless, 57, 59, 72, 76, 123–4
homelessness, 157 n13
homophobia, 80, 106, 123
homophobic American culture, 106
honor killing, 166 n12
hooks, bell, 6
Howe, Florence, 33, 156–7 n4
humor, 19–21
Hurston, Zora Neale, xix, 3, 29–30, 51, 54,
    69, 84, 142, 151–2 n34, 153 n3;
    Their Eyes Were Watching God, 3, 54,
    69, 84, 151–2 n34, 153 n3, 156 n3
Hutcheon, Linda (Bartalotti), 21, 85, 161
    n21; "Crypotoethnicity," 85; *The
    Politics of Postmodernism,* 21
hyphenation, 73–4

iconography, religious, 96
icons, 99
    Catholic, 114
    cultural, 105
    of saints, 102
identity
    African American, 74
    class, 106, 125
    cross-cultural, 55
    ethnic, 77, 109, 115, 125
    fragmented, 78
    Italian American, 1
    political, 21
    politics, 161 n20
    Southern Italian, 2
    working-class, 77, 88
illness, mental, 106
immigrants
    experience, 35
    history, 90
    Southern Italian, 65
    working-class Italian 114
Inada, Lawson Fusao, 27; *Aiiieeeee! An
    Anthology of Asian American Writers,*
    27

inherited poverty, 154 n10
initiatives, cultural, 31
"intellectual unemployment," 25
intellectual voices, 90
intellectuals,
    public, 122–3, 124, 131, 135
    transformative, 133
    working-class, 26, 96
interconnections, food and violence, 165
    n29
intergenerational female relationships, 39
International Woman's Day, 117
intersections, ethnic, 161 n25
invisibility
    cultural, 24, 67
    ethnic, 86
Irish American characters, 89
Irish heritage, 144
isolation, cultural, 125
Italian American
    becoming, xiii–xiv
    cultural worker, xxi, xxii
    cookbooks, 165 n24
    gays, 106, 166 n7
    lesbians, 80, 106, 166 n7
    material culture, 163 n7
    positionality, 8
    studies, xvi
    Writers Association, xxii
Italian feminist movement, 48
Italophobic American culture, 106

James, Henry, 45; *The Portrait of a Lady,* 46
Jewish heritage, 144
Jones, Gayle, 6
Joyce, James, xvii–xx, 37, 158 n21

Kadi, Joanna, 6, 27, 38, 95, 120; *Food for Our
    Grandmothers: Writings by Arab-
    American and Arab-Canadian
    Feminists,* 27, 95
Kahlo, Frida, 102, 164 n17
Kincaid, Jamaica, 6
Kingston, Maxine Hong, 30, 38, 120
Kirschenbaum, Blossom, 147 n22
kunstlerroman, 39, 49, 80, 155 n23

La Barre, Adele Regina, 11
La Capra, Dominick, 21, 85
La Spina, Silvana, 143

Labozzetta, Marisa, 20; *Stay with Me, Lella,* 20
Lagier, Jennifer, 32
language, xv
    secret, 109
Lanzillotto, Annie, xxii, 11, 105, 167 n20; "Confessions of a Bronx Tomboy," 105
Latin American Catholicism, 102
Latina
    characters, 89
    women, 125
    writers, 24
Latinos, 69
Laub, Dori, 120
Laurino, Maria, 4, 10, 20, 22, 23, 32, 33, 63, 73, 88, 105, 121, 128, 147 n2; *Were You Always an Italian? Ancestors and Other Icons of Italian America,* 4, 20, 32, 63, 73, 121, 128, 147 n2
Lee, Spike, 18, 148 n5; *Jungle Fever,* 18, 148 n5
Legas, 29
legitimation, cultural, 83
legitimization, 30
    authorial, 27
legitimize, 43
Lentricchia, Frank, 85, 160 n6, 161 n24
Leonardi, Susan, 109
lesbians
    Italian American, 106, 166 n7
    love 156 n3
    Sicilian Neapolitan American, 106
    writers, 80, 96, 123, 151 n32
Leto, Denise Nico, 27, 29; *Hey Paesan: Writing by Lesbians and Gay Men of Italian Descent,* 27, 151 n32
life, domestic, 102, 109
life-writing, 105
Linfante, Michele, 165 n30; *Pizza,* 165 n30
Ling, Amy, 7
linguistic assimilation, 141
Lipari, Loryn, xxii, 19, 105; "Cracked," 19
Lisella, Julia, 29, 31, 147 n22
literature, 96
    working-class, 48, 157 n12
Lloyd, Susan Caperna, 31, 81, 96, 98, 121, 148 n6, 166 n4; *The Baggage,* 121, 148 n6, 166 n4; *No Picture in My Grave: A Spiritual Journey in Sicily,* 31, 98–9; *Processione,* 98–9

Lorde, Audre, 5, 6, 44, 117, 121, 127; *Sister Outsider,* 44; "The Transformation of Silence Into Language and Action," 117
Louima, Abner, 150 n22
Lupino, Ida, 31

Macari, Anne Marie, 33, 163 n12
mafia, 17, 21
mafiosi, 107
Maggenti, Maria, 18; *The Incredibly True Adventure of Two Girls in Love,* 18
Maggio, Theresa, 4, 5, 32, 33; *Mattanza: Love and Death in the Sea of Sicily,* 5, 32
Mairs, Nancy, 127, 134; *Waist-High in the World: A Life Among the Non-Disabled,* 127
Majozo, Estella Conwill, 120
Malafemmina: A Celebration of the Cinema of Italian American Women, 148 n6
malafemmina press, 29
male violence, 164 n15
Mallett, Kim, 156–7 n4
Manfredi, Renée, 33, 75; "Running Away with Frannie," 75
Mangione, Jerre, 53–4, 104; *La Storia: Five Centuries of Italian American Experience,* 53–4; *Mount Allegro,* 53–4
Mannino, Mary Ann, 147 n22, 152 n40, 155 n27
Maraini, Dacia, viii, 143; *La lunga vita di Marianna Ucrìa (The Silent Duchess),* viii
Marazzi, Martino, 31, 147 n22
Marcus, Jane, 37; *The Languages of Patriarchy,* 37
marginal status, 38
marginalization, cultural, 134
Marian cult, 164 n14
Marinoni, Rosa, 31, 151 n34
Masini, Donna, 33
Maso, Carole, viii, xvi, 10, 18, 24, 27, 33, 59, 76–7, 90, 139, 141, 151 n31, 160 n12, 164 n17; *The American Woman in the Chinese Hat,* viii, 76, 77; *Break Every Rule,* 59; *Defiance,* 90; *Ghost Dance,* 151 n31; "The Shelter of the Alphabet," xvi, 59, 139
Mason, Alane Salerno, 33

material culture, 11, 95–6, 100, 109, 114
  Italian American, 163 n7
maternal
  figures, 81
  silence, 81
matriarchal
  cult, 98
  roots, 99
Mattera, JoAnne, 19, 96
Mazza, Cris, 10, 18, 24, 33, 75; *Your Name
  Here_____, 75*
McDaniel, Judith, 121; "Taking Risks: The
  Creation of Feminist Literature," 121
McKeon, Laura, 135
Mecca, Tommi Avicolli, 27, 29; *Hey Paesan:
  Writing by Lesbians and Gay Men of
  Italian Descent,* 27, 151 n32
Medina, Tony, 167 n16; *In Defense of
  Mumia,* 130
MELUS, 54
memoiristic fiction, 80
memoirists, 119–37
memoirs, 63, 79, 98, 106, 128, 167 n22
  contemporary, 119–37
  familial, 128
memory, 129
  cultural 44, 95
  ethnic, 89
mental illness, 106
Messina, Annie, 143
Messina, Maria, 143
Micallef, Gabriella, 27, 128; *Curaggia:
  Writing by Women of Italian Descent,*
  27, 29, 128, 151 n32
middle-class context, 49
migration, class, 49
Minasola, Giuseppe, 145 n7
Minasola, Laura Emanuelita, 145 n7
minorities, 146 n11
minority students, 132
misogynist American culture, 106
Miuccio, Giuliana, 3–4, 12, 72, 147 n23;
  "Apolide," 3–4, 72
Modern Language Association (MLA)
  Conference, 85
Monardo, Anna, 27, 31; *The Courtyard of
  Dreams,* 31
Moonstruck, 18, 112–3, 148 n6
Moraga, Cherríe, 2, 5, 27; *Loving in the War
  Years: lo que pasó por sus labios,* 2–3;

*This Bridge Called My Back: Writings
  by Radical Women of Color,* 27
moral standards, 28
Morante, Elsa, 143
Morrison, Toni, xix, 5, 6, 38, 51
movement
  artistic, 98
  cultural, 98
  Italian feminist, 48
Mulas, Franco, 147 n22
multigenerational stories, 38–9
multiple origins, 140
mysticism, 102, 109, 163 n11, 163 n12
  Franciscan, 100
  Southern Italian, 113
mythical, 57, 98
mythology, 101
myths, 44, 58, 60, 81, 98, 110, 143, 154 n12,
  154 n13
  Southern Italian, 98

name-calling, political implications, 160
  n10
names, in an Italian American context, 160
  n8
naming, 75, 85
  in an Italian American context, 160 n8
  political implications, 160 n10
narrative
  recovery, 126
  tapestry, 39
nationals, foreign, 133
Native Americans, 69
  heritage, 144
  women, 125
  writers, 24
Nelli, Humbert, 159 n28, 159 n29
Nerenberg, Ellen, 31
New York Times, 15, 122
Nocerino, Kathryn, 33
Norton, 33
Noschese, Christine, 19, 148 n6; *Mary
  Therese,* 19, 148 n6
Notari, Elvira, 143
notions of community, 166 n6

oppression
  class, 128
  ethnic, 128
  female, 80

sexual, 128
origins
    African American, 88
    multiple, 140
    working-class, 7, 151 n30
Orleck, Annelise, 118
Orsi, Robert Anthony, 11
outsiders, 24–5, 71–2

Pagani, Dalia, 18, 33, 75; *Mercy Road,* 75
Pallotta, Lina, 19
Parenti, Michael, 93, 97; *Dirty Truths,* 93, 97;
    "*La famiglia:* An Ethno-Class
    Experience," 97
Parini, Jay, 32, 104
Parker, Roszika, 163 n5; *The Subversive
    Stitch,* 163 n5
Paterson, New Jersey, 77, 79, 130
Patriarca, Gianna, 81; "Daughter," 81;
    "Italian Women," 81; "My Birth," 81
patriarchal
    hierarchy, 99
    strictures, 97
    structures, 97
Pearlman, Mickey, xvi; *A Place Called Home:
    Twenty Writing Women Remember,* xvi
pedagogy, political, 133
Pelton, Ted, 75
Penguin, 33
Penzato, Sadie, 29
Penzato Enterprises, 29
people, working-class, 112
performance poet, 167 n20
Perillo, Lucia, 24, 71, 105; *The Oldest Map
    with the Name America,* 71
Perrotta, Tom, 104; "The Wiener Man," 104
Persephone, 44, 50, 81, 98, 99, 143, 154
    n12, 154 n13
perspective, female, 35
photographer, 98
Pipino, Mary Frances, 147 n22, 152 n40,
    155 n27
Pirandello, xiii; *Uno, nessuno, e centomila,* xiii
Poetry Center at Passaic County
    Community College, 129
Pola, Antonia, 27, 30, 30–1, 153–4 n9; *Who
    Can Buy the Stars?,* 30–1, 153–4 n9
political
    pedagogy, 133
    recovery, 118

politics
    identity, 161 n20
    of recognition, 166 n5
    of the publishing world, 28
poverty, inherited, 154 n10
power of silence, 76
prayers, 102
Pretolani, Luisa, 8, 19, 123, 145 n1; *Things I
    Take,* 19, 145 n1
Prose, Francine, 102
public health, 166 n3
public intellectuals, 122–3, 124, 131, 136
Puzo, Mario, 67, 107, 122

quilting, 163 n5

race, 48
racism, 19, 132, 150 n22
    environmental, 120
Radio Gela, xix
Ragusa, Kym, xxii, 6, 8, 10, 11, 19, 23, 74,
    88, 96, 103, 105, 106, 121, 123, 124,
    131–2, 148 n6, 166 n4; *fuori/outside,*
    23, 88, 103, 106, 121, 131–2, 166
    n4; *Passing,* 19, 74, 166 n4
Ramholz, Jim, 55, 157 n5
Rando, Flavia, 97
Raptosh, Diane, 105
reauthorization, 87
recipes, 105, 109, 165 n23
    food, 102
reclamation, cultural, 24, 95, 131
recovery narrative, 126
recovery, 111–2, 114, 115, 126, 130, 131
    cultural, 103
    ethnic, 125
    historical, 118–9
    political, 118–9
    recreating, 114
Redmond, Layne, xvi; *When the Drummers
    Were Women,* xvi
regionalism, Sicilian, 142
relationships, 64
    between sisters, 158 n21
    father-daughter, 57, 81
    intergenerational female, 39
religion, 103, 114
    Sicilian, 99
    woman-made, 97
religious iconography, 96

repetto, Vittoria, xxii, 10, 32, 123, 150 n22
representations of working class, 167 n17
revival, ethnic, 39
Rhys, Jean, 158 n21
Rimanelli, Giose, 20, 21; *Benedetta in*
    Guystersland, 20, 21, 148 n3
rituals
    Catholic, 99
    food, 104
    self-deprecating, 103
Roediger, David, 155 n20
role, cultural, 82
Romano, Rose, 4, 10, 23, 28–9, 68, 73, 74,
    90, 105, 106, 107, 115, 121, 122, 123,
    149 n15, 151 n32, 165 n28; "And
    She Laughs," 106; "Confirmation
    (AKA The Sauce Poem)," 106;
    "Dago Street," 149 n15; "Ethnic
    Woman," 106, 115; "Grandmother
    Cooking," 106; "Italian Bread," 106;
    la bella figura: a choice, 151 n32 "A
    Little Spaghetti," 106; "Mutt Bitch,"
    23, 90; "Native Language 101," 106;
    "Only the Americans," 106; "That
    We Eat," 106; "Vendetta," 106–7;
    Vendetta, 90, 165 n28; *The Wop Factor,*
    74, 165 n28
Romeo, Caterina, 140, 143, 147 n22, 151
    n32, 152 n40, 155 n27
Ronquillo, Annalisa, 133
roots
    matriarchal, 99
    Southern Italian, 100
Rossellini (Roberto), xix; *Roma, città aperta,*
    xix
Rossi, Agnes, 9, 10, 24, 28, 33, 77–91, 160
    n15, 162 n27; *Athletes and Artists,*
    81; *The Houseguest,* 28, 78, 79, 160
    n15, 162 n27; "The Quick," 78, 81,
    84; *The Quick,* 81; *Split Skirt,* 78,
    84–5, 86–7, 88, 89
Rushdie, Salman, 90
Russo, John Paul, xvii, 85, 145 n4, 147 n22
Ryan, Michael, 128; *My Secret Life,* 128

Sacco, Nicola, 149 n15
Said, Edward, 122–3
Salerno, Sal, 119
Sand, George, 28
Sankaran-Lazarre, Anuradha, 117

Santa Lucia, 16–7
Santiago, Esmeralda, 5, 48
Sapphire, 5, 134
Saracino, Mary, 6–7, 10, 33, 44, 88, 105,
    121, 122, 123; *No Matter What,* 121,
    122; "Sunday Rounds," 44
Savarese, Julia, 30, 158 n25; *The Weak and*
    the Strong, 30, 158 n25
Savoca, Nancy, xix, 10, 18, 19, 96, 102, 105,
    106, 123, 148 n6, 149 n11, 164 n16,
    166 n4; *Dogfight,* 18; *Household*
    Saints, 19, 102, 106, 149 n11, 164
    n16, 166 n4; *The 24 Hour Woman,*
    18; *True Love,* xix, 19, 106, 148 n6,
    164 n16, 166 n4
Scalabrini, Bishop, 55
Scalapino, Leslie, 27
Schiavon, Caterina, 110
scholars
    feminist, 38
    working-class, 38
scholarship, feminist, 95
Sciascia, Leonardo, 17, 148 n4; *La Sicilia*
    come metafora, 148 n4
Sciorra, Annabella, 18
Sciorra, Joseph, 11
Scorsese, Martin, xix, 105, 107;
    Italianamerican, 105; *Raging Bull,* xix
sculptures, 97
    wood, 98
Seaview, 153 n4
secret language, 109
Segale, Sister Blandina, 27, 31, 103–4, 151
    n34, 166 n8; *At the End of the Santa*
    Fe Trail, 166 n8
self-
    articulation, 109
    assertion, 80
    centered monologues, 89
    creation, 37
    creation, authorial, 115
    definition 69, 80–1, 86, 115, 131, 157
        n11
    denial, 130
    deprecation, 25
    deprecating rituals, 103
    doubt, 45
    erasure, 80
    examination, 82
    exposure, 85

fashioning, 58
identification, 1
hatred, 25, 73
legitimization, 27, 36
less conversations, 89
perception, 21
presentation, 85
publish, 15, 28–9
revelation, 85
sacrifice, 102
silencing, 21, 29, 72, 73, 75, 76, 86
understanding, 103
valorization, 36
self, hidden, 63
selfhood, 30, 50, 83, 135
Sereni, Clara, 143
sewing, 163 n5
sexual
    abuse, 103
    oppression, 128
Sicilian
    American women, 143
    custom, 108
    Neapolitan American lesbian, 106
    regionalism, Sicilian, 142
    religion, 99
    writers, 109
Sicily, 107, 140
Signorelli-Pappas, Rita, 81
silence, 43, 46, 50–1, 54, 55–6, 63, 69, 115,
    123, 132, 136
    and ethnicity, 71–91
    cultural 86, 149 n9
    heritage of, 46
    historical, 128
    maternal, 81
    of critics, 27, 28
    power of, 76
    struggles, 24
    voices, 49–50, 130
Silko, Leslie Marmon, 5, 30, 38
Sinisi, April, 134
Smith, Barbara, 27; *Home Girls: A Black
    Feminist Anthology,* 27
Smith, Sidonie, 134, 165–6 n1; *Getting a
    Life: Everyday Uses of Autobiography,*
    165–6 n1
social
    activism, 118
    history, 129

Sollors, Werner, 2, 146 n5, 146 n6, 157 n10;
    Multilingual America, 146 n6
Southern Italian, 7–8, 66
    ancestry, 104
    Catholicism, 97, 104
    culture, 71
    descent, 94
    immigrants, 65
    mix, 113
    mysticism, 113
    myths, 98
    roots, 100
    superstition, 113
Southern Italy, 58, 97
spaces
    cultural, 136
    domestic, 46, 97, 105, 109
    ethnic, 89
spazio/space, 12
Spinelli, Rose, viii, 5, 105, 167–8 n21;
    Baking Bread, viii, 167–8 n21
spirituality
    feminine/feminist, 102
    women's, 98
standards, moral, 28
status, marginal, 38
Stefanelli, Filomena Lo Curcio, 15–6, 29;
    *The Stromboli Legacy: My Voyage of
    Discovery,* 15
Stein, Gertrude, 157–8 n16
stereotypes, 18, 19
stories, multigenerational, 38–9
strictures, patriarchal, 97
Strom, Linda, 151 n30; "Reclaiming Our
    Working-Class Identitites: Teaching
    Working-Class Studies in a Blue-
    Collar Community," 151 n30
Stromboli American Heritage Society, 29
structures, patriarchal, 97
struggles
    quotidian, 39
    silenced, 24
students, 134, 135
    African American male, 134
    minority, 132
    working-class, 132, 133
superstition, 102
    Southern Italian, 113
Symposium on Italian and Italian American
    Women, 151 n29

Talese, Gay, 122, 150 n25; "Where Are the Italian American Novelists?," 150 n25

Tamburri, Anthony, xx, 39, 46, 147 n22, 151 n32, 155 n27, 160 n5; *From the Margin,* 43, 151 n32; *FUORI,* 151 n32; *A Semiotic of Ethnicity,* 153 n7, 154 n18

Tan, Amy, 6, 38, 84, 89; *The Joy Luck Club,* 84; *The Kitchen God's Wife,* 84

tapestry, narrative, 39

teach, 115

teachers, 119–37

teaching, 132

Temple, Shirley, 67

Terrone, Maria, 120

text, autobiographical, 109

Therese of Lisieux, 102

Three Guineas Press, 29

Timpanelli, Gioia, 4, 17, 25, 27, 31, 32, 81, 117, 151 n29; *Sometimes the Soul: Two Novellas of Sicily,* 5, 32

Tomasi, Mari, 30, 151 n34; *Deep Grow the Roots,* 30; *Like Lesser Gods,* 30

Torgovnick, Marianna De Marco, 22–3, 25–6, 28, 32, 75, 85, 161 n21, 161 n24; *Crossing Ocean Parkway: Readings by an Italian American Daughter,* 25–6, 32, 75, 85; *Primitive Obsessions: Men, Women, and the Quest for Ecstasy,* 160 n9

Torre, Roberta, 17, 21, 143; *Tano da morire,* 21

tradition, 115

Anglo-American, 107

transformation, 126, 131, 132, 134

cultural, 144

transformative intellectual, 133

translating, 47, 140, 141–2

Triangle Shirtwaist Factory Fire, 117–9, 120, 163 n6

Trinh T. Minh-ha, 6, 15; *Woman, Native, Other,* 15

Tucci, Stanley, 19

Tusmith, Bonnie, 87, 161–2 n25

tutteStorie, 140, 143, 151 n32

Vacirca, Clara, 31

Valerio, Anthony, xxii–xxiii, 104; *Anita Garibaldi: A Biography,* xxii; *The Mediterranean Runs Through Brooklyn,* xxii; *Valentino and the Great Italians,* xxii

Vanzetti, Bartolomeo, 149 n15

Vecoli, Rudolph, 21–2

Verdicchio, Pasquale, 154 n11

Versace, Gianni, 17, 147 n2

victims, 149 n15

video, 98, 103

autobiographical, 76

Vinciguerra, Francesca (Frances Winwar), 24

violence, 107, 111, 128, 132

and food interconnections, 165 n29

Viscusi, Robert, xxii, 45, 147 n22, 155 n27, 162 n4

"Debate in the Dark: Love in Italian-American Fiction," 162 n4

Vitiello, Justin, 32

voices

authorial, 39

ethnic, 85

intellectual, 90

silenced, 49–50

Voices in Italian Americana (VIA), xx, xxiii, 9, 151 n32, 157 n14

Vuocolo, Jeanette, 105, 167 n14; *Three Graces,* 167 n14

Waldo, Octavia Capuzzi, 30; *A Cup in the Sun,* 30

Walker, Alice, xix, 5, 6, 7, 29–30, 35, 38, 51, 84, 89, 95, 134, 151–2 n34, 153 n3; *The Color Purple,* 10, 84, 89; *In Search of Our Mother's Gardens,* 35, 153 n3

Watson, Julia, 134, 165–6 n1; *Getting a Life: Everyday Uses of Autobiography,* 165–6 n1

Weiss, Penny A., 157 n11; *Feminism and Community,* 157 n11

Wertmuller, Lina, 143; *Pasqualino Settebellezze,* xix

Wharton, Edith, 45; *The House of Mirth,* 45

white ethnicity, 161 n17, 161 n20

Williams, Patricia J., 18

Wine Press, 53, 55

Wing, Daine Yen-Mei, 27; *Making Waves: An Anthology of Writings by and about Asian American Women,* 27

Winwar, Frances, 24, 27, 28, 31, 86, 150–1
   n27, 151 n34
The Wizard of Oz, 67, 158 n22
woman-made religion, 97
women
   African American, 51, 95, 125, 129, 142
   Chicana, 51
   Latina, 125
   Native American, 125
   Sicilian American, 143
women's spirituality, 98
Women's Words, 29
Wong, Nellie, 71; "Where is My Country?,"
   71
Wong, Shawn Hsu, 27; *Aiiieeeee! An Anthology
   of Asian American Writers,* 27
wood sculptures, 98
Woolf, Virginia, xx, 26, 125, 158 n21
work
   archival, 136
   domestic, 95
workers, cultural, 119–37
working-class
   academics, 96
   artists, 96
   authors, 57
   filmmakers, 96
   histories, 120
   identity, 77, 88

intellectuals, 26, 96
Italian immigrants, 114
literature, 48, 157 n12
origins, 151 n30
people, 112
representations of, 167 n17
scholars, 38
students, 132, 133
writers, 26–7, 48, 59, 96
writerly strategies, 19
writers, 98, 105
   African American, 24, 29–30
   Asian American, 24
   cultural minority, 27
   ethnic, 87
   gay, 96, 123, 151 n32
   Latina, 24
   lesbian, 10, 80, 96, 123, 151 n32
   Native American, 24
   Sicilian, 109
   working-class, 26, 48, 59, 96

Zandy, Janet, 7, 8, 26, 27, 48, 49, 66, 75–6,
   88, 120; *Calling Home,* 26; "My
   Children's Names," 75–6; *Liberating
   Memory,* 26–27, 66
Zora Neale Hurston Multimedia Center in
   Rome, 143–4
Zancan, Marina, 143